QUOTA

ON BOBBY KENNEDY:
"He's the one I'd put my hand in the fire..."

ON ARISTOTLE ONASSIS:
"His constant attention is wonderful. Last Thursday morning, for example, he told me I looked quite pale and needed a bit of a change. He suggested we fly to Paris and have dinner at Maxim's."

ON BOOK PUBLISHING:
"I'm drawn to books that are out of our regular experience. To me, a wonderful book is one that takes me on a journey into something I didn't know before."

ON SAVING NEW YORK LANDMARKS:
"I'm passionate about architecture. We are the only country in the world that trashes its old buildings. Too late we realize how very much we need them."

ON MEETING MADONNA:
"Jackie reportedly stared at the sex queen when John brought her home, said little to her while she was there, and berated her son for even entertaining the notion of an alliance with her. She ordered John to stay away from her, and he did."

—Lester David

JACQUELINE KENNEDY ONASSIS

A Portrait of Her Private Years

LESTER DAVID

ST. MARTIN'S PAPERBACKS

Published by arrangement with Carol Publishing Group

JACQUELINE KENNEDY ONASSIS: A PORTRAIT OF HER PRIVATE YEARS

Copyright © 1994 by Lester David.

Cover photograph by Bettina Cirone.

Library of Congress Catalog Card Number: 93-45492

ISBN: 0-312-95546-4

Printed in the United States of America

Birch Lane Press hardcover edition published 1994
St. Martin's Paperbacks edition/June 1995

St. Martin's Paperbacks are published by St. Martin's Press, 175 Fifth Avenue, New York, NY 10010.

10 9 8 7 6 5 4 3 2 1

*To Irene, my wife and collaborator on two children,
several books, and scores of magazine articles,
who contributed so much wisdom and editorial expertise
to this project. With love and gratitude.*

Throughout my life, I have always tried to remain true to myself. This I will continue to do as long as I live.
—JACQUELINE KENNEDY ONASSIS

Women and music should never be dated.
—OLIVER GOLDSMITH
She Stoops to Conquer

Contents

Preface   xi
Prologue   xv

Part One
Supernova

1. The Woman Who Invented Herself   3
2. The Importance of Being Jackie   14
3. Love Her, Love Her Not   23

Part Two
One Brief Shining Moment

4. Young Jackie, Young Jack   29
5. The Truth About the Marriage   41
6. Jackie and Politics   57
7. Days of Glory   66
8. Fears for Her Sanity   77

Part Three
Out of the Abyss

9. A Greek Bearing Gifts   101
10. The Truth About *That* Marriage   121
11. Jackie's Children—Caroline   132
12. Jackie's Children—John   152

Contents

Part Four
New Horizons

13. Close-up   167
14. Her Mysterious Significant Other   176
15. Working Woman   189
16. Jackie and the Kennedys   206
17. A Woman of Independent Means   215
18. Crusader   226
19. Her Passing   235
    Coda   248
    A Garland of Tributes   255
    Notes on Sources   261
    Bibliography   273
    Index   277

Preface

In this book, I attempt to cut through the layers of legend, undocumented "facts," and sensation-seeking "exclusives" to tell what I believe to be the truth about Jacqueline Kennedy Onassis.

The book I have written is drawn from interviews over the years with persons who have had close contacts with Jackie. Many of these interviews are new; others have been in my files for some time. As a journalist, I have covered the Kennedys for more than three decades. I did not attempt to obtain interviews with Mrs. Onassis for two reasons: One, the possibility that she would grant any for a book about her life in maturity is less than zero. Second, even if she did, judging by the very few she has given in almost forty years, the restrictions she would have imposed would have sanitized the facts out of all resemblance to the truth.

Mostly, then, I have relied on my "contacts," as journalists and journalist-biographers call their sources. These are numerous: my file of persons whose lives have touched those of the Kennedy family over the years is extensive, for I have covered the clan ever since the election of John Kennedy as president in 1960.

I have printed the observations of those I considered to be accurate and ignored the others.

I offer profound thanks to those members of the Kennedy family, their friends and associates who agreed to be interviewed. Each is duly identified in the text. I am deeply grateful to the following who have helped me in my quest for the essential Jackie as she enters her seventh decade of life: John F. Baker, executive editor of *Publishers Weekly;* Luella Hennessey Donavan, the Kennedy family nurse; fashion expert and editor Rosemary Kent; Edwin Schlossberg, Caroline Kennedy's husband and father of her three children; Richard Reston, editor of *The Vineyard Gazette;* Lily Tempelsman, wife of Maurice Tempelsman; James Brady, former publisher of *Women's Wear Daily;* John Mack Carter, editor-in-chief of *Good Housekeeping* magazine; Mary Lynn Kotz, coauthor of *Upstairs at the White House;* authors Nena O'Neill and Frances Spatz Leighton; Sandy Boyer, head of the Irish Arts Center; photographer Brian Quigley; and the friendly residents of the lovely town of Chester, Massachusetts. Others who have offered substantive information—too numerous to mention here—are acknowledged in the text or notes.

My files on the Kennedys have yielded a treasure trove of information about Jackie from persons no longer alive, such as Kenneth P. O'Donnell, one of John Kennedy's close associates and a staunch friend of Jackie; author Joe McCarthy; lawyer Roy Cohn; and Doris Cerutti of Cerutti Children Enterprises.

I owe much to the archivists and librarians for their unstinting and time-consuming help in locating research materials I requested. The staff of the John F. Kennedy Memorial Library at Columbia Point in Boston responded patiently to my Oliver Twist-ish pleas for "more." Grateful acknowledgment is made to chief archivist William Johnson, and to Maura Porter, June Payne, and Ron Whealan, and to audiovisual archivist Allan Goodrich for his help in locating photographs.

I must make mention, and offer a special indebtedness,

to the reference staff of the Hewlett-Woodmore Public Library, headed by Jeffrey Mason. I was truly astonished by the extent of their reach; they obtained for me materials that I had despaired of finding. Thanks, too, to the Municipal Art Society in New York, especially to Douglas Cogan and Ann Anereski; also thanks to Christopher E. Bowen, researcher and librarian, who gave so graciously of his time and expertise to ferret out needed information; and to Eulalie Regan, *Vineyard Gazette* librarian.

Also consulted were newspaper and magazine files, in particular those of *The New York Times, Washington Post, New York Herald-Tribune* (now defunct), *Los Angeles Times, Boston Globe, Boston Herald,* and *Springfield Union. The Ladies' Home Journal, McCall's, Look,* and *Life* were also consulted. Citations of material drawn from these sources appear in the Notes.

My gratitude extends also to Hillel Black, my editor, for his guidance through the gestation of this project. My agent, Anita Diament, was with me every step of the way, holding my hand when necessary, which was often. The manuscript was typed on a mechanical upright, but Bonnie-Ann Black brought me into the 1990s with her masterful use of a word processor.

Prologue

IN THE HARSH WINTER of 1994, Jacqueline Kennedy Onassis faced yet another challenge in her extraordinary life.

Early in January, suffering flulike symptons, she visited her doctor, who discovered suspicious nodules in her neck. Further examination at New York Hospital—Cornell Medical Center on East 68th Street in New York revealed that she had lymphoma, cancer of the lymph nodes or glands.

Rumors about Jackie's health had been growing since the turn of the year. Newspaper, television, and radio journalists were interviewing everyone from nurses and doctors to parking-lot attendants at the major medical centers, seeking leads.

Finally, Jackie decided to make the disclosure. She was indeed a cancer victim.

On February 10, her longtime friend and spokesperson, Nancy Tuckerman, who first told the world that Jackie would wed Aristotle Onassis, made the stunning announcement: Jackie had lymphoma and had been having chemotherapy since the middle of January. Her first major illness in a lifetime of excellent health came only six months before her sixty-fifth birthday.

"There is every expectation that it [the course of treatment] will be successful," Ms. Tuckerman said. "There is an excellent prognosis. You never can be absolutely sure, but the doctors are very, very optimistic."

Jackie's malignancy was not Hodgkin's disease, though the two are similar. Both are cancers arising in the lymph nodes, the catch basins in the body's drainage system, where harmful bacteria are trapped and destroyed by the body's defense system. A definitive diagnosis, Hodgkin's or lymphoma, is made by microscopic testing of the affected tissues.

In recent years, medical science has made amazing progress in the treatment of malignancies affecting the lymph glands. While, as Ms. Tuckerman correctly stated, one could not be certain, the statistics seemed in Jackie's favor, since the cancer was caught early. Dr. Robert N. Taub, professor of clinical medicine at the Columbia University College of Physicians and Surgeons, said, "If the disease is diagnosed in an early stage, patients with these cancers can survive for five or more years."

The world had watched Jackie ever since she was the beautiful young wife of a youthful senator and president, through her bereavement after his assassination, through her second marriage to Aristotle Onassis, through her emergence as a social superstar, through mothering of her two children, Caroline and John, and it was still watching as she entered her mature years.

By mid-May, a great many stories—very few of them authenticated—were published in the newspapers and magazines and discussed by "experts" on television, spurred by a scare about her condition. On April 14, she had felt weak in her Manhattan apartment. Her doctor was summoned. He advised that she be taken to New York Hospital—Cornell Medical Center. There she was placed in a private room on the fourth floor, and two burly security guards were posted outside. Maurice Tempelsman, her longtime friend, counselor, and protector, to whom she was devoted, was at her side almost constantly.

Doctors reported that she was suffering from a bleeding ulcer. One week later she was discharged and driven home. Unaided, she walked from the car into the apartment building. Two days later, wearing a gray trenchcoat, her head covered by a gray-and-gold scarf, she took a forty-five-minute walk in Central Park with Tempelsman, then sat with him on a bench in the warm sunshine.

Cindy Adams, the widely syndicated columnist who writes for the *New York Post,* said in the *Ladies' Home Journal:* "One cancer specialist treating Mrs. Onassis says the condition is very serious. He has given friends to understand that is a 'fast-moving' case." Ms. Adams, who lives near Jackie, is generally acknowledged to have excellent sources of information. But at the same time, she pointed out that Nancy Tuckerman was on record as saying the prognosis was "excellent."

Photographs of Jackie following the April surgery showed her looking drawn, even haggard. Before the operation, indeed, before her illness, she looked as people had always remembered her, dazzling, beautiful. She had that same mysterious smile, that same will-o'-the-wisp quality of always appearing beyond reach, and she spoke in that same little-girl voice she affected in public.

Nobody expected that the cancer would claim the life of Jacqueline Kennedy Onassis on May 19, 1994.

What I have written about Jackie Kennedy in this book was set down in the belief that she would have a long and happy life; that expectation informed every word of it. And so it was doubly shocking, not only that she should have become ill but also that she should have been carried off so quickly. Though I might have revised the text to reflect her death, I have decided to keep the text as it was to preserve the sense of her living presence, of the immediacy of the woman she had become. It was this sense of the vibrant, alive, active woman that I wanted to convey to my readers. And so the passages in this book that describe these times must, of course, be considered in that light.

This, then, is the story of Mrs. Onassis, who in her maturity was not the same woman she was in her youth. She had changed so utterly that people who thought they knew and understood her will discover that they never really did.

PART ONE

⁓

Supernova

1

The Woman Who Invented Herself

Jacqueline invented Jacqueline—from her hair, which was originally kinky and had to be straightened regularly, to her seductive, breathy, whispery voice. Psychohistorian Nancy Gager Clinch called it "her deliberately little-girl voice," adding, "She had spent years cultivating this voice until it was second nature." But as Alexander and Boxendale stated in their book, *Behind Every Successful President:* "Merely because the smile and the voice were artifices did not mean they were artificial. Rather, they were *art.*"

Consider her voice, as much a part of Jackie's persona as her wide smile. It is not an actress's voice, because she lacks lung power. Nor does it display that cultivated way of speaking that makes graduates of exclusive finishing schools sound alike. The voice is a perfect accessory to Jackie's appearance as a worldly-wise girl-woman. The combination went together like a silver purse with a black evening dress. Jackie knew it, and the voice became her trademark.

The comparison that comes to mind is Maurice Chevalier, the one-time celebrated French movie star and music hall performer. Chevalier spoke English with only a slight accent, but on the stage and before the camera he deliberately adopted that distinctive Gallic manner of speaking that he knew charmed audiences.

Jackie, too, can alter the voice. She is all business at functions, such as book-and-author luncheons where writers of newly published books are introduced to journalists, editors, and critics. In 1993, Rosemary Kent, the first editor of Andy Warhol's *Interview* magazine and a leading fashion journalist, attended a luncheon in the Park Lane Hotel in Manhattan to herald the publication of a book. Jackie circulated among the guests, chatting informally. "I didn't hear that breathy voice at all," said Ms. Kent. "She was very much the editor, competent, professional and, of course, very gracious."

In 1993, she gave one of her rare interviews to John F. Baker, editorial director of *Publishers Weekly,** the trade journal of the book industry. "Her voice was not really whispery at all," Baker said. "It was low, quiet but fully produced, with plenty of chest tones and deeper than you might expect in a woman with such a slight build."

When she began work as an associate editor at Doubleday and Company in 1978, she joined the other dozen editors at their weekly meetings where new projects were discussed around a square table. The first day, she offered a book in the whispery voice but the others complained they could not hear her. Jackie spoke up in her normal tones.

Jackie can be imperious and demanding when secretaries, servants—and husbands—annoy her or fail to do what she wishes. She will substitute a loud voice for the junior-high tones. Witnesses who overhear her at these tempestuous times, unavoidable because Jackie becomes incautious about her image when she becomes angry enough, report that she is as intimidating as a Marine drill instructor.

One afternoon, at a horse-country event in Upperville,

---

* See chapter 15.

Virginia, where she maintains a weekend retreat, a man approached her, apparently seeking an autograph. "I don't want to bother you, but . . ." he said. Jackie cut him off, snapping out a reply that was anything but whispery: "Well, then, don't!" and turned away.

Years before, when Jackie deposited Caroline at Concord Academy in Massachusetts, they had an argument in public about the size of Caroline's allowance. Students passing by heard the discussion, which escalated into an argument on both sides. Jackie ultimately gave in, agreeing to give her daughter slightly more than the ten dollars a week she originally intended. During the mother-daughter argument, Jackie's voice was clear and authoritative.

These were mild responses compared with the way she would sometimes talk to her two husbands.

Once, in 1962, Jack upbraided her for remaining less than a quarter of an hour at the Washington Flower Show, a major annual springtime festival at which first ladies are always honored guests and stay several hours chatting with the sponsoring political wives. Jack knew wives can influence husbands, whose help hers needed to get his legislation passed on Capitol Hill.

Jackie's temper flared. "Why scream at me?" she shot back in a voice loud enough to be heard by people nearby. Then she reminded him of a dumb mistake he had made a few weeks previously. He had eaten bacon with his poached eggs on a Friday and Pierre Salinger, his press secretary, had dutifully reported the presidential fare, unaware of the then-existing Catholic prohibition against eating meat on Friday. The media forced Salinger into the embarrassing position of saying he had misunderstood the president.

Another time, she and Jack argued about a political situation in which the President had become enmeshed. William "Fishbait" Miller, the doorkeeper of the House of Representatives, said two Secret Service men recalled the conversation they overheard when JFK and Jackie left the church.

Jackie, her voice rising, angrily said to her husband: "Come on now, you son of a bitch. You got yourself into this and you know your public demands it. So get your damned tie and coat on and let's go."

Her blowups with Aristotle Onassis, the Greek shipping magnate she married in late 1969, were monumental —and loud. In January 1972, the two were in the Clipper Club, the Pan American Airways VIP lounge at Heathrow Airport outside London, waiting for a flight. An argument broke out, the cause unknown, which soon escalated into a heated verbal brawl. No other passengers were present, but a Pan Am employee told a London newspaper, which headlined the battle: "It sure was a flaming row. She was shouting at him to be quiet and listen for once. It wasn't at all one-sided, take it from me. It got so loud I don't think they could hear each other."

Jackie stormed out of the lounge and almost ran to her limousine, parked on the tarmac. She sat there, angrily thumbing a magazine until an airline official approached and told her it was time to board. Stalking toward the plane, she told Ari, in a sharp, and loud, voice, "I'm going home to America!"

Her sense of public relations is finely tuned. When Caroline married Edwin Schlossberg on Cape Cod on July 19, 1986, Jackie emerged from the little white church in Centerville and, facing a battery of photographers, put her head on Ted Kennedy's shoulder. Wrote the *Washington Post*: "Didn't she know [it] would make an exquisite photo op?"

She has ordered Caroline and John to say nothing to the media at any time unless under special circumstances. John ducks the press, smiling graciously and offering flippant comments. Caroline is like a frightened doe when confronted by a reporter. One day I met her on Main Street in East Hampton, Long Island. She was wheeling her oldest daughter, Rose, in a stroller; Ed Schlossberg, whom I knew slightly, was at her side. "Hi, Ed," I said as they drew alongside. He stopped to chat, but Caroline, a startled look on her face, walked quickly on.

When Harrison Rainie was compiling material for *Growing Up Kennedy*, a book about the grandchildren of Joe and Rose, he called John and asked for a brief interview. According to Rainie, "He was very nice. He knew I was talking to some of his cousins and friends, and he said, 'I'm sorry, I can't talk. My mother would kill me.' "

She stage-manages her publicity masterfully, trying to control every word attributed to her. That is why every biography of Jackie, whether labeled so or not, is "unauthorized," as this one is. Authors know that an authorized biography would be gone over with infinite care and anything that might tend to disturb the legend would be excised.

It is clear she would insist upon a sanitized version of her life, as Rose Kennedy did in her memoirs, *Times to Remember*, published in 1974. Rose set down the Kennedy family legend in 522 pages glowing with adulation for every member, omitting anything that would spoil the carefully created fable that entranced America and the world.

Take, for instance, the description of Gloria Swanson, whom Rose knew was her husband Joe's mistress, having given him tacit permission to roam after she left his bed following the birth of Ted. Rose treated her as a good friend with whom she went gaily shopping for clothes in Paris. This shopping venture followed an ocean voyage during which Joe spent more time in Swanson's cabin than in theirs. Teddy, with whose notorious womanizing she was entirely familiar, was "extraordinarily thoughtful and understanding . . . a loving guiding influence for all the grandchildren." Joan Kennedy, already a hopeless drunk, "managed well."

Jackie is fully in charge of anything she authorizes to

be written about her, as she showed in the interview she gave to John Baker. Baker told me: "The interview was circumscribed with extreme thoroughness." He had to agree to an extraordinary set of limitations:

• He was forbidden to tape-record her remarks, presumably because she did not want a recording of her voice to wind up in some auction house.
• No photographer could be present.
• She would entertain only questions about her work as a book editor, none about her personal life or lifestyle.
• She must have the right to refuse to answer questions if she chose.
• She must have complete editorial approval of the article, which most authors resist.
• Finally, there must be a "trusted associate" present to make certain all the rules were observed. Jackie chose Marly Rusoff, vice president and associate publisher of Doubleday & Company, where she worked.

All this, of course, was to preserve the Jackie mystique. Following this public appearance in print, she secluded herself once again.

Her actions over the years provide convincing evidence that she loves the spotlight, courts it, and, as one long-time Jackie watcher said, "would be hurt and disappointed if it gets turned off."

Her talent for self-promotion is masterful. One major public-relations executive in New York said: "She couldn't have maximized her appeal any better if she had hired a team of the most high-powered professionals in the business of celebrity promotion and paid them a fortune." Her only media "contact" is Nancy Tuckerman, a friend and former private secretary who is now employed at Doubleday. Tuckerman's sole function in Jackie's behalf is to politely turn down all requests for interviews.

When her public career began, Jackie, encouraged by Jack, gave interviews freely to journalists but ever since the late 1970s she has never talked to any journalist, no matter how celebrated, about her personal life.

And therein lies one answer to her eternal fascination. In an era of tell-alls, stars of every magnitude reveal everything—the men and women with whom they have slept, how much or how little their partners satisfy them, their sexuality, the abuse they have suffered at the hands of parents or relatives who beat, raped, or neglected them, the emotional illness they have overcome, or not overcome. In contrast Jackie has said nothing, keeping her secrets.

Excessive exposure to the media will erode public interest in a short while, so Jackie offers just enough to make the public crave more. She goes to restaurants and theaters, and attends social functions, offering "photo ops" to the paparazzi and the women's fashion publications.

But then she will disappear, remaining inaccessible in her well-guarded homes. "It's a lot like Gypsy Rose Lee," the publicist said. "Gypsy never stripped completely but revealed just enough of herself to make her the most celebrated stripper of her time. Jackie has apparently adopted the same formula."

There are times when she would go jogging in Central Park at odd hours to foil the photographers. During these excursions she would wear sweats, one of her son's old T-shirts, or anything nondescript that would hide her identity. She would also wrap a kerchief around her head. But at other times, she dressed in a way that would make a flattering photograph in a newspaper. On these occasions she may wear a catsuit—a tight-fitting leotard that covers her body but still reveals her trim figure.

She would not jog counterclockwise in the park, as others do, but in the opposite direction, said Shaun Considine, a journalist, ardent runner and Jackie-watcher. Considine quotes a friend, whom he calls Doris, who explains why. When she runs clockwise, she can always see photographers who may be lying in wait for her to appear. "She *wants* to be recognized," Considine quotes Doris. "When she does spot a camera, she suddenly straightens up, smiles broadly, and jogs smartly."

Despite her insistence on privacy, Jackie went to midnight mass at St. Patrick's Cathedral in New York, one recent year. She did not sit in the middle of the great church, as someone who does not want to be recognized might do, but took a front pew with her two children. The photographers, of course, somehow were there to record the scene.

"She wanted publicity but on her own terms," said James Brady, the former publisher of *Women's Wear Daily*. "When Jackie mania was at its height in the post-Camelot years, we would get calls from Nancy Tuckerman alerting us that she would be attending some function or other wearing a Galanos, or whatever it was, on Thursday, and lunching with Babe Paley on Monday wearing some other creation. We would thereupon assign our best photographer to cover her appearances."

However, Brady declares, "At other times we would call her to solicit information and get a complete turndown."

This trait of ducking into, and out of, the spotlight is repeated, fuguelike, in her behavior. Throughout her public life, she has been a study in contradictions, which is another part of our continuous fascination with her.

Oleg Cassini, her personal designer for years, said: "She is an original and difficult to decipher. She might be very warm one day and freeze you out the next; she did this to everyone, even her closest friends. She even perplexed the Kennedys."

Note some more contradictions:

Despite the huge sums she spends on clothes and accessories for herself, she is stingy with her employees. The woman who did not blink an eye at spending twelve thousand dollars for a dress designed for her, balked at paying that same amount as a yearly salary to her old and trusted private secretary, Mary Barelli Gallagher, who worked for her from 1957 to 1964. When Gallagher suggested that twelve thousand dollars would be a reasonable wage as part of the fifty-thousand-dollar annual federal appropriation authorized for Jackie, Jackie pleaded with Mary to accept part-time work and scale down her salary request.

Bills submitted by employees for overtime work infuriated Jackie. "Do you mean to say," she asked Mary, "that for every little thing extra someone does around here, I have to pay them?" Mary reminded Jackie that was how the U.S. labor system worked.

She made good use of resale shops. Much of her clothing, accessories, and other possessions would end up in the secondhand market.

One buyer for a Manhattan store said:

> Jackie has been dealing with us for a long time. It started when Jack was a senator, continued when he became president, and went on during the Onassis marriage. She still does business with us.
>
> The way it works is like this—she'll telephone and we'll go to her apartment on Fifth Avenue to look over the items she wants to sell. We'll agree on how much they should sell for, and then we'll send over a truck to pick up the clothes. When they are sold, Jackie gets half the proceeds.

And yet, when Mary Gallagher resigned in September 1964, Jackie presented her with a beautiful golden brooch surrounded by exquisite turquoise stones, which doubtless cost a great deal of money.

Imperious Jackie can care little about whom she hurts.

In 1961, she humiliated Mrs. Villeda Morales, wife of the president of Honduras, by refusing to receive her at the White House. Her official explanation was that Mrs. Morales was not on a state visit. Her real reason: she knew she would be bored by pretending to be nice to someone she neither knew nor cared about.

Yet, the year before, she was moved by the poverty she saw while campaigning for Jack in the Appalachian region of West Virginia. One of her first acts after moving into the White House was to order the purchase of handmade crystal from a factory in Morgantown, in the northern part of the state, just below the Pennsylvania border. Said J. B. West, the chief usher: "She wanted not only to bring to the White House an authentic piece of traditional American craftsmanship, but also to symbolize the president's interest in the economic problems and potential of Appalachia."

She disliked Ethel Kennedy, yet was responsible for obtaining a special church dispensation for her from Francis Cardinal Spellman. Ethel had requested a choir of nuns from the Manhattanville College of the Sacred Heart, from which she had graduated, to sing at Bobby's funeral in St. Patrick's Cathedral. Strict rules forbade singing by women inside the great cathedral. Jackie, learning of Ethel's wishes, called Cardinal Spellman, head of the New York archdiocese, who granted an exemption for the nuns. It is doubtful that Ethel ever knew what Jackie had done.

Again, in 1983, Jackie learned that J. B. West had died. He had served six presidents and their wives in his twenty-eight years as chief White House usher. His family and friends wanted him to be buried in Arlington National Cemetery. Regulations prevented this: only military veterans are to be buried there. Jackie called James S. Rosebush, chief of staff to Nancy Reagan, then first lady. Two days later, Mrs. Reagan telephoned Jackie, telling her the rules had been waived. Mr. West now rests at Arlington.

Despite harsh disagreements she had with her mother, Janet Auchincloss, Jackie was at her bedside almost constantly when Janet fell victim to Alzheimer's disease. "I feel like I am now the mother and my mother is my child," she said as degeneration of nerve cells in the brain caused Janet to slip further into irrational and childlike behavior. Jackie read poetry to her, spoon-fed her, sent her flowers and gifts, and paid for round-the-clock nursing until her death in 1989.

Will Jacqueline Onassis ever publish her own memoirs? Hidden away in the JFK Library is a twelve-hour oral history she made following the assassination. She has stipulated that it must not be made public until fifty years after her death.

That is as far as she will ever go in telling the world about herself. Were she to agree today to expand her recollections into a book, publishers would pay any price for it. As it is, her version, albeit an abbreviated form, will be known solely to future generations.

She won't ever write her memoirs. Because if she did, Mona Lisa would have to explain what lies behind the enigmatic smile—and the world would conjecture no more.

2

The Importance of Being Jackie

She has never been a head of state like Britain's Margaret Thatcher or Israel's Golda Meir, she has never been involved in a scandal, royal or common, like Diana, Princess of Wales, or Elizabeth Taylor. She has never triggered a war like Helen of Troy, won a Nobel Prize like Marie Curie, or pioneered in nursing like Florence Nightingale.

Yet Jackie Onassis has received more public attention than most of them. It is difficult to think of another woman whose every movement has been followed and recorded so completely, who has been talked about and argued about so much. Indeed, one biographer called her "the most famous woman in history since Cleopatra."

John McCormack, speaker of the House of Representatives during John Kennedy's administration, paid her the extraordinary compliment of describing her as a major influence around the world. "She was a great diplomat and a great ambassador who has given an image of America which has made the world smile again," he declared. And Dr. James F. Giglio, professor of history at Southwest Missouri State University, said, "Americans, without knowing much about her personal life, proudly perceived her as more than a match for European royalty."

"Over the past thirty years," said Clark Clifford, counsel to John Kennedy and six other presidents, "more words have been written about her than any other woman in the world."

Every newspaper morgue, or library, has cabinets filled with clippings about her; there are more envelopes labeled JACQUELINE KENNEDY ONASSIS in the library of the *Boston Herald,* for example, than there are for Queen Elizabeth or, for that matter, Nikita Khrushchev, the former Soviet leader, President Gerald Ford, or Princess Diana.

The printout of books about Jackie at the Online Computer Library Center, a database that records all books in the catalogues of major libraries around the country, is forty-four inches long and lists fifty-seven separate titles published in the United States alone, and another thirty in foreign languages for American ethnic groups. Scores of the books about her have been written in nations throughout the globe.

She is a prime subject for gossip columnists. Free-lance photographers scour the newspapers for events where she is scheduled to appear, then show up in droves.

Brian Quigley, a free-lance photographer who has snapped the world's superstars for fifteen years, said:

Jackie is the most sought-after celebrity in the world today. She's more in demand by editors, even as a grandmother, than Elizabeth Taylor, Bruce Springsteen, Sylvester Stallone, Arnold Schwarzenegger, and even Madonna.

Every time we hear of an event she is likely to attend, from twenty to thirty of us show up. That doesn't happen with any of the others. We love her because she is a photographer's dream. She's got that dazzling smile, those large expressive eyes and, even when wearing jeans, looks impeccably groomed. But beyond her appearance, there is a kind of strangeness about her, a depth that she does not reveal, that the camera can often capture.

When newsstand sales of popular magazines falter, editors will commission articles on Jackie and, more often than not, circulation rebounds. John Mack Carter, who has been editor-in-chief of *McCall's, Ladies' Home Journal,* and *Good Housekeeping* in a career spanning more than thirty years, said: "In the decade of the sixties whenever Jackie was featured on the cover, she sold more copies than any other personality in the world." And that was the decade when Sophia Loren, the Duke and Duchess of Windsor, Richard Burton and Elizabeth Taylor, Robert Redford, and all the other Kennedy wives and women were the media stars.

"Even today," Carter adds, "Jackie matches sales with any other Hollywood celebrity." She holds her own, and frequently outsells, such luminaries as Barbra Streisand, Cher, and members of the British royal family.

Reporters for the more sensational publications and television shows have staked out her homes around the clock, stationed themselves on boats where they watched through powerful binoculars, disguised themselves as joggers, even flown over her houses in helicopters to catch her in a sexual indiscretion.

The only time Jackie was caught with her pants down by the media—literally, unfortunately—was in 1971 when she was married to Aristotle Onassis. Feeling secure in the knowledge that Ari's private island of Skorpios was indeed private, she removed her bathing suit and stretched out nude on the beach for a sunbath.

She was wrong. A team of ten photographers, equipped with underwater cameras and telescopic lenses, watched her from a boat in the Ionian Sea. They took pictures of a naked Jackie, fourteen of which were published in the Italian magazine *Playmen* and subsequently circulated worldwide. Jackie was furious, but Ari simply shrugged and told reporters: "I have to take my pants off to put on my bathing suit. Well, so does Jackie." And, with more than a touch of pride, he told friends: "She looks so lovely without clothes. Just look at that figure. I think I'll get an artist to paint her. She makes all the other nude ladies look like a bag of bones."

Jackie endured teasing for a long time, even from her good friend John Kenneth Galbraith, who had been ambassador to India in Jack Kennedy's administration. At a dinner, he looked down at her from his towering six-foot-six height and exclaimed: "Why Jackie, I didn't recognize you with your clothes on."

Jackie's impact on fashion from haute couture to bargain basement off-the-rack has been unequaled.

Edith Head, who designed clothes for most of the Hollywood stars, said she was "the greatest single influence [on fashion] in history."

Said James Brady, the former editor of *Women's Wear Daily:* "As a consumer, as distinguished from a designer, Jackie has been the greatest influence of any woman of her time."

Oleg Cassini, a transplanted European aristocrat, was astonished that an American president's wife, dressed by an American, would become the most emulated fashion figure in the world. Cassini disclosed that Jackie, too, was surprised by the power she had over what women wore. Said the *Philadelphia Inquirer:* "She has been enshrined in fashion annals as America's most influential style-setter."

If Jackie was surprised by her influence, clothing manufacturers and retailers were not. They rooted hard for the election of Jack Kennedy in 1960, some contributing heavily to his campaign fund because they knew she would create an earthquake in their industry.

The trade knew that Pat Nixon, campaigning for her husband Richard, had bought five simple ready-to-wear dresses in one fast hour of shopping, guided only by whether they were conservative enough and how well they would pack. She would do nothing for their business. In contrast, Jackie gave interviews in her Georgetown home wearing chic purple Pucci slacks. Pat talked about homemaking as a practicing housewife with full credentials. Jackie couldn't make a bed, handle bills, iron anything, and she insisted on having her sheets changed after an afternoon nap. But she was hip, elegant, and loaded with "class."

The fashion businessmen were right. They made fortunes by rushing into production whatever Jackie was wearing.

One day a photograph of her appeared in *Women's Wear Daily.* She wore a skirt cut to three inches above the knees. Within weeks, women appeared in offices and at social events in the shorter skirts, later to be called miniskirts.

She was the pied piper who led women to wear pillbox hats, sunglasses atop their heads, and even to go to church bare-armed and bare-legged. Wrote Marilyn Bender: "All the arguments for adjusting one's hemline to one's physical dimensions and taming one's coiffure to the limits of one's age fell apart when Jacqueline Kennedy went girlish."

When a youthful hairdresser named Kenneth Battelle, then thirty-four, whom she had patronized for five years, came to Washington to set her hair for the inauguration, he suggested, and she approved, a daring bouffant style. Within days, women asked hair stylists across the nation for a change to the new fluffed-out hair.

It was hardly a coincidence that the models in newspaper advertisements were slender young women with broad smiles, widely spaced eyes, and hair that looked as though it had been blown up by bicycle pumps. Department stores on Fifth Avenue in New York, Michigan Avenue in Chicago, Rodeo Drive in Los Angeles, and the famous shopping streets in Rome and London featured models resembling Jacqueline Kennedy.

Women bought Jackie-type sunglasses by the millions. When she decided to wear clothes with belts, the sales graphs of the flagging belt industry shot sharply upward.

None of this came about haphazardly.

James Brady believes that Jackie's flawless sense of style was both inborn and honed and cultivated. She just *knew* what was right for her at an early age. When she was fourteen and a new student at Miss Porter's School for Girls in Farmington, Connecticut, she was told that the unofficial but rigidly followed uniform for students included a short mink coat and a white raincoat. Jackie wore neither, not out of stubborn rebellion, but because she simply did not like the look. Instead, she wore sheared beaver, and did not care what the other girls said or thought.

Later, at Vassar and thereafter, she became an avid student of fashion, eagerly reading magazines on the subject. She has also understood that dressing down can be even more important than dressing up at certain times. As first lady, she was never seen in a mink coat, though she owned several. On Inauguration Day in 1961, she sat between the outgoing president, Dwight D. Eisenhower, and Mrs. Lyndon B. Johnson, wife of the new vice-president, wearing a simple beige woolen coat with a tiny fur collar. In a week, cloth coats with narrow fur collars were being delivered to stores and sold as quickly as they arrived.

Jackie reportedly spends from seventy-five thousand up to one hundred thousand dollars annually on her wardrobe. It is a large amount of money to spend on clothes and sometimes triggers criticism by the press and public, not to mention her two husbands.

But look at the expenditure in another light. Jackie is

very rich.* Said James Brady: "First, I doubt strongly that her clothing bill is quite that high, but consider that she is Jackie and that she loves fine clothes, and original designs are extremely costly."

Of course, Jackie can, and certainly does, buy inexpensive things. She will pick up a thirty-dollar T-shirt that she likes, or pantyhose for less than twenty dollars, pajamas for under fifty or a hundred dollars. She shops at the Gap, a trendy clothing chain, which caters to middle-income and lower-income shoppers and sells stylish, good-quality clothes, where she will buy sweatpants (size small), a rayon vest (medium) or a pair of medium-size jeans for about seventy-five dollars, play shorts or a denim workshirt.

In the fine stores in New York, Los Angeles, Palm Beach, Paris, Milan, and other great fashion centers, a designer evening dress can cost between one thousand and ten thousand dollars—or more than double that if it is an exclusive creation. A dress of linen or silk for daytime wear is now priced from five hundred to one thousand dollars; shoes from $160 to $275 (if made of rare skin like crocodile skin, up to a thousand or more) according to a salesperson at Gucci, the exclusive Fifth Avenue shop. Undergarments, scarves, and other accessories can run into hundreds of dollars. At such prices it does not take a great deal of shopping to reach a high figure.

"Look at the major Hollywood stars or sports figures who earn millions a year," said fashion journalist Rosemary Kent. She added:

They buy luxury cars that cost eighty or ninety thousand dollars or more. Is that so outrageous when compared to their salaries?
Scaling Jackie's clothing costs down to a propor-

* See chapter 17 for a discussion of her wealth.

tion of her income makes sense. If a sports lover wants to spend five hundred dollars or higher to attend an event that will decide a championship, or a tycoon spends a hundred thousand for his daughter's wedding, takes his family on a world cruise for which he pays a huge sum, spends an enormous amount on a weekend party, *and he can afford the expense,* who has the right to say he cannot, or should not, or that he is too extravagant?

In the Camelot years, the criticism of Jackie's spending was justified. According to a survey by Charlotte Curtis of *The New York Times,* her expenditure of fifty thousand dollars for clothes in sixteen months after Jack Kennedy's election was about two-thirds of his income from the trust fund his father had set up for him and his other children.

Joe McCarthy, the author who had known the family since the early 1950s, told me. "The President blew a gasket. 'God,' he said, 'she's driving me crazy.' "

Early in JFK's term, Benjamin C. Bradlee, then Washington bureau chief of *Newsweek* magazine, came to the White House when the President "boiled" at a forty-thousand-dollar department store bill. Jackie, wide-eyed, was unable to explain the charge because, she said, she hadn't purchased any furnishings, nor a sable coat, "or anything." Kennedy groused to Bradlee: "This [the White House] is a place where a fellow should at least break even, with all the services provided."

In 1962, the president's personal fortune was $2.5 million after he had received three more trust funds. If he invested the entire capital in tax-free municipal bonds, which were then paying three percent for a twenty-year bond in New York, his annual income would have been only seventy-five thousand dollars. This, of course, was 1962 dollars, when a steak dinner was under five dollars in New York, a loaf of bread cost twenty cents, and a split-level in the suburbs could be had for about twenty-five thousand.

Still, Jackie's personal expenses were far too high for her husband's income, especially since he was donating his annual hundred-thousand-dollar salary to charity.

Kennedy, like any husband in a similar bind, not only complained loudly and often to his wife, with small success, but also tried to economize elsewhere. The United States government picked up the bill for state functions, but when private parties were given the president had to pay the costs himself.

JFK, who loved people and entertaining, soon discovered that parties were expensive indeed. After his inauguration, he received the bills for the first few months and, as Chief Usher West said, "went through the ceiling." Kennedy told West to buy food henceforth from a local market instead of an exclusive French merchant in Georgetown. Once, after he saw that champagne bottles were only half consumed after a private party, he told West that a new bottle must not be opened until a waiter brought an empty one to the pantry.

Never, during his entire short administration, was Jack Kennedy able to staunch the financial expenditures that could be traced to the first lady.

But none of this mattered to the public. People would experience her spending in their imaginations. As Marilyn Bender of *The New York Times* said: "The public does not begrudge their gods and goddesses their extravagances."

Even at sixty-five-plus, she continued to capture the public's fashion imagination. At age sixty, she was a cover girl for *Life, Vogue,* and *Vanity Fair.* "For thirty years she has been fashion dynamite, setting trends, breaking rules, and putting her stamp on American style," said the *Philadelphia Inquirer.* "And judging from the public's ongoing fascination, she will continue to do so."

3

Love Her, Love Her Not

While America made her into a virtual national monument before she was thirty-five, and while she has charmed heads of state from former Soviet Premier Nikita Khrushchev to France's Charles de Gaulle, from Cambodia's Prince Norodom Sihanouk to India's Jawaharlal Nehru, Jackie is not a beloved celebrity in the United States. She has never been revered like Mary Martin, Helen Hayes, or Judy Garland. She has inspired a broad spectrum of feelings that include admiration, envy, contempt, and anger—but not love.

Indeed, love is not an essential factor in determining the level of public fascination with celebrated persons. Consider Frank Sinatra, Madonna, and Fergie, the estranged wife of Prince Andrew of England, all of whose flaws have been extensively chronicled yet who remain objects of intense interest nonetheless.

Over the years Jackie has received many critical letters, even ugly ones. She has been accused of hauteur, a cavalier attitude toward people of lower social rank, cupidity, an obsession with clothes, pseudointellectualism, and of possessing a superambition as intense as that of the Kennedys themselves. Not least, she has been charged with flirting openly and outrageously with other women's men and, on occasion, appropriating them for herself.

Despite her beauty, exquisite taste, dignity, and courage in the face of calamity, her public approval rating has not been as high as that of others.

In the 1961 Gallup Poll, which asked respondents to name the women they most admire in any part of the world, Eleanor Roosevelt, widow of President Franklin D. Roosevelt, won first place. It was the thirteenth time she had led the polls since they began in 1947. Jackie placed second that year and was first from 1962 to 1966.

But since then she has never ranked higher than fifth, dropped to tenth in 1977 and 1979, and did not make the top ten at all in 1968, the year she married Aristotle Onassis. She was also out of the running in 1982 and 1984, and in subsequent years trailed behind Jeane Kirkpatrick, Jane Fonda, Barbara Walters, Oprah Winfrey, and Margaret Thatcher. In 1992, when the top four were Barbara Bush, Mother Teresa, Margaret Thatcher, and Hillary Clinton, she came in eighth.

Jackie fared dismally in another poll of "most admired" women, this one conducted by *Good Housekeeping* magazine. Not once has she ranked among the top ten since the poll began in 1969. Pat Nixon, Mamie Eisenhower, and Nancy Reagan, three other first ladies, won much higher ratings. Mrs. Nixon was in first place in 1973, '74, '75 and '77, was second to Betty Ford in 1978 and never dropped out of the first ten through 1987.

In 1981, Jackie placed twenty-eighth, beaten by her sister-in-law, Joan Kennedy, then in the process of divorcing Senator Edward M. Kennedy of Massachusetts. Joan placed twenty-first. In 1982, Jackie sank to number thirty-seven, topped by Rose Kennedy, her former mother-in-law, who was nineteenth. And in the 1993 poll, Barbara Bush was first, Mother Teresa second, Princess Diana third, while Jackie was far down the list.

Madame Tussaud's waxworks, a two-hundred-year-old exhibition of models of famous people, asks its visitors every year to vote on women they consider the most beautiful in the world. Jackie won in only one year, 1972, and was thereafter beaten by Sophia Loren, Raquel Welch, and Elizabeth Taylor, among others.

But these surveys leave nagging questions unanswered. If people do not universally approve of this Jackie, why do they dislike her, resent her, lament her lifestyle? Opinion, or quantitative studies, measure preferences but—a crucial point—not the reasons for those preferences.

Since neither the Gallup nor *Good Housekeeping* polls rating Jackie's popularity asked the question why, I enlisted the help of Bernard Engelhard & Associates, one of the country's leading focus group specialists, to find out how people feel about her, everything from her appearance and behavior to lifestyle, personality, and character.

The focus groups, developed as a marketing tool in the 1970s, target individuals the researchers want to reach, to explore their feelings on various aspects of an issue, product, or individual. Assured of anonymity, the group members can express their feelings freely.

Usually between seven and twelve people sit around a table and, in a relaxed, informal atmosphere, engage in a freewheeling discussion, led by an experienced leader. The respondents exchange ideas and explore issues and attitudes that might ordinarily go undetected by other types of approaches, such as quantitative research.

Engelhard conducted three separate focus group sessions on Jackie—in San Francisco, the San Fernando Valley, and New York—carefully choosing people representing a cross-section of middle America—teachers, plumbers, house painters, businessmen, personnel administrators, and others. Afterward, Engelhard studied the audiotapes of the proceedings and arrived at these findings:

- The vast majority of respondents held Jackie in high esteem because of how she has raised her children. There was virtually unanimous agreement that, although Caroline and John, Jr., were in the public spotlight even more than the twenty-seven other grandchildren of Joseph P. and Rose Kennedy, they haven't had any of the problems, some serious, that a large number of the others have had in their growing-up years.

• Most men thought that while Jackie was beautiful she lacked sex appeal.

• Everyone agreed that JFK was the archetypal unfaithful husband, but that Jackie had never strayed.

• Whether Jackie was ever in love with Jack was hotly debated, with inconclusive results. Half of all respondents believed she was, the other half felt just as strongly that she was never in love, even when she married him in September 1953.

• Most men and women expressed admiration for her because all through her life she has been an independent woman, remained strong in the face of tragedy, never sinking but always forging forward, knowing what she wanted and achieving it, and—important in the view of most—changing with the passing decades.

• Strong sentiment still persists that Jackie married Aristotle Onassis for his money and, to a lesser extent, power.

• The three most prevalent attributes that come to mind when her name is mentioned are, in this order: character, charisma, money.

The study results are significant for what they tell us about people's perceptions of Jackie.

But perceptions can be misleading. As we will see in later chapters, a number of these findings are correct, but because she has subsumed her thoughts and feelings throughout her life, the world has accepted as gospel "facts" about her that, in a large number of instances, are wildly inaccurate.

PART TWO

∞

One Brief Shining Moment

4

Young Jackie, Young Jack

The best times of Jackie's life were the 1,002 days she spent as the wife of John F. Kennedy and the mistress of the White House.

The worst was the 1,003rd.

At the age of thirty-one, she became the country's thirty-first first lady, the youngest except for Frances Folsom Cleveland, who married Grover Cleveland in the White House, and Julia Gardiner, the second wife of John Tyler, both of whom were twenty-one.

Jackie was born in Southampton, Long Island, New York, on July 28, 1929, the eldest of two daughters of John Vernou Bouvier III and Janet Lee Bouvier. She was a privileged, pretty child and a first-class brat.

By the time she had turned five, she had gone through governesses almost as fast as she had gone through diapers; none of them would put up with her. She was willful, stubborn, and intractable—the kind of child mothers adore for their beauty and charm and throw up their hands because of their orneriness.

"Oh, she'll grow out of it," her mother was told by her friends, but she didn't. After spending a year in a preschool program, she was enrolled in Miss Chapin's School in New York. She was classed as a problem child by her teachers. An early biographer wrote:

"She was an outlaw. She did everything that drives teachers mad: she stood up in class and mimicked other pupils and the teacher herself; she roamed around the room, annoyed other students, made faces and at one time pretended to vomit."

Her mother explained her mischief-making by saying that Jackie was too smart, and she may have been right. "Her brightness, almost precocity, made school too easy," Janet said. "She finished studying before her classmates and then found nothing but mischief to occupy her mind and energies."

Still, Janet was not prepared for the remark one of Jackie's classmates made one day when, volunteering as class mother, she watched over a group of Miss Chapin's students in a Central Park playground. Jackie was obstreperous—and Janet, in an offhand way, said to one of the children: "Isn't she a naughty girl?"

The child replied, "She's the worst kid in school. Jackie does something bad every day. She gets sent to Miss Stringfellow every day—well, almost every day."

Ethel Stringfellow, the formidable headmistress, cowed her students, except for Jacqueline Bouvier. That evening, Janet asked her daughter, then nine, "What does she say to you?"

Jackie replied, "Oh, lots of things. But I don't listen."

Her father, known as Black Jack because of his perennial tan, expected his baby daughter to be a mischief-maker, but her mother surely did not. Black Jack was ornery himself, a rounder, a lout, a roué, a gambler and womanizer; and because he adored his dark-eyed daughter, he did little to stop her from becoming a holy terror. As quiet and reserved as Black Jack was boisterous, Jackie's mother could not control her eldest daughter, and hardly did better with her younger one, Lee, born on March 3, 1933.

Janet Lee was rich, refined, and ambitious for social success. Jack Bouvier's forebears arrived in the colonies to fight for American independence with the Marquis de Lafayette, the French general and statesman who became a major general in George Washington's army. Janet's family was "new money." Her grandfather had been a poor Irish immigrant, like the Kennedys. He had settled in New York City. His son, James, a lawyer, speculated in real estate and built a great fortune, married a girl who was also of Irish immigrant stock. Janet Lee was their daughter. She counted on Jack Bouvier to introduce her into high society and, for a while, he did.

Black Jack's grandfather, Michael, was once many times a millionaire through real-estate and import interests in Philadelphia, but by the time Bouvier inherited the family wealth, it had declined to about $250,000, even though he continued to move in high society and spend lavishly. But Jackie had a home in Manhattan, a summer place in the Hamptons, horses to ride, and fine schools to attend.

However, in 1936, when Jackie was only eight, Janet had had enough. She left her husband, taking Jackie and Lee with her. Jack visited his daughters only on weekends, an arrangement he could not oppose because his fortunes, such as they were, were dwindling.

Janet had hoped that life in a lavish Manhattan apartment with servants and luxuries would suit Jackie and Lee admirably, but it did not. Actually, living with Janet, who insisted on propriety, was excruciatingly dull for both girls, but the weekends were deliriously happy. Jack Bouvier, at his most charming, took his daughters to the best toy stores and boutiques and bought them everything they wanted and could carry and had the rest sent. He dined with them in the swankiest places, took them to theaters, and everyone laughed a lot. How he managed to pay for the purchases was another matter. He ran up a considerable debt.

Predictably, when it came time to return to Janet's apartment, the laughter turned to sour looks and, too often, tears. The two days of bounty were over until the next weekend.

It was during these years, between the ages of eight and twelve, that Jackie learned a significant lesson. While she surely was not consciously aware of it at the time, the discovery she made was momentous. John H. Davis, a distant relative, encapsulated it best in his admirable story of the Kennedy family, *The Kennedys: Dynasty and Disaster, 1948–1983.* Jackie learned, he said, "that with a little charm and a little cunning, you could get almost anything you wanted out of a man."

A sharp, perceptive preteenager, Jackie was also well aware that Jack Bouvier had many girlfriends. He certainly made no secret of it. This knowledge did not lessen her adoration of her father. There were never any father-daughter quarrels, naturally enough, because he permitted her to do anything she wished; but Jackie and her mother squabbled almost continuously.

In 1940, Janet went to Nevada and obtained a divorce, the details of which were chronicled in the tabloids and which were devoured by Jackie, then eleven. Two years later, Janet married Hugh Dudley Auchincloss—"Hughdie" to his friends and his stepdaughters as well—a prosperous Washington broker. She took the girls to live with them at his Newport, Rhode Island, estate, Hammersmith Farm, and his Georgian manor house, Merrywood, on the Potomac River in Virginia, just outside Washington, D.C. Auchincloss, a staid and proper gentleman, could trace his social lineage back seven generations and was, of course, listed in the social register. Stephen Birmingham notes that the Astors had a mere two listings in the register, the Vanderbilts just eight, the Rockefellers forty-two, and the Auchinclosses forty-seven. Janet was delighted.

Meanwhile, Jack Bouvier could only afford a room now at the Westbury Hotel in Manhattan. Dejected and despairing, he drank more and more, and soon was drunk all day long.

Jackie's schooling continued to be very upper class. Between the ages of thirteen and fourteen, she went to a fashionable private school in the capital, Holton Arms. At fifteen, she was sent to the famous Miss Porter's School in Farmington, Connecticut, where she studied fine arts, became active in the drama society, worked as a reporter for the school newspaper, and spent as much time as she could caring for a horse Hughdie bought her, a mare she named Danseuse.

By then, Jackie was a lovely girl, the envy of her classmates because of the hordes of boys she attracted from neighboring schools and colleges. Her name appeared with increasing frequency in the society columns and, in 1947, the Hearst society columnist, Cholly Knickerbocker, whose real name was Igor Cassini, dubbed her Deb of the Year when, at the age of eighteen, she came out at the Clambake Club in Newport, a rambling wooden structure on Eaton Point overlooking Long Island Sound.

In 1947, she enrolled in Vassar College near Poughkeepsie, New York, where she studied Shakespeare and the history of religion, her tuition paid by Jack Bouvier from his ever-decreasing funds. Jack, who still adored her, was delighted she lived some fifty miles from the city and he visited often. Though already fifty-five, he still looked dashing, despite his continual drinking, and Jackie proudly showed him off to her friends at the college.

Europe beckoned. The following summer, she and three friends, Judith and Helen Bowdoin and Judith Bissell, toured the continent. In her junior year, she studied at the University of Grenoble in southeastern France and at the Sorbonne on the Left Bank in Paris, living with a French family part of the time. Returning to the United States, she decided not to complete her undergraduate studies at Vassar, and enrolled instead at George Washington University, where she graduated in 1951 with a bachelor of arts degree.

She was almost twenty-three, with no money of her own and no employable skills. Bouvier was broke and Auchincloss was leaving everything to his children by his previous marriage. She was devoted to the study of France, its language, history, and art, but finding work with those credentials would prove a daunting task. Hughdie opened a door for her at the *Washington Times Herald* by calling an old friend, Arthur Krock, the influential columnist of *The New York Times,* who persuaded the *Times Herald* to hire her as its inquiring "camera girl" at $42.50 a week.

And she did well, devising provocative questions. Wandering through antique stores, she asked owners if they had to make a choice, which single piece would they keep. She went to Capitol Hill to ask senators and representatives about current topics. She asked dental aides at a clinic which sex was braver when undergoing treatment. Shortly after the election of President Eisenhower in 1952, she interviewed two of his nieces, Mamie and Ellen Moore, asking their reactions. That story was published on the front page.

Soon after she got her job, Jackie became engaged to a young broker named John Husted, whom she had met in her senior year at George Washington University. Husted, who worked in New York, belonged to the social register. His affluent family lived in Washington and was acceptable in the eyes of Janet Auchincloss.

The courtship with John Husted soon ended. He could only see her in Washington on weekends, and in between they corresponded, but soon her letters became fewer and shorter. Husted suspected what was coming, and he was right.

One day, when he arrived in Washington, Jackie met him at the airport and quietly dropped the sapphire-and-diamond ring he had given her into his jacket pocket.

She was without a beau, but not for long. The next man who entered her life, and who would change its course, was the eldest surviving son of Rose and Joseph P. Kennedy.

At this time, John Fitzgerald Kennedy was a thirty-four-year-old congressman from the Eleventh Congressional District in Massachusetts. His flashing smile, unruly auburn hair that glinted orange in sunlight, his Irish charm and quick wit made him a favorite of Washington hostesses, especially since he was rich and unattached.

Girls fell for young John Kennedy, and he accepted all who did, but until then he had only been in love once.

Ten years before, at twenty-four, he had begun a relationship with a twenty-eight year old Danish journalist, a beautiful blonde named Inga Arvad. Some biographies of the late president gloss over his involvement with "Inga Binga," his pet name for her, but it was hardly a momentary interlude in his life. The affair lasted three years, during which he was deeply in love. Jack Kennedy never forgot Inga and what she had meant to him.

Jack met Inga in 1941 when he was stationed in Washington as an ensign in the Office of Naval Intelligence. The affair plunged him into a mess that almost got him thrown out of the Navy, which would have wrecked his career before it had started.

They lived together openly in the capital. At the time not only was Inga married to a Hungarian named Paul Fejos, but she was under surveillance by the Federal Bureau of Investigation, suspected of being a German spy. Reportedly she had close ties with high Nazi officials, had been a guest of Hermann Goering at the 1936 Summer Olympic Games in Berlin, and had been introduced to Adolf Hitler, who termed her "a perfect example of Nordic beauty."

Jack had seriously considered marrying Inga, which infuriated his father, who loudly pointed out that she was already married. Inga's phone was tapped by the FBI, which also placed bugs in every room of her apartment, thereby revealing her relationship to the young naval officer. Her affair with Jack was duly reported to the Office of Naval Intelligence.

Intelligence officers listening to the goings-on in Inga's apartment were treated to the sounds of the bed creaking, her moans of pleasure, and Jack's instructions on positions he wanted her to take during sex.

The information, duly typed up in sanitized Navalese, was forwarded to Captain Howard Klingman, assistant director of the Office of Naval Intelligence, who decided that Jack Kennedy should be discharged from the Navy forthwith. Joe, Sr., however, made some telephone calls to persons in high places and, on January 15, 1942, Jack was reassigned to the Sixth Naval District Headquarters in Charleston, South Carolina, where he instructed workers in the defense plants around the state on how to protect themselves against bombing attacks, a subject about which he knew almost nothing. He soon developed a stock answer to questions he could not answer. Looking earnestly at the questioner, he would say: "Now that's a good point. I'll have a specialist come down from Washington next week to explain it thoroughly."

Jack and Inga corresponded often, she writing much more frequently than he, but when he wrote, his letters were passionate declarations of love, and she responded with equal fervor. Her letters to him from Washington, on the stationery of the *Washington Times Herald,* where she worked as a reporter, are a tender admixture of love and poesy, plus a remarkable insight into Jack Kennedy's personality and character.

On January 28, 1942, a little more than a week after his transfer, she wrote:

> I think I will always know the right thing for you to do. Not because of brains. Not because of knowl-

edge. But because there are things deeper, more genuine—love, my dear.

Two months later, on March 11, she wrote to Jack:

You did want to ask me to come down this weekend, didn't you? It is not because I am stubborn that I am not going. My impulse is to throw everything overboard and get away. Not because I want you to make love to me and say charming things. Only because I wish more than anything to be with you when you are sick . . .

Once I said, "If you ever need me Jack, call me." It still holds good. It wasn't said in a flippant mood. It was really written with heartblood if that doesn't sound too drastic and repulsive. So, it stands. If ever I can ease you a pain, physical or mental, come to me, or I will go to you. It won't be a matter of petty pride. It won't be, "I can't go to you, but if you come to me, it is all right." Pride is fine. Too much spoils one's own and others lives. Please don't ever let pride ruin a friendship which started, which I hope wasn't ruined because you had me too easily. If you feel anything beautiful in your life—I am not talking about me—then don't hesitate to say so, don't hesitate to make the little bird sing. It costs so little; a word, a smile, a slight touch of a hand . . .

My dearest the very best to you including my love,

Binga.

Inga understood Jack Kennedy well, and was supremely confident that one day he would ascend to the top. In April 1942, she wrote:

Maybe your gravest mistake handsome . . . is that you admire brains more than heart, but then that is necessary to arrive. Heart never brought fame—except to Saints—nor money—except to the women of the oldest profession in the world, and that must be hard earned.

I can't wait to see you on top of the world. That is a very good reason why war should stop, so that it may give you a chance to show the world and yourself that here is a man of the future.

Should I die before you reach to the top step of the golden ladder, then Jack dear,—if there is a life after death, as you believe in—be I in heaven or hell, that is the moment when I shall stretch a hand out and try to keep you balancing on that—the most precarious of all steps . . .

Your Binga.

Joe Kennedy convinced Jack that marriage with Inga would be a dreadful mistake. Finally, the affair flickered out. Inga went to Hollywood, where she married Tim McCoy, the cowboy movie star. She died at the age of sixty in 1973, but all his life Jack Kennedy remembered his relationship with her as his first truly passionate involvement with a woman.*

In March, 1943, Kennedy finally got his wish, a chance at sea duty. Assigned to the Solomon Islands, he was given the command of a PT boat, a motorboat, the smallest vessel in the Navy. PT–109 has gone down in history as the ship that earned a future president the Navy and Marine Medals and the Purple Heart after it was rammed

---

* No evidence that Inga was disloyal to the United States ever came to light. Jack Kennedy learned years later that she had been under surveillance and never forgave those responsible, even after he was elected president. When he spoke at Harvard University's graduation ceremonies during his administration, he was introduced to an industrialist who had once been an FBI agent assigned to watch Inga. Jack knew his background. The man extended his hand but Kennedy ignored the gesture, leaning over to whisper: "You son of a bitch!"

on August 2, 1943, by a Japanese destroyer. Ensign Kennedy and ten of the twelve surviving crewmen clung to the wreckage until morning, when they swam to a nearby island, Kennedy towing one seaman five miles despite an injured back, which would plague him for the rest of his life. After back surgery at Chelsea Naval Hospital in Boston, Kennedy received a medical discharge from the service on March 16, 1945.

He ran for Congress the following year and won easily, defeating nine other candidates, and began eyeing a Senate seat.

After Inga, Jack concentrated on one-night stands, mostly with large-bosomed young women who heralded their availability. Jacqueline was nothing at all like the others. Her forehead was too high and sloped. Her eyes were too far apart, her neck too long, and in a low-cut gown her collarbones protruded unattractively. Her mouth was too wide, her bust was small even though augmented by padded brassieres, and her upper arms too bony. Her calves were thin and the legs slightly bowed. She stood five feet seven and one-half inches and her feet, size ten and one-half, were exceptionally large even for a fairly tall woman.

Yet by some curious alchemy, the sum was more attractive by far than the parts. They all came together in the body of an enchantingly beautiful woman.

Jack was intrigued.

He knew at once that Jacqueline Bouvier was not someone who could be forgotten in a few hours or, at the latest, by morning, but a woman of refinement with an enigmatic personality that was, for him, new and exciting.

They met in a time-honored way—through a fix-up.

Charles Bartlett, a columnist for the *Chattanooga Times,* and his wife Sylvia believed that Jack Kennedy and Jackie would be well suited for each other. They gave a small dinner party at their Georgetown home May 8, 1952. Jack was thirty-five, Jackie, twenty-three.

Bartlett recalled, "I walked her out to the car and Jack Kennedy came sort of trailing after and he was muttering shyly, 'Can we go someplace and have a drink?' But Jackie knew that one of the other guests was waiting in the car for her, so she declined Jack's invitation."

He phoned the next week and she accepted a dinner date. A courtship of sorts began, with a tougher obstacle than the one with John Husted. Jack, then running for the Senate, could spend far less time in Washington and he had to travel extensively. Still, there were numerous telephone calls and, on his infrequent return to the capital, cozy dinners at suburban restaurants, strolls along the streets of Georgetown, and hand-holding at the movies. Nobody paid much attention; Washington was full of pretty young girls and handsome young men on dates.

After Jack defeated incumbent Henry Cabot Lodge by 70,737 votes in 1952, Jack and Jackie saw each other more and more frequently.

He doesn't remember when the romance became serious and neither does anyone else. But he did enjoy the good times with her. Once she called and said she wanted to interview him for her column on senatorial pages. Because of his youthful appearance, Kennedy was often mistaken for one, and they had a grand time bantering about the problem. He told her that, a short while before, he had tried to board the subway car that shuttled all day long between the Senate Office Building and the Capitol, a journey of only a few minutes. It's free to tourists as well as officials. When Kennedy stepped forward to get on the car, a guard stuck out a beefy arm, saying: "Just a minute, young fellow. Let the senators go first." Kennedy also told Jackie that it mightn't be a bad idea if pages and senators switched jobs.

Jackie was John Kennedy's date to President Eisenhower's inaugural ball in January 1953; and before spring the young senator found himself in love for the second time in his life.

5

The Truth About the Marriage

Myths and misconceptions have surrounded the marriage of Jack and Jackie Kennedy to such an extent that the truth has been all but obscured.

It is *not* true that their marriage had been shredded beyond any hope of repair when they flew to Dallas in November 1963.

It is *not* true that Jackie had been smiling for the camera during most of the Camelot years to keep alive an illusion that America was being led by a happily married president and a first lady who were parents of two adorable children.

It is *not* true that Jack Kennedy, a world-class womanizer, was so self-involved in satisfying his sexual needs that he was unable to make a serious commitment to a permanent relationship with the woman he married.

It is *not* true that Jack Kennedy resented his wife's independence and her desire to go her own way rather than submit to his.

And, perhaps most important, it is *not* true that her husband's womanizing destroyed Jacqueline Kennedy's love for him.

Evidence follows, but first, details of the courtship and marriage.

* * *

Four months after Jack was sworn in as the junior senator from Massachusetts, Jackie, promoted to reporter, was assigned to cover the coronation of Queen Elizabeth II in London because her editor felt her social connections could generate good inside stories.

Not many men propose by transatlantic telephone, but Jack Kennedy did in May 1953. The call was marred by static but was just clear enough for Jackie to hear that he wanted to marry her and for him to hear her acceptance. They were officially engaged in June that year.

They obtained a marriage license at the Newport City Hall on September 3 and a striking photograph of the couple appeared in many newspapers, Jackie in a summer print with a fitted bodice, Jack in a sports jacket, shirt, and tie. Below the waist, however, he wore shorts. The jacket and tie were loaned to him by the photographer after Jack refused to pose, explaining it would not be proper for a United States senator to be snapped in such informal attire. The photographer was careful to take the picture from Jack's waist up.

Jack's bachelor party at the Clambake Club in Newport turned into a raucous affair, ruefully recalled by Hugh Auchincloss for the costliness of smashed stemware he had to replace. Before the dinner of boiled lobster, clams casino, clam chowder, and cornbread, all Jack's favorites, his friend Paul (Red) Fay, later assistant secretary of the navy in his administration, proposed a royal toast, which traditionally called for the emptied glasses to be smashed, never to be used again.

The toast was given, the champagne drunk, and the glasses were tossed against the brick-and-stone fireplace. Auchincloss, counting the two dozen crystal pieces he would have to replace, ordered the waiters to bring another set. Jack rose again, announcing that Mr. Auchincloss's stepdaughter was the most beautiful girl he had ever known and insisting that another royal toast must be drunk to her. It was, and again the stemware was shattered.

So was Hugh's patience. "Bring some plain water glasses," he told the waiters.

At the celebrity-studded wedding on September 12, 1953, at St. Mary's Roman Catholic Church in Newport, Hugh gave the bride away. Black Jack Bouvier, who had arrived in Newport the night before, was too drunk to appear. He had begun drinking the previous evening at the Viking Hotel, and by ceremony time was found lying across his bed in a drunken stupor.

After a two-week honeymoon in Acapulco, Mexico, the couple lived for two years in several rental apartments in Georgetown, a mile from downtown Washington. Jackie signed up for history courses at Georgetown University, and Jack, under her tutelage, began to paint as a hobby. Their home lives were uneventful; when there were no social engagements, they filled a scrapbook with clippings about themselves, went to the movies, where they stood in line to buy tickets, and, occasionally, flew to New York to see a Broadway show.

They wanted a large house where they hoped to raise a family. Jack and Jackie searched the Virginia countryside. In 1955, they found an estate on six and one-half acres of rolling pastureland not far from the Potomac River and only some thirty minutes from downtown Washington. This was Hickory Hill, at Number 1147 Chain Bridge Road above the small town of McLean. It later would be sold to Ethel and Robert and become, after the White House, the second best known place in America during the New Frontier years. A fine old Georgian house, it was rich in history. In the early years of the Civil War it had been the headquarters of Gen. George McClellan, then commander of the Union Army. Kennedy paid $125,000 for the estate and spent a large sum renovating it.

Jackie became pregnant in the spring of 1956, a few months before the August opening of the Democratic

Convention in Chicago. Young Senator John Kennedy, only thirty-nine, stood high on the short list of hopefuls for the vice presidential nomination. He eventually lost to Senator Estes Kefauver of Tennessee, who ran with Adlai Stevenson at the top of the ticket; Dwight D. Eisenhower and Richard Nixon defeated them easily in November.

Exhausted after the hectic politicking, they agreed to separate for a short while; Jack would fly to the French Riviera for a brief rest and Jackie would go to Newport to await the arrival of the baby, due in September, at Hammersmith Farm, the home of her mother and stepfather.

On August 23, Jackie began hemorrhaging and was rushed to Newport Hospital where an emergency caesarian was performed. The baby, a girl, was born dead.

Jack had been sailing on a yacht in the Mediterranean Sea, with his pal George Smathers, with no radiotelephone. He didn't hear about the tragedy until he docked. He flew home to be at her side, and when she had recovered, returned with her to Hickory Hill.

Jackie entered the house and, followed by Jack, went directly to the large, sunlit nursery. The walls had been beautifully decorated for the infant's arrival and there was a ribboned canopied crib in a corner. Glancing at it, she turned away and sobbed uncontrollably in Jack's arms.

Unable to remain in the house where her dreams of rearing a family had exploded, depressed by the bigness and loneliness of the home and grounds, she wanted to return to Georgetown. Jack sold Hickory Hill to Bobby and Ethel, who by then had five children, for the $125,000 he had paid originally, and he and Jackie moved into a small furnished house at 2808 P Street.

Jackie loved the little house, filling it with her own personal touches; eighteenth-century furniture, which she adored, and framed drawings she had collected. She didn't want a home so elegant that she would have to tell children, "don't touch," but a house where her politician-husband could be comfortable. She said, "While there are lots of little things around [i.e.: decorative objects] there are also big chairs and the tables every politician needs next to his chair, where he can put papers, coffee cups, and ashtrays. So it's a little bit of everything."

Caroline was born on November 27, 1957, while the Kennedys were living in the P Street house. Everything went well, and Jack and Jackie, like most new parents, were proud and happy.

Three years later, Jackie had a more difficult time with her next baby. John, Jr., was born November 25, 1960, just seventeen days after his father had been elected president of the United States. Once again, Jackie, eight months pregnant on Election Day, had begun hemorrhaging, and she was rushed to Georgetown University Hospital. The new president had just landed in Palm Beach, where he and aides were to confer on the transition and cabinet appointments.

Word came that Jackie was in the hospital. Kennedy and his staff boarded a plane and took off for Washington. At 12:22 A.M., while the plane was flying over Virginia, he received word that he had become the father of a healthy six-pound, three-ounce baby boy. The U.S. Census Bureau heralded the arrival with the announcement that America's population had risen to 182,000,267. The Internal Revenue Service sent out a press release that John F. Kennedy would now be entitled to an additional tax deduction of six hundred dollars a year. Of somewhat more interest to historians was the fact that John F. Kennedy, Jr., was the first baby to be born to a President-elect and his wife.*

---

* Soon after the inauguration, after a long search, the president and Jackie found what they considered an ideal weekend retreat. Called Glen Ora, it was a four-hundred-acre estate in the midst of the rolling Virginia hunt country near Middleburg, to the west of Washington and only about an hour's drive away. It afforded peace, privacy, charm, and plenty of space in which Caroline could romp. They signed a lease.

* * *

Was it indeed a bad marriage?

Books and magazine articles have labeled the union a sham, even a disaster. It was a marriage of convenience to both parties, said Kitty Kelley, in her 1978 "exposé" *Jackie Oh!* Stephen Birmingham, in his biography the same year, declared that less than two years after their marriage Jackie might have begun to wonder if he had wanted a wife "mostly as decoration" and the "touch of class" she could provide.

After they entered the White House, Birmingham said, "The marriage had become, by now, little more than a mutual convenience. . . . Any romantic love that might have existed between them had long since evaporated . . . and all that was left was a need to put the best public face on things."

C. David Heymann, in his biography, *A Woman Named Jackie,* refers frequently to their domestic "hostilities" and the game of one-upmanship they played, seeking to make the other jealous by flirting openly, behavior that is a clear sign of an unhealthy union.

Indeed, there were strains. They quarreled about her spending habits, her associations with gay men, whom he despised; her preoccupation with redecorating the White

---

Much had to be done to get the large stucco house ready for a presidential tenant. New carpeting was laid, furniture reupholstered or changed, rooms were painted and papered, and curtains were hung. By late February, the place was ready and the Kennedys came down for their first weekend.

When John Kennedy met his landlord for the first time, he committed a gaffe. Upon his introduction to Gladys Tartiere, who had purchased Glen Ora with her late husband, Raymond, two decades before, he remarked, "Your house cost me a lot of money."

Mrs. Tartiere was astonished and annoyed. A year later, Clark Clifford, Jack's personal lawyer, told Mrs. Tartiere that the president might want to renew his lease on the property and even purchase it eventually.

According to Mary Van Rensselaer Thayer, Jackie's lifelong friend, Gladys Tartiere turned him down.

House. She disliked being confined to the Executive Mansion for long periods, told him so and, he felt, fled too often and for too long, to Hyannis Port, Europe, and India. There were times when she was away so much that the media coined the phrase: "Good night, Mrs. Kennedy, wherever you are," a spoof of the comedian Jimmy Durante's farewell to his audience at the end of his TV shows: "Good night, Mrs. Calabash, wherever you are." Jack Kennedy fumed and laced into her upon her return.

When Jackie accepted an invitation for a lengthy cruise aboard Aristotle Onassis's palatial yacht, the *Christina,* the reporters sent accounts of her ultraluxurious vacation. Jack called her by radiotelephone and angrily yelled: "I know you're on the high seas, and I don't care how you get off that yacht, but get off!" When Jackie wanted to know how she was expected to leave the vessel while it was in the middle of the Aegean Sea, Jack retorted: "Jackie, you're a good swimmer."

These and other marital spats are, of course, titillating, but the disagreements between the two have been sensationalized far out of their true significance in their relationship.

As a Kennedy family chronicler, I have heard and read them all, plus others that have not been recorded by the media. But many, if not most, quote persons who overheard what he said to her and what she said to him, often colored by the listeners' interpretation of the decibel count of their voices and the degree to which their faces were inflamed by anger.

Assuming the accounts to be accurate and that the comments were recalled correctly—a big assumption—does that mean the marriage had gone irreparably bad?

Jackie was more independent that the other Kennedy wives and women. Was this quality a marital flaw, as some have suggested?

What must be understood is that a new concept of marriage was spreading throughout the nation. The sexual revolution, which would have a seismic impact in the 1970s and 1980s, had already started by the late 1950s, bringing with it an altered moral climate that would markedly lessen society's disapproval of live-in relationships outside of marriage, single motherhood, and other taboos.

Women like Jackie were beginning to develop strong desires for freedom, for the right to express themselves as individuals, spurred in part by Betty Friedan's landmark book, *The Feminine Mystique,* published in 1963.

John Kennedy understood rebelliousness. He himself parted ideological company with his father before he was twenty. "He knew in his gut that Jackie, a free spirit, could not be tamed to behave like the other Kennedy wives and women," said George Smathers, who knew them both well. Even Robert Kennedy, who wanted a wife at home and not on a career path, acknowledged her independence. "Jackie always kept her own identity," he said.

Was it, in part, a marriage of convenience? No argument here. Jack Kennedy was very conscious of the asset that the beautiful and cultured Jacqueline would be to his rising career. And there is hardly any doubt that Jackie was well aware that he was the catch of the decade. Her own two families, the Bouviers and the Auchinclosses, may have had deeper roots in high society, but Black Jack had dissipated his fortune and her stepfather, Hugh, could not match Joe Kennedy's wealth.

But to cite the "marriage of convenience" argument as evidence that the union was a hollow one, and to ignore the other elements is sophistry. It is illogical to claim that romance cannot blossom and bloom between two people who are aware of what the other can contribute to a marriage. After all, this was not an Old World, prearranged choice of mates who had never set eyes on each other. It was a marriage of two people who met, parted, met again and, after a while, fell in love.

The infidelity factor could be the most potent argument advanced as proof that the marriage failed.

But this may be the most astonishing fact of all: It was not.

It would be foolish, of course, to state that Jackie accepted her husband's incorrigible womanizing as a mere breach of etiquette.

She hated it. And she let him know that she was perfectly aware of what he was doing, and even where.

One story that appears in virtually every biography asserts that by 1958 the marriage had crumbled so badly that the patriarch Joseph P. Kennedy offered Jackie a million dollars if she would not divorce his son. (Jackie, having heard the story, confronted Joe at the Big House in Hyannis Port. "Cheapskate," she reportedly teased him.)

This incident has never been documented. And even though writers have been careful enough to say that Joe's offer was only a "report," it has appeared so many times and in so many places that most people have accepted it as fact.

The only "fact" is that it never happened.*

Scarcely naive, Jackie knew about John Kennedy's infidelities. Once, while escorting an Italian journalist named Benno Graziani around the mansion, she pointed to two young secretaries and said: "Those are my husband's lovers." She knew that when Jack disappeared from a reception, and an attractive guest exited very soon afterward, that he wasn't going to the Oval Office to study state papers. She knew about his affairs with movie queens Jayne Mansfield and Marilyn Monroe. Frequently, ac-

---

* After decades of writing about the doings and undoings of the Kennedys, I have noted that when an item is described in one book and stated as "fact," various journalists, historians, biographers, and assorted other writers pick it up and duly cite it in their notes and documentation as "fact."

cording to Patricia Seaton Lawford, Peter's third and last wife, Jackie would answer the telephone in the upstairs family quarters to find that Marilyn was on the line from Hollywood to speak to Jack. It didn't take Jackie long to figure out that her husband had given Marilyn his private number. She would hand the phone to Jack, who would, in her presence, chat with the movie star.*

Jack, cautious in his approach to weighty matters such as civil rights, was indiscreet in his own home. The nude swimming parties he gave from time to time in the White House pool, attended by close friends and at least one girl for each, are legendary. Trusted aides would make the arrangements for times when Jackie was away for the weekend. A frosted glass door to the pool was installed so that passersby could not see the goings-on.

One day, while a party was in full swing in the pool and upstairs, the White House sounded the alarm. Traphes Bryant, the White House kennel keeper, was in the mansion. He found himself in the midst of a Georges Feydeau farce, with naked men and women scurrying through corridors and in and out of doors.

Mr. Bryant is now dead, but Frances Spatz Leighton, who cowrote his memoirs, *Dog Days at the White House,* said that while Jackie never actually saw the action, she strongly suspected what Jack was up to in the White House during her absence. "She would find hair pins and bobby pins in his bedroom and, of all things, a radio under his bed." Apparently, Jack liked sex with musical accompaniment.

One afternoon she found a woman's undergarment beneath a pillow in his bedroom.* She removed it, held it

---

* In his 1993 book, *Marilyn Monroe: The Biography,* author Daniel Spoto disputes the oft-repeated assertion that the star and the president had a lengthy love affair, saying that they had but one sexual encounter. Anthony Summers, Dr. Thomas C. Reeves, C. David Heymann, and others, claim there were many more.

* The Kennedys slept in separate bedrooms.

between her thumb and forefinger and told the startled president, who was reading in the family room outside, "Would you please shop around and see who these belong to. They're not my size."

Whether Jackie knew about one of her husband's most notorious affairs is unknown. This romantic interlude involved Mary Pinchot Meyer, sister of Tony, then Ben Bradlee's wife. Jack had known Mary since his school days but, said Carol Felsenthal, "their affair did not blossom until January 1962," and was conducted mostly in the White House during Jackie's absence. Mary had been divorced from Cord Meyer, Jr., a former military aide of Harold Stassen, governor of Minnesota, later a founder of the United World Federalists. Mary had a distinguished ancestry: Gifford Pinchot, a great uncle, founded the Yale School of Forestry and was twice governor of Pennsylvania, from 1923 to 1927 and again from 1931 to 1935. She was also beautiful and rich. In October 1964, the body of Mary Meyer, then forty-three, was found on the Chesapeake and Ohio towpath in Georgetown. She had been murdered. The crime has never been solved.

That Jack Kennedy, for some reason buried deep in his psyche, had a need for sexual experience with women outside of his marriage, and that he satisfied this need, is indisputable.

That Jack did his womanizing flagrantly, often crudely, is unarguable.

His father, Joe, told his sons that "if there's something on your plate, take it"—referring to the availability of women—and he showed by personal example that such behavior was perfectly acceptable.

Blame the credo of one of the most celebrated, yet dysfunctional, families that this country has produced—a family whose patriarch made his own rules about morality, who gauged his manliness by the quantity of his conquests, rarely by the quality of a relationship.

Blame the arrogance of Kennedy males, who believe

the family can do no wrong and the public will continue to adore them and elect them to high office.

What *is* important is how Jackie looked upon her husband's skirt chasing.

She accepted Jack's infidelities as a significant percentage of today's parents have been forced by changes in the moral codes to accept their children's live-in arrangements with boyfriends and girlfriends.

For Jackie, understanding and acceptance came earlier than for most. In 1951, when she was still an undergraduate at George Washington University, she entered a contest sponsored by *Vogue* magazine. Entrants were required to write dissertations on high fashion, plus an essay on the topic, "People I Wish I Had Known." Jackie wrote on Charles Baudelaire, the French poet; Sergei Diaghilev, the Russian ballet impresario; and Oscar Wilde, the British playwright, novelist, and wit. In her essay on Wilde, she quoted this epigram: "The only difference between a saint and a sinner is that every saint has a past and every sinner has a future."*

Mary Lynn Kotz, who cowrote West's memoirs, *Upstairs at the White House,* revealed information that she had not included in the chief usher's book.

"Mr. West told me," Ms. Kotz said,

that Jackie was in love with President Kennedy the entire time. He was closer to the first lady than any other person in the White House. He saw her countless times during the day, received all kinds of notes from her, some with funny little drawings. She confided in him and he saw them together in private moments. There was no doubt in his mind that the

* Jackie won, beating out 1,279 other entrants, but she declined the prize, which was first a six-month trip to Paris and then a six-month internship at the magazine.

rumors, then and afterward, that the marriage had deteriorated, were totally untrue.

Mr. West told me that Jackie made a great effort to be a good wife. She worked hard to create an atmosphere that would help him relax from his arduous duties. She played the kind of soft music she knew he liked, insisted they have quiet, restful dinners, sometimes alone, sometimes with old and close friends.

She also saw to it that he had time with his children, whom he adored, giving them naps so that they would be able to stay up later to see him when he returned from the Oval Office.

During their marriage, she made it plain that she could ignore her husband's roving eye.

"I don't think there are any men who are faithful to their wives," she said. "Men are such a combination of good and evil."

She had been brought up to believe this. From her earliest years, Black Jack Bouvier, her father, had told her there was nothing wrong with loving a man who sleeps with other women. Indeed, when Bouvier and Jack Kennedy met for the first time, Jackie said, "they talked about sports, politics—and women." These, she declared, were subjects that "all red-blooded men like to talk about."

According to Frances Leighton, who also spent a year with Jackie's private secretary, Mary Gallagher, coauthoring her memoirs, "Of course, Mary never spoke about it and we did not say it in the book, but it was plain to me from my long interviews that Jackie was sophisticated enough to rise above the husband's infidelity. Marital straying was a way of life in her set. She knew it, and she accepted it."

White House aides saw and heard no evidence of a failing marriage. Traphes Bryant's anecdotes of sexual goings-on were given wide publicity, but his observations of Jack and Jackie's intimate moments were not. "They both loved their kids," he said, "and, I think, each other, very much. They were always looking out for each other, sometimes protectively, sometimes trying to think up little surprises." The two were seen strolling around the White House grounds, hand in hand, in all sorts of weather, sometimes walking one or two of the dogs.

A heartbreaking event in the summer of 1963 drew the Kennedys even closer together.

Jackie and Caroline and John were at their rented home on Squaw Island in Hyannis Port, a mile across the causeway from the compound. Jackie was pregnant with her third child, who was not expected for almost two months. But at 11 A.M., on August 7, while she was in Osterville, seven miles away, with Caroline and John, she felt pains and, after asking a Secret Service man to call her obstetrician, began driving back to the house.

Dr. John Walsh, who had been vacationing at the Cape, met Jackie at Squaw Island and, following an examination, advised her to fly by helicopter to Otis Air Force Base near Falmouth on Cape Cod, where a fully equipped four-room suite had been made ready for her.

At Otis, a caesarian was performed, and Jackie gave birth to a boy who weighed only four pounds, ten and one-half ounces.

The president had been informed and was airborne when a radio call gave him the news. He grinned broadly.

But only a few hours after the baby was born, doctors noted that he was having trouble breathing; he was suffering from hyaline membrane disease, or respiratory distress syndrome, which can occur in premature infants with insufficiently developed lungs. At that time, the disease proved fatal to between twenty-five thousand and thirty-thousand babies every year, a mortality rate of 75 percent.

The baby boy, who had been named Patrick Bouvier Kennedy, lived only thirty-nine hours.*

A letter from Jackie, doubtless expressing her love, is buried with her slain husband at Arlington. After Jackie flew back from Dallas on *Air Force One* with his body, she wrote the lengthy letter to him following her arrival at the White House. Next day, she asked Caroline, then six, to write a message to her daddy, telling of her love for him and what he had meant to her. Even young John, only three, solemnly scribbled some marks on a page because his mother had said it was his message to his father.

The contents of Jackie's letter have not been revealed, nor will they be. The treasured gifts in the casket of the president at Arlington National Cemetery must reflect the deep love Jackie bore him.

Then, shortly after noon, she went downstairs to the East Room where the president lay in a flag-draped casket. Brigadier General Godfrey McHugh, Air Force aide to the president, apprised of Jackie's intention to place something inside the coffin, opened the top and folded it back. With Robert Kennedy next to her, Jackie knelt and placed inside the three sealed letters, a pair of gold cuff links she had given him before their marriage, and another gift she knew he loved and had placed on his desk, a carved whale's tooth, or scrimshaw. She also took something—a lock of his hair.

There is also this poignant story:

On November 29, a week after the murder of the president, the journalist Theodore A. White sat with Jackie at her Hyannis Port home, listening to her anguished story of what had happened that fateful day and how she felt about her husband. (It was during this interview that Jackie, sitting on a small sofa and clad in a beige sweater

---

* Today better treatment methods, involving the use of carefully measured concentrations of oxygen and intravenous fluids, have reduced the mortality rate sharply to about 25 percent.

and black-trimmed slacks, asked Teddy White, when he wrote his story for Life magazine, to call the thousand days of JFK's administration "Camelot.")

What emerged from that four-hour talk with unmistakable clarity was not just Jackie's grief and anguish, not just her wish to spare her husband from being analyzed by historians who would write about him coldly and impassionately, but her desire to have him remembered as a father and a husband, a living being who knew love of wife and family and children.

Over and over, she pleaded with Teddy White, "Don't leave him to bitter old men to write about."

Were they madly, passionately, hopelessly in love? As with many couples, the heat of romantic love had simmered down as they passed the "seven-year itch" on September 12, 1960. They had arrived at the point where they had discovered one another's flaws and understood and accepted them. In short, they were, along with most other couples, settled, married folks.

There was passion still in their relationship, all who knew them well have asserted, and absent a videocamera in their bedroom, one must believe these friends. But sex was not everything any longer. "Love implies . . . the esteem and recognition of another individual as a separate personality," wrote Dr. Percival M. Symonds, formerly of Teachers College, Columbia University.

The bottom line is that Jack and Jackie were comfortable with each other, enjoyed each other's company, were devoted to and contented with each other, which is as good a definition of married love as one can find.

6

Jackie and Politics

People have come to believe Jacqueline Kennedy Onassis always despised politics and politicians and was far more concerned with fashion, social life, and the jet-set celebrity world.

A distinction must be made between disliking the *atmosphere* of politics and its *substance*. Certainly she hated the way her homes looked during and after a political meeting: papers strewn all over, cigar and cigarette ashes on the tables and floor, smoke sweeping into the fabric of her sofas and chairs, glasses and half-empty coffee cups everywhere.

She fervently disliked her husband's too-frequent absences from home to meet with political leaders around the country.

She had little use for such JFK cronies as Torbert MacDonald, a Harvard classmate; Lem Billings; and Paul B. (Red) Fay, an old Navy friend who served with Jack in the Solomon Islands during World War II. She rolled her eyes heavenward when Jack, leaving the house one morning, said that he had invited some forty people to lunch— that day! Author Ralph G. Martin said that at dinner parties Jack Kennedy would always steer the conversation to politics, "and politics bored Jacqueline into nearly total silence."

But the strategy employed by political hopefuls seeking to be elected to office, and what the political process could accomplish, did not bore Jackie at all.

She was not like Eleanor Roosevelt, whose political activity made her the most controversial first lady of all who had preceded her, who spoke her mind at her weekly press conferences, and who served in her later years as a delegate to the United Nations and chaired its Human Rights Commission. She was not like Rosalynn Carter, who sat in on her husband Jimmy's cabinet meetings, nor was she as immersed in politics as is Hillary Rodham Clinton.

But never, at any time in her marriage to John Kennedy, did she turn her back on politics or ignore what a politician could do.

In 1958, Dave Powers said, Jackie campaigned for her husband's reelection to the Senate "in every single district of Massachusetts, from Cape Cod to the Berkshires." A novice at delivering speeches, she approached her first one with high anxiety, especially since she was to deliver it in French to the Worcester Cercle Français. But after only a few moments, she confessed that public speaking in French "was not as frightening as it would have been in English."

However, when she did speak in English, the people loved her. She explained compellingly why Jack Kennedy would make a great senator, and with an endearing naïveté that enraptured the audiences.

During Jack Kennedy's Senate years, Jackie attended many hearings of the African subcommittee of the Foreign Relations Committee of which he was a member. Back home, she did not hesitate to voice her views on the McCarran Immigration Act, sponsored by Patrick McCarran, the Democratic senator from Nevada, which would place harsh limitations on immigration. Jackie bristled with indignation. She told Jack that under tight immigration policies her own family, the Bouviers, who had come to the United States from France, and the Kennedys themselves, immigrants from Ireland, might not have been allowed to enter the country.

In 1959, the historian Arthur Schlesinger, Jr., who was closer to the Kennedys than was any other historian or biographer, was invited to dinner at the compound. He had met Jackie a few times before but had only chatted with her briefly, not long enough to form any opinion about her except that she was exceptionally attractive and personally charming.

But on that mid-July evening, he said, after a long and leisurely talk with her, he came to realize that "underneath a veil of lovely inconsequence, she concealed a tremendous awareness, an all-seeing eye and a ruthless judgment."

Schlesinger declared that the widely accepted notion that Jackie had no interest in politics arose because Jackie herself pretended to have a "total ignorance" of the subject, and, additionally, would "impose a social ban on politicians."

Actually, said Schlesinger, she retreated into this world of disinterest as a means of preserving her own identity in the Kennedy family, whose aggressive athleticism she knew she could not match and because she feared she would not be able to hold her own in the often loud and rambunctious political discussions.

During their courtship, Jack had asked her to translate about a dozen French books dealing with Indochina, a task that took an entire summer and provided him with considerable information about how France viewed the conflict in Southeast Asia. In the Senate years, she was an invaluable speechwriting aide, going over his talks, eliminating some material and suggesting additions; Jack approved of most of her editorial changes.

According to Charles Bartlett, the journalist at whose dinner party Jack and Jackie had first met: "It's possible to love a politician without loving politics, but it's impossible to marry one without becoming part of his career." Bartlett added that it was surely not possible to be close to JFK without absorbing politics by osmosis.

In the race for the presidential nomination in 1960, Jackie astounded Jack Kennedy not only by her campaigning skills, but with the compassion she so clearly showed to the people left behind by the march of progress. In West Virginia, she insisted on going into the areas hardest hit by poverty. The elegant, artistic, well-bred young woman went to the miners' shacks and talked to the wives and children. One woman put it best after she had left: "That woman cares, she really *cares.*"

What she saw and heard in West Virginia was an epiphany for Jackie. The poverty affected her more than the conditions she had witnessed in India. She wrote to a friend, "Maybe I just didn't realize it existed in the U.S."

In Wisconsin one day, Jack received a call to rush back to vote on civil-rights legislation. Jackie, unfazed, made all his scheduled speeches, and in between she insisted on touring dairy farms, asking such knowledgeable questions that the farmers were convinced she had been raised on a farm.

Jackie remained home a great deal of the time during the campaign, giving rise to criticism, repeated even now in books and articles, that she disliked the race for office. In truth, Jackie was pregnant when her husband was nominated and, considering her history of miscarriage, her doctors had ordered her to rest as much as she could.

She disobeyed too often, though, turning up at many rallies. Early in the race, she delivered a graceful talk to newspersons, afterward inviting them to her home at the Hyannis Port compound where, she said, she would answer any and all questions. They came and she did.

One of the points she stressed was the subject of her wardrobe. Yes, she said, she liked to look good. Yes, she admitted frankly, she paid a great deal of attention to her hairdo. But, she added, wasn't that a woman's right?

Moreover, what was the connection between the way she dressed and looked and Jack Kennedy's ability to run the country?

In bed, she studied Jack's schedule of campaign appearances and her logical mind saw serious mistakes that could cost him money and energy. "You can get from City A to City B and then to City C a whole lot faster without detouring hundreds of miles to speak at Cities D and E," she explained. Jack, who had never paid attention to his schedule but went where he was told, agreed that Jackie was making an important point. He called Robert Wallace, his aide in charge of setting up his campaign itinerary, and instructed him to streamline the schedule as Jackie had suggested.

Jackie began writing a syndicated newspaper column from home called "Campaign Wife" in which she explained her views on issues from teachers' salaries ("more teachers must be trained and must be paid for") to the critical importance of health care for the elderly. In the latter column she argued that the problem affects not only older persons, as many might believe, but younger people as well. She wrote that they must face the agonizing choice between spending their limited resources for the education of their children and the care of their elderly parents. The solution, she argued, was care for the elderly, paid for by the government. She called for more classrooms and better schools, making it clear that the U.S. must assist local governments in improving the quality of education.*

Said author Carl Sferrazza Anthony: " 'Campaign Wife' proved that this was not a woman consumed with fashion. In fact, Miss Bouvier's *own* newspaper stories

---

* In his campaign, Kennedy pledged to move forward on legislation to establish Medicare and increase federal aid to education. In July 1965, President Johnson signed a Medicare bill into law. Shortly afterward, Johnson signed a huge aid-to-education bill.

[her Camera Girl articles, ed.] had never focused on fashion. Still, the 'women's page' reporters of the national press harped on that traditional topic in covering political wives. It was easy to see why Jackie began to resent many women reporters."

On September 25 and October 7, 1960, when the first two of the four Kennedy-Nixon debates were held, she invited groups of people to watch and listen with her. After the opening debate, in which John Kennedy's graceful ease contrasted sharply with Richard Nixon's drawn, pale, and almost sickly appearance, she could barely contain her pride and enthusiasm for his performance, bouncing up and down and clapping her hands like a teenager. When she talked to him on the telephone after the debate, she told him, "You were wonderful, Jack!" Kennedy "could not suppress his delight," said Ralph Martin.

She was in the studio audience for the October 13 and 21 debates. What struck her most forcibly, she said, was that while Nixon offered little or no view of the future, Jack Kennedy demonstrated his vision by challenging the nation to "move forward," adding, "I do not want future historians to say, 'These were the years when the tide ran out for America.' "

Jackie's greatest influence on her husband, said Arthur Schlesinger, was "to confirm his feelings about the importance of living his life according to the values he honored most."

With her help—Schlesinger called it her "complicity" —he learned that total immersion in politics was self-defeating. If politics and politicians were all that mattered, he would have no time or energy to develop new views, new visions, new ideas of what the country and the world needed and wanted. Jackie could separate herself and was surprised to discover that so many of her husband's associates and even their wives could not. "It was as though they were on television all the time," she remarked one day after party leaders and their spouses had spent most of a day at the compound when Kennedy was preparing his campaign.

Kennedy learned through Jackie's example as well as the many talks they had, that his world was not bound on all sides by politics. And so he declined to yield himself to it. And because he made that critical decision he was able to change his life.

Even after her husband's assassination, Jackie's interest in, and contributions to, solving worldwide political problems did not lessen. She did not retreat completely into the jet-set whirl of parties, fashion, and art.

As late as November 1967, Jackie traveled ten thousand miles to Cambodia to visit Prince Norodom Sihanouk, chief of state of the Buddhist kingdom. At the time, the United States had no diplomatic relations with the remote Asian country, which was clearly hostile to America. Jackie, traveling without diplomatic status, remained for six days, puzzling Americans worldwide, who wondered: Was it a vacation-sightseeing journey? If so, why did she fly on a United States Air Force plane? And, most important, why would she agree to receive high-level honors from a nation widely reported to harbor supply depots for the soldiers of North Vietnam.

The answers were suggested by Marvin and Bernard Kalb, then television journalists. "Jackie," the Kalbs said, "was on a subtle, probing mission camouflaged as a tourist trip . . . to pave the way for further diplomatic exchanges between Phnom Penh [Cambodia's capital] and Washington."

Jackie's unprecedented journey resulted from the recognition by President Lyndon Johnson's administration of her standing in the international community. If she had been only an airhead beneath the bouffant hairdo, with no political savvy or ability to dampen the anger of an important foreign leader against the United States, she would not have been selected for this delicate assignment.

While the details of the trip were never revealed. Jackie succeeded in winning over Prince Sihanouk, who said when it ended that her visit had produced "a lessening of the tensions between our two peoples." He added: "Cambodia was able to appreciate a very charming person of the American people. Thanks to this visit and her very charming presence amongst us, we can appreciate fully the charm of America so far as her ablest representative is concerned." Although the prince was not similarly charmed by America's policies in Asia, said the Kalbs, her visit "took the chill out of Cambodian-American relations and by so doing, opened the door to an improvement."

It was during the Camelot years that Jackie, at last, became her own woman. And more: she was also becoming a "force—a woman to be reckoned with," said Stephen Birmingham.

She suffered setbacks: a grievous one when baby Patrick died, another when Joe Kennedy, whom she had come to regard as a substitute father, suffered a disabling stroke in December 1961. She liked Joe. Despite his financial manipulations he was a strong man and, as we shall see, Jackie admired forceful men with drive and initiative who would not allow themselves to be fazed by adversity. For his part, the Kennedy patriarch had grown to respect her spirit and intelligence, and even to love her. Jackie was one of the first to know of her father-in-law's stroke. When he was carried to the mansion, she telephoned Jack in Washington to tell him the news. (Joe Kennedy died in 1969, aware of three more tragedies that battered his family: the murders of Jack and Bobby, and the drowning of Mary Jo Kopechne.)

For most of the time she was America's first lady, Jackie was a happy woman, and she had reason enough:

• She had accomplished her purpose to make the Executive Mansion the country's finest house.

• She had won the respect and admiration of her husband.

• She was of significant help to him on domestic and foreign issues.

• She was responsible, almost single-handedly, for a cultural revival throughout the United States. She invited the world's greatest musicians, singers, actors, and dancers to appear at the White House, among them cellist Pablo Casals, composer Igor Stravinsky, and painter Andrew Wyeth. Nobel laureates graced one entire evening. But this interest in the arts was not confined to the president's home. Because of these evenings—and because the White House came to be a center of cultural activity—"a wave of intellectual interest and excitement rippled out all across America," said Theodore C. Sorenson, John Kennedy's special assistant.

• And she enjoyed a personal popularity unmatched by any other first lady or, in fact, by any other woman in the world.

7

Days of Glory

As first lady, Jackie had a mission. She had long since been bored by journalism, writing dainty bits of poetry and painting watercolors she knew were mediocre at best. None of these activities provided enough of an outlet for her considerable creative energies. While her interest in fashion had not waned and probably never would, she searched for a way to make a lasting contribution.

She could turn the White House not only into the kind of home she wanted for herself and her family but a source of pride for all Americans.

It was here that she shone, said Clark Clifford, special counsel to John Kennedy, "When her husband reached the White House, Jacqueline Kennedy truly came into her own."

Late in November 1960, soon after JFK's election, Jackie had been invited by Mamie Eisenhower for a basement-to-top-floor tour of the Executive Mansion. Jackie accepted eagerly. In her eighth month of pregnancy, she had consulted with her obstetrician, who ordered her to use a wheelchair for the visit. Jackie arrived at the White House, looked around for the chair, saw none, and walked the entire distance with an exuberant Mamie, who kept saying how much she and Ike loved the place. The wheelchair was there, but it was hidden behind an elevator and not seen by either woman. The White House servants had been given orders to bring it out as soon as the new first lady asked for it. Jackie never did. "I was too scared of Mrs. Eisenhower," she admitted later. As a result, her doctor ordered her to bed for the next two weeks.

During the tour, Jackie exclaimed at how beautiful everything appeared to be, when inwardly she felt dismayed. The décor was homespun, with the heavy, solid drapes and furnishings that Mamie preferred. Carpeting covered the lovely flooring and pink could be found everywhere. The living quarters had pink walls, pink curtains, pink slipcovers on the furniture, a pink cushioned headboard on Mamie's bed, a pink wastebasket—and even a pink toilet seat in the chief executive's private bathroom.*

Mamie showed Jackie a tiny kitchen Ike had installed where he could cook his famous chicken-vegetable soup, which took two days to prepare.

She also saw something else but never let on. When she peeked into the upstairs pantry, she caught a glimpse of several cockroaches.

John Fitzgerald Kennedy was inaugurated as the thirty-fifth president on January 20, 1961, the day after one of

---

* When Eisenhower suffered a heart attack on September 25, 1955, at Mamie's girlhood home in Denver, which served as a vacation White House, he recuperated at Fitzsimmons Army Hospital in Aurora, seven miles east of the city. Mamie stayed in a nearby suite consisting of a sitting room, bedroom, and sun porch. But it did not have a pink toilet seat, so Mamie asked aides to supply one. The first lady's request, relayed downstairs, caused consternation. There were plenty of extra toilet seats in the hospital, but none were pink—nor did Denver stores stock any. A call was made to the White House in Washington, and two days later Mamie got her pink seat by airmail. It still rests on the toilet in the suite, now a hospital office.

the heaviest snowstorms in the memory of Washingtonians had hit the city.

The evening before, all traffic had come to a virtual standstill. A preinaugural concert had been planned for Constitution Hall, which adjoins the Ellipse at the rear of the White House. The journey from Georgetown ordinarily took less than five minutes, but the limousine carrying the new president and first lady arrived forty minutes after they started out. William Walton, an artist and friend of the Kennedys, noted that only a few hundred people were in the vast hall. He told the Kennedys to remain in a side room until more people appeared. "People had fought like tigers to get tickets," sighed Walton, "and nobody was there."

However, the concert went on and afterward the official car plowed through the heightening drifts to the Armory, where Frank Sinatra and Peter Lawford had worked for weeks to arrange a program featuring glittering Hollywood celebrities. The storm made havoc of this event too, and it wound down after midnight, long past its scheduled end. Before the final artists appeared, Jackie decided to leave for home to rest for the hectic ceremonies planned for the inauguration itself, but Jack and his father Joe, each smoking long black cigars, remained to the end, watching and applauding Ethel Merman, Bette Davis, Sir Laurence Olivier, Harry Belafonte, and others who kept showing up at odd intervals.

The next evening, following the inauguration and parade, the new president went to every one of the inaugural balls grinning happily at the cheering crowds.

Old Joe Kennedy, who had been conspicuously absent during the convention and the campaign the year before (though he gave many of the orders) now moved into the spotlight, since his ultraconservative views could no longer harm his son's chances of election. He drew gales of laughter when he removed his topcoat at one of the balls, accidentally taking off his tailcoat and standing before thousands of guests in shirtsleeves and brightly colored suspenders.

Leonard Bernstein, composer and conductor, told of a gaffe he committed when he spotted a pretty girl dancing with the president. Said Bernstein: "He was dancing with a friend of mine with whom I wished to dance, and since people were cutting in all over the floor, I thought nothing of doing likewise, except that I had forgotten that I was cutting in on the president of the United States. He looked pale for a moment but he got over it and it did not injure our relationship."

And the young woman? "She was furious," Bernstein admitted.

By Monday morning, both Kennedys were hard at work, he in the Oval Office, she on the monumental task of redecorating the White House. "It was a toss-up whose job presented more challenges or would arouse more public furor," said one former New Frontiersman, exaggerating, of course, but not as wildly as one might think, because Jackie's ideas for change incensed many Americans who objected to any tampering with the historic house.

Jackie had begun to make plans immediately after her postelection tour of the White House with Mamie Eisenhower. She asked the Library of Congress to send her everything they had on the mansion. Day after day she pored over the books and files, jotting down notes. At first, she thought she would renovate only the seven rooms that the first family occupied on the second floor, then realized that the entire house had to be redone. "The White House contained almost nothing of historical importance," she said. "Everything looked like it came from B. Altman" (a Fifth Avenue department store that has since gone out of business). Her overall design was to redecorate the entire Executive Mansion, using historic furnishings and paintings, either belonging to the government or donated privately.

As soon as John Kennedy went to work on Monday morning following the inauguration, Jackie began to have the family quarters disassembled. Kennedy had been in the Oval Office less than an hour when carpenters began to tear the rooms apart, electricians started to rewire, plumbers change pipes and painters mix paints, all under the direction of Jackie who, in jeans and a T-shirt, strode about the growing shambles like a foreman on a construction job, assisted by Mrs. Helen (Sister) Parish, a New York decorator she had engaged.

Jackie had instructed J. B. West, the White House chief usher, to put the president in the Lincoln bedroom and herself in the Queen's Room for the duration. When Mamie Eisenhower read that Jackie was sleeping in the Queen's Room, she became outraged. Calling Mr. West, she demanded to know who had suggested the idea. When West told her, Mamie replied that she had kept that room as a very special place, "and you had to be a queen to sleep there." Tartly, Mamie added that she "didn't think Jackie fit that requirement."

At lunchtime, hamburgers, ordered by Jackie, were brought in by four liveried servants as solemnly as though they were serving pheasant under glass. While the women ate, two servants stood at attention behind each of them. Jackie was not prepared for this. She giggled all through the meal.

About 1 P.M., the president, who had a glass of Metrecal for lunch, went upstairs for a brief nap. Some forty-five minutes later, he rose refreshed and, on his way downstairs, passed the table where the two women had dined. Metrecal, apparently, hadn't been enough. Noting that the hamburgers were only partly consumed, he finished them, along with some of the vegetables the ladies had left, and went back to the Oval Office.

Jackie had not realized that the dining arrangements

for the first family were also inadequate. She and Jack were served elegantly enough in their new dining room, but since the food had to be carted from the kitchen below it always arrived tepid at best. And late as well. She had Ike's tiny kitchen enlarged, and she turned an unused bedroom into a cozy dining room. Thereafter the family's meals were served hot, and promptly.

To legalize the restoration project, Jackie asked Clark Clifford to draw up a legal document creating a committee empowered to conduct the operations of the restorers, and, at the same time, keep the public informed of what was happening.

Only $100,000, the amount Congress permitted a new first family for refurbishing of its family quarters, came from the U.S. Treasury. The rest had to come from private donations, government warehouses, and dusty back rooms of museums. In the three years of John Kennedy's administration, 240 pieces of furniture and assorted artworks were given, gratis, to Jackie's cause. She herself discovered portraits of American Indians, several paintings by Paul Cézanne, the French Impressionist, and even a few pieces of china that had been used by Abraham Lincoln.

Jack was delighted by one of his wife's finds, a desk that had been carved from timbers of a British warship, the *Resolute*, and presented by Great Britain in 1877 to Rutherford B. Hayes, after he had won the office in a close election against his Republican opponent, Samuel J. Tilden.*

Every so often, Jackie would get an urge to wander some more through the mansion, to see what lay hidden beneath layers of dust in some unused corner. One day,

---

* President Kennedy used the beautiful old desk during his administration. John, Jr., would often open the little secret door that swung open in the back and hide there; JFK would pretend he didn't know his son was there. President Clinton uses the same desk.

while walking through the basement with a secretary, she entered a room with the indistinct sign Men on the door. When the aide knocked loudly and they were sure no male was within, they entered and Jackie was aghast. She was staring at magnificent marble busts of two former presidents, George Washington and Martin Van Buren, and another of Christopher Columbus, stored there by a previous administration and long since forgotten.

Jackie ordered them polished until they gleamed, and placed in one of the galleries of the White House. Visitors would admire their beauty and craftsmanship, unaware that for scores of years they had been no more than decorations for an unused men's room.

With her friend Jane Wrightsman, whose husband was a Texas oil tycoon, she toured Winterthur Museum in Wilmington, Delaware, whose one hundred rooms contained the finest collection of American furniture and decorative arts made or used in the United States between the mid-seventeenth and mid-nineteenth centuries. They had been collected by Henry Algernon du Pont of the E.I. du Pont de Nemours chemical company and installed in the family's stately home on its two-hundred-acre estate. The women returned with a sheaf of notes and a commitment from Henry du Pont, a descendant of the family, to chair the new Fine Arts Committee.

As the project got underway, the donations—furnishings, paintings, sculptures, and objets d'art—began arriving from all over the country. Pierre Salinger, JFK's press secretary, said the committee's staff cringed whenever another package arrived, "knowing that Mrs. Kennedy would be there five minutes later wondering why the box was not unpacked."

Jackie's elaborate project, unfortunately, did not go smoothly. In redoing the family dining room, she had ordered dainty chairs for the table. They looked lovely but were, it turned out, insubstantial for sturdy backsides.

Every Tuesday morning, President Kennedy had a

breakfast meeting in the dining room at which his congressional leaders mapped their strategy. Until the renovation of the room could be finished, the meeting was held elsewhere. Finally, word came it was ready.

Promptly at 8:45, the administration's top guns trooped in. First to enter was Lawrence F. O'Brien, a special assistant to the president, who pulled out a chair and sat on it. It promptly broke under his weight and Larry found himself sitting on the floor. John W. McCormack, the Speaker of the House, was halfway down to his seat but quickly stood up and helped pick up O'Brien. Mindful of Kennedy's chronically bad back, McCormack said, "It's a good thing it wasn't the president."

All the others were seated safely when John Kennedy walked in and everyone rose. As he eased into his chair, an ominous cracking sound was heard. Mike Mansfield, the Senate majority leader, and McCormack grabbed his arms in time to prevent the president of the United States from being deposited ignominiously on the floor. Pierre Salinger said, with pardonable understatement, "It is rumored that this particular aspect of Mrs. Kennedy's renovation program was the subject of some discussion that night at their dinner table."

So was Jackie's decision to put white drapes, with just a touch of blue, on the walls of the Blue Room on the main floor. The president, logically enough, argued that the Blue Room had acquired its name because its décor was predominantly blue, but Jackie, whose own logic was based on historical fact, showed him that the room was not all blue. Jack, knowing when he was beaten, conceded, but Jackie had to yield on one point. He asked that a large blue rug be placed on the floor.

But the media representatives did not yield so readily. They gave Pierre Salinger a tough going-over at a press briefing. Usually concerned with weighty matters of state, the questions that day dealt entirely with Jackie's color scheme. Salinger attempted to answer them, with indifferent success. In retrospect, he considered the briefing one of the funniest of the administration. Here are some of the questions and Salinger's brave responses:

Q: Is there anything to the story that the Green Room is going to be chartreuse and the Blue Room is going to be white on white?

A: I am glad that you brought that up.

Q: What was the question?

A: The question was whether the Green Room was going to be chartreuse and the Blue Room is going to be white on white. I would like to deal with this matter within the limitations of my own knowledge, but I can state equivocally that—

Q: You mean unequivocally.

A: Unequivocally, that the Blue Room will continue to be the Blue Room.

Q: You didn't answer someone's questions. What is chartreuse?

A: I couldn't tell you that. The Green Room will remain the Green Room and the Blue Room will remain the Blue Room.

Q: Pierre, I want to ask you two questions. Are these rooms going to be done over? Is the fabric going to be removed?

A: The fabric in both rooms is old and soiled and will be replaced. That is accurate. That is the only part, and virtually the only part of the story that was accurate.

To raise still more money for the project, Jackie devised the idea of publishing a new White House guidebook, selling it to visitors and using the proceeds to acquire even more objects. Purists in and out of the administration were horrified. *Selling* a guide to the mansion would appall the nation, they said. After all, the place was America's house, and hawking a book for profit, no matter how the money would be used, was un-American.

But Jackie persisted. Mrs. Lorraine Pearce, the White House curator, was assigned the job and, with considerable help from the first lady, who helped choose the illustrations and even the typeface, completed the book, which was published in July 1962 by the National Geographic Society.

Once again, Jackie's instincts were correct. Visitors to the mansion happily paid one dollar for a copy, which contained a foreword by the first lady herself. Within sixteen months, more than six hundred thousand were sold.

Eight years later, in a nasty display of vindictiveness, the Nixon White House published a brochure describing the mansion room by room, and handed it out to tourists. It was not Jackie's book but a new one, well and even lyrically written, but while it told all about the appearance of the great rooms, no mention was made of Jackie Kennedy, whose imagination and ingenuity was more responsible than anyone else's for the décor.

In 1962, for example, Jackie discovered an extremely rare type of wallpaper in a Maryland house that was about to be demolished. She persuaded the National Society of Interior Designers to purchase it for $12,500 and donate it to the White House. The paper, called "Scenic America," was removed piece by piece and painstakingly transplanted to the diplomatic reception room in the mansion. At the time, the story of the discovery and removal of the wallpaper was national news. But the new brochure ignored the fact that Jackie was responsible for this masterstroke of decorating.

Other rooms, such as the Treaty Room, Blue Room, and Red Room, are described in thorough detail in the Nixon brochure, but Jackie's contribution is nowhere mentioned. Richard Nixon's staff knew he hated and feared the Kennedys. Wrote journalist Isabelle Shelton: "It would appear that somebody in the Nixon White

House—not necessarily, nor even probably, First Lady Pat Nixon herself—still feels haunted by the looming shadow of the beautiful, tragic widow Kennedy."

Neither Jack nor Jackie was able to complete their work. Two years and ten months after the restoration was begun, Jackie left for Dallas with her husband. Only three more projects remained: she had ordered heavy golden draperies to be hung in the East Room, but the weaving of the fabric had taken longer than expected; upholstery for the chairs in the State Dining Room had not yet arrived; and she was still awaiting the new chandeliers for the ground floor.

But she knew she had done well. "The White House is as it should be," she wrote Clark Clifford. "It is all I ever dreamed for it. There are only a few things left to be done. I know we are in the red, but after this year we will not be."

She left for Texas glowing with satisfaction for having applied her "sense of what was right" (as Jane Wrightsman put it) to America's house. Her achievement was "superb," said Mary Van Rensselaer Thayer, who had Jackie's full cooperation in writing her book on her White House years.

Little wonder Jackie's self-esteem racheted up several notches.

The Jacqueline Bouvier Kennedy legend was created in the 1,002 days of the Kennedy administration. It still endures and will surely become a permanent part of this nation's social history.

8

Fears for Her Sanity

The murder of John Kennedy came close to destroying Jackie. Her despondency was so deep that friends feared for her sanity, pointing out that severe psychoneurosis and alcoholism ran in the family. Her aunt, Edith Beale, "crazy Aunt Edith," she was called, lived surrounded by dozens of cats in her decaying mansion in East Hampton, Long Island. Jackie's father, Black Jack Bouvier, and his younger brother, William S. Bouvier, had sunk into alcoholism.

There were even worse fears.

One afternoon in 1970, when I was researching a biography of Ethel Kennedy, I went to Lem Billings's small apartment on Fifth Avenue on Manhattan's Upper East Side to ask him how Ethel had coped after the assassination of Bobby.

Emotionally strong, Ethel had made up her mind that her family's lives must be kept as normal as possible. She would not allow any sadness to be expressed or manifested in her presence. She insisted that when the children spoke about their father, they should talk, without emotion, about his career, his goals, and their recollections of the good times they had together. Several of her children later developed problems; one, David, died of a drug overdose at the age of twenty-eight in a Palm Beach motel on April 25, 1984.

The conversation turned to Jackie. I said, "I have heard that she was deeply depressed after the assassination of Jack Kennedy. Was she depressed to the point of doing away with herself?"

Billings replied, "Nobody has asked me that before. In the months after Jack's murder, the thought that she might try did cross my mind."

How much credence can be given to Billings's comment about Jackie's contemplation of suicide? Lem, who died in May 1981, devoted his entire life to the family.* He never married, made a living in the advertising business, and was as thoroughly loyal to the Kennedys as if he had been a member of the clan himself. He loved Jack, wept inconsolably after the assassination, revered him all his life. Never in our conversations through the years had Lem Billings told anything but the truth as he saw it. He never was a "P.R. man" for Jack or anyone else in the family, although he defended them against what he considered unfair attacks. In short, Lem was too honest to be devious.

By the time he said this to me, Billings was a heavy drinker and on his way to becoming a drug addict. The conversation about Jackie came after his fifth or sixth trip to the kitchen of his apartment to replenish his glass. Was it a case of *in vino veritas,* that truth emerges under the influence of liquor?

Luella Hennessey Donavan, the Kennedy family nurse who also lost a husband, said that in profound grief a new widow may indeed feel like joining her husband in death

---

* In his eulogy, Bobby Kennedy, Jr., said, "He felt pain for every one of us—pain that no one else would have the courage to feel . . . I don't know how we'll carry on without him." Eunice Shriver said, "Jack's best friend was Lem and he would want me to remind everyone of that today. I am sure the good Lord knows that heaven is Jesus and Lem and Jack and Bobby loving one another."

because she believes nothing is left in life for her, but this bleakness passes and the life force reasserts itself, as it did in her own case. For Jackie to have planned suicide, then gone ahead to complete the act of self-destruction, Luella said, was totally absurd, particularly since she was clearly aware of how much her children relied on her.

Similar thoughts about Jackie may have occurred to Bobby Kennedy because he was hearing reports daily from friends and family members of Jackie's agony. He telephoned her every day and, whenever he could, visited her for long periods.

Jackie's mother, Janet, was also deeply concerned about her daughter. She told author Stephen Birmingham when he was a weekend houseguest at her Newport home, "I'm afraid Jackie will have a nervous breakdown."

Ominous signs would soon appear that Jackie was slipping into a depression.

The worst period in the life of Jacqueline Bouvier Kennedy began at 12:30 P.M. on Friday, November 22, 1963, as she rode with her husband in the rear seat of a blue Lincoln convertible.

A loud report came from a building eighty-five feet away as the president's automobile made the turn around Dealey Plaza in Dallas, Texas. Kennedy, a dazed, uncomprehending look on his face, reached both hands up to his throat. An instant later came another loud pop, then a third.

Some of the Secret Service men and witnesses close by thought they were car backfires; others believed they were firecrackers. But Texas Governor John B. Connally, Jr., in the jumpseat with his wife, recognized the sounds immediately as rifle fire. John Connally knew because he was a hunter.

Slowly, Jack slumped toward Jackie, who stared at him.

"Jack, Jack!" she cried out. "What are they doing to you?"

The first shot, coming from the sixth floor of the Texas School Book Depository, had ripped a hole in the president's throat, after entering through the back of his neck. The third shot sheared off the side of his head, sending bone and brain tissue throughout the rear seat, onto Jackie's hands and into her lap, staining her strawberry-pink wool suit.

Only a few seconds before, Mrs. Connally had leaned toward the president and said, "Mr. Kennedy, you can't say Dallas doesn't love you."

Dallas did. The Kennedys had been receiving a tumultuous welcome in the city where the president had gone in an effort to mend the feud between two bitterly opposing Democratic factions. Governor Connally's conservative backers were not on speaking terms with Senator Ralph Yarborough's liberal forces and with the 1964 elections coming up, the schism could seriously hurt the Democrats.

The unconscious president, rushed to Parkland Memorial Hospital four miles away, was pronounced dead at 2 P.M. by Dr. William Kemp Clark, chief of neurosurgery. JFK had never regained consciousness. Jackie remained in the emergency operating room, refusing to leave.

"I want to be there when he dies," she said to Doris Nelson, the hospital's supervisor of nurses.

Unable to sleep that night after Jack's body had been flown to Washington, Jackie called her stepbrother Hugh Auchincloss, son of her stepfather, who rushed to the White House, and held the weeping young widow until she fell into a fitful slumber. Bobby Kennedy came over and slept that night in the Lincoln bedroom.

The next morning, Jackie appeared confused and disoriented. After a 10 A.M. mass in the East Room, where John Kennedy was lying in state, Jackie embraced Chief Usher West and asked him to come with her to the Oval

Office. Workers were already dismantling the room, removing Jack's rocking chair, the paintings and the bric-a-brac on his desk, putting them into crates.

Jackie watched for a few minutes, then walked across the hall to the cabinet room. Motioning to West to follow, she opened the door and stepped inside the larger rectangular chamber.

She sat at the mahogany table and looked at the center, where one leather-upholstered chair was two inches higher than the others. That was where the president sat. She stared at it for long minutes, then went to the tall window and looked out at a trampoline and sand pile where Caroline and young John usually played in the afternoon.

West recalled that dialogue that ensued.

Jackie: My children, they're good children, aren't they?

West: They certainly are.

Jackie: They're not spoiled?

West: No, indeed.

Jackie (coming close to West and staring into his face): Will you be my friend for life?

West, so wracked by emotion that he was unable to offer an answer, nodded his head. Silently, Jackie returned to the family quarters.

The evening before, Ben Bradlee had gone to the White House, finding Jackie still in her bloodstained suit. "She moved in a trance," Bradlee said, "to talk to each of us there and to new friends as they arrived, ignoring the advice of the doctors to get some sleep and to change out of her bloody clothes. When she saw her personal secretary, the faithful Mary Barelli Gallagher, she rushed to embrace her and cried, 'Why did Jack have to die so young?'"

In the days that followed the assassination, Jackie gave

the country and the world an unforgettable image of
courage that will remain etched forever in the minds of
the estimated one hundred million persons who watched
her on television and read about her in newspapers and
later in history books.

While Lynn Kotz interviewed West for his book, she
told me that the chief usher wondered, "How could a
woman function so well, act so bravely under these circumstances? How could she plan the details of a funeral
so carefully, so meticulously?" (West did not want these
questions to appear in his memoirs.)

Jackie was fully in charge. She chose the smaller St.
Matthew's Cathedral for the mass over the larger Shrine
of the Immaculate Conception because that was her husband's church. She had the private mass for the family
and close friends moved from the family dining room to
the more spacious East Room and ordered that the
honor guard at the catafalque include members of the
Special Forces, or the Green Berets. She convinced
the rest of the family that Jack should lie in Arlington
National Cemetery on the slope below the Lee mansion,
which commands a view of all Washington, instead of in
the family plot in Brookline, Massachusetts. She wanted
the members of the family to walk the eight blocks to the
cathedral behind the cortege, along with the kings,
princes, queens, prime ministers, and other great world
figures. She asked that "Hail to the Chief" be played at
St. Matthew's in slow, funeral cadence and Irish Guards,
Black Watch, and Infantry troops line the graveside at
Arlington. She ordered the eternal flame to be lit there,
she herself bending over with a torch to light it.

Most of the ceremonial details were her idea, many of
them taken from a close study of the funeral of Abraham
Lincoln, which she had studied carefully on Saturday and
Sunday. She even wrote a note to herself to send condolences to the wife of Officer J. D. Tippet, who had been
shot to death by Lee Harvey Oswald, while Oswald was

trying to escape after firing the three shots that killed the President.*

Intrigued by West's questioning how Jackie could think so clearly and perform with such skill and assurance after such an overwhelming tragedy, I sought out experts in human behavior for an answer.

Two Jackies were functioning that weekend from Saturday, November 23, to Monday the 25th, the day of President Kennedy's burial. One part of her was able to stand apart from the other because of the phenomenon called dissociation, which occurs in many persons following extremely stressful events.

One leading psychiatrist, who requested anonymity because he had not examined Jackie and therefore could not ethically evaluate her mental state, explained how the dissociative reaction is manifested.

* As the reader doubtless knows, a number of "conspiracy" theories have been advanced in the years following the assassination. The author makes no attempt to deal with these, except to note that William Manchester, who wrote the definitive account of the murder, as well as Robert Kennedy, believed there was only one killer: Lee Harvey Oswald. In 1964, only a year afterward, Bobby was stunned when, during a visit to Poland, the head of the Polish Student Union in Cracow, Hieronym Kubiak, asked him for his version of the assassination. Kennedy's aides held their breaths because Bobby had never before spoken in public about the tragedy. Then quietly, he said: "It is a proper question and deserves an answer. I believe it was done by a man with the name of Oswald who was a misfit in society, who lived in the United States and was dissatisfied with our government and our way of life, who took up communism and went to the Soviet Union. He was dissatisfied there. He came back to the United States and was antisocial and felt that the only way to take out his strong feelings was by killing the president of the United States." Three months later, after the Warren Commission had issued its report in which it named Oswald as the sole killer, Bobby was again asked by a student at Columbia University for his views. Again he was stunned. Tears flooded his eyes, but he responded: "As I said when I was asked this question in Poland, I agree with the conclusions of the report that the man they identified was the man, that he acted on his own."

An individual who has experienced a terrible event will most likely be in shock for a few days. In this state, he or she may be able to view the event as something that didn't happen to him or her at all. The person may be saying: "Not me, oh, not me! This didn't happen to me at all!"

The condition, well known in psychiatry, is like combat fatigue in soldiers after a battle. While the shells are flying and his friends are being killed or wounded around him, the soldier does his duty ably, sometimes brilliantly, even though he is in extreme danger. Then, when the battle ends and he is out of harm's way, a reaction sets in.

He may have a wide range of emotional problems. A deep depression may set in. He may sob, have terrifying nightmares, or develop any number of psychoneuroses.

This, essentially, is what happened to Jacqueline Kennedy.

On Monday, November 25, after Richard Cardinal Cushing completed the requiem mass for the departed president, Jackie, fully composed, stood outside St. Matthew's Cathedral as Kennedy's casket was borne down the steps. Cardinal Cushing, watching young John salute his father at Jackie's whispered suggestion, was overcome with emotion. "Oh, God," he said, "I almost died." The little boy had been taught the military salute by Dave Powers, an assistant to JFK. Little John had liked to take a sword from the Oval Office and, playing a soldier game, march his one-boy army through the corridors. John was also a parade buff. He had also liked to watch as soldiers marched outside the White House. When they saluted their commander-in-chief, he would come to attention and imitate them.

After the funeral, "combat fatigue" set in and Jackie fell apart. She was unable to speak of the events in Dallas without crying. "Her speech slurred, her eyes darted, she seemed frightened of everyone and anything that moved," Birmingham said. Friends and relatives became alarmed at how she looked and acted. "I'm a freak now," she said to them. "I'll always be a freak."

For ten minutes on Friday, June 5, 1964, Jacqueline Kennedy testified before the President's Commission on the Assassination of President Kennedy, headed by Chief Justice Earl Warren.

Her graphic account has been largely ignored by biographers. She was questioned by J. Lee Rankin, the commission's general counsel, at 3017 N Street in Washington. Chief Justice Warren was present, along with all the members of the commission. Robert Kennedy, then still attorney general, was also there, ready to come to Jackie's aid if emotion overcame her as she recalled the terrible moments. Jackie, however, speaking in a monotone, was composed throughout.

Here is her testimony:

Mr. Rankin: Can you go back to the time that you came to Love Field on November 22 and describe what happened there after you landed in the plane?

Mrs. Kennedy: We got off the plane. The then Vice President and Mrs. Johnson were there. They gave us flowers. And then the car was waiting, but there was a big crowd there, all yelling, with banners and everything. And we went to shake hands with them. It was a very hot day. And you went all along a long line. I tried to stay close to my husband and lots of times you get pushed away, you know, people leaning over and pulling your hand. They were very friendly.

And, finally, I don't know how we got back to the

car. I think Congressman Albert Thomas somehow was helping me. There was lots of confusion.

Mr. Rankin: Then you did get into the car. And you sat on the left side of the car, did you, and your husband on your right?

Mrs. Kennedy: Yes.

Mr. Rankin: And was Mrs. Connally—

Mrs. Kennedy: In front of me.

Mr. Rankin: And Governor Connally to your right in the jump seat?

Mrs. Kennedy: Yes.

Mr. Rankin: And Mrs. Connally was in the jump seat?

Mrs. Kennedy: Yes.

Mr. Rankin: And then did you start off on the parade route?

Mrs. Kennedy: Yes.

Mr. Rankin: And were there many people along the route that you waved to?

Mrs. Kennedy: Yes.

Mr. Rankin: Now, do you remember as you turned off the main street onto Houston Street?

Mrs. Kennedy: I don't know the name of the street.

Mr. Rankin: That is that one block before you get to the Depository Building.

Mrs. Kennedy: Well, I remember whenever it was, Mrs. Connally said, "We will soon be there." We could see a tunnel in front of us. Everything was really slow then. And I remember thinking it would be so cool under that tunnel.

Mr. Rankin: And then do you remember as you turned off of Houston onto Elm right by the Depository Building?

Mrs. Kennedy: Well, I don't know the names of the streets, but I suppose right by the Depository is what you are talking about?

Mr. Rankin: Yes; that is the street that sort of curves as you go down under the underpass.

Mrs. Kennedy: Yes; well, that is when she said to President Kennedy, "You certainly can't say that the people of Dallas haven't given you a nice welcome."

Mr. Rankin: What did he say?

Mrs. Kennedy: I think he said—I don't know if I remember it or I have read it, "No, you certainly can't," or something. And you know then the car was very slow and there weren't very many people around.

And then—do you want me to tell you what happened?

Mr. Rankin: Yes; if you would please.

Mrs. Kennedy: You know, there is always noise in a motorcade and there are always motorcycles besides us, a lot of them backfiring. So I was looking to the left. I guess there was a noise, but it didn't seem like any different noise really because there is so much noise, motorcycles and things. But then suddenly Governor Connally was yelling, "Oh, no, no, no."

Mr. Rankin: Did he turn toward you?

Mrs. Kennedy: No; I was looking this way, to the left, and I heard these terrible noises. You know. And my husband never made any sound. So I turned to the right. And all I remember is seeing my husband, he had this sort of quizzical look on his face, and his hand was up, it must have been his left hand. And just as I turned and looked at him, I could see a piece of his skull and I remember it was flesh colored. I remember thinking he just looked as if he had a slight headache. And I just remember seeing that. No blood or anything.

And then he sort of did this [indicating], put his hand to his forehead and fell in my lap.

And then I just remember falling on him and saying, "Oh, no, no, no," I mean, "Oh, my God, they have shot my husband." And "I love you, Jack," I remember I was shouting. And just being down in the car with his head in my lap. And it just seemed an eternity.

You know, then, there were pictures later of me climbing out the back. But I don't remember that at all.

Mr. Rankin: Do you remember Mr. Hill [Secret Service Agent Clinton J. Hill] coming to try to help on the car?

Mrs. Kennedy: I don't remember anything. I was just down like that.

And finally I remember a voice behind me, or something, and then I remember the people in the front seat, or somebody, finally knew something was wrong, and a voice yelling, which must have been Mr. Hill, "Get to the hospital," or maybe it was Mr. Kellerman [Secret Service Agent Roy Kellerman] in the front seat. But someone yelling. I was just down and holding him.

Mr. Rankin: Do you have any recollection of whether there were one or more shots?

Mrs. Kennedy: Well, there must have been two because the one that made me turn around was Governor Connally yelling. And it used to confuse me because first I remembered there were three and I used to think my husband didn't make any sound when he was shot. And Governor Connally screamed. And then I read the other day that it was the same shot that hit them both. But I used to think if I only had been looking to the right I would have seen the first shot hit him. But I heard Governor Connally yelling and that made me turn around, and as I turned to the right my husband was doing this [indicating with hand at neck]. He was receiving a bullet. And those are the only two I remember.

And I read there was third shot. But I don't know.

Just those two.

Mr. Rankin: Do you have any recollection generally of the speed that you were going, not any precise amount.

Mrs. Kennedy: We were really slowing turning the corner. And there were very few people.

Mr. Rankin: And did you stop at any time after the shots, or proceed about the same way?

Mrs. Kennedy: I don't know, because—I don't think we stopped. But there was such confusion. And I was down in the car and everyone was yelling to get to the hospital and you could hear them on the radio, and then suddenly I remember a sensation of enormous speed, which must have been when we took off.

Mr. Rankin: And then from there you proceeded as rapidly as possible to the hospital, is that right?

Mrs. Kennedy: Yes.

Mr. Rankin: Do you recall anyone saying anything else during the time of the shooting?

Mrs. Kennedy: No; there weren't any words. There was just Governor Connally's. And then I suppose Mrs. Connally was sort of crying and covering her husband. But I don't remember any words.

One day shortly after the assassination, Caroline walked to the beach at the compound and sat on the sand looking out over the sound, recalled Rita Dallas, Joe Kennedy's private nurse during his illness. The little girl, Dallas said, "made a desolate picture huddled so alone in deep despair." Jackie joined her, sitting with her; and both stared for a long time at the choppy waters.

They rose, Dallas recalled, and strolled along the beach in the face of a cutting December wind. They presented a picture of utter desolation as they walked together,

Jackie's arms around Caroline, pressing close to protect her from the piercing wind.

To Dallas, the scene was a metaphor for what would follow. "I knew," she said, "she would provide the child with the strength that is necessary to suffer a great loss. She shielded her until the sharp pain had settled into a dull, eternal ache. She set an example for her, and as the years passed, the little girl was able to pick up the task of living . . ."

Ten days after Jack was buried, Jackie moved out of the White House, declining the invitation of Lady Bird Johnson, the new first lady, to remain longer. W. Averill Harriman, · the former New York governor and John Kennedy's Undersecretary of State, offered her the use of his mansion on N Street in Georgetown, and she gratefully accepted.

In the bleak months after Jack's death, the presence of her children, their need for her and the conviction that nothing else mattered very much if she failed them, sustained Jackie. For their sake, she made a supreme effort to maintain some degree of normalcy in their lives. And by doing so she herself found a lifebuoy to which she could cling while trying to put her own life in order.

At the Harriman home, she was dismayed by the attention her presence in the area caused. Peering from a front window, she saw tourists, cameras poised, as well as Washingtonians in the street hoping to catch a glimpse, and a snapshot of her or Caroline or John when they emerged.

She shrank back, leaving only when the crowds were thinnest. "The world is pouring terrible adoration at the feet of my children and I fear for them, for this awful exposure," she confided to a friend. "How can I bring them up normally?"

She used family and friends in an effort to brighten the children's day. Dave Powers came by daily to play soldiers with John, when he was approaching three. Bobby, undergoing his own period of grief, was very concerned about Caroline. Overnight she had been transformed from a sunny, vivacious little girl into a solemn-faced, joyless child. Unable to comprehend what had happened in her life, she withdrew into herself. Her eyes took on a blank, expressionless look.

Many times Bobby invited Caroline and John to Hickory Hill to play with his children but he could not get Caroline to join in their hectic activities. She would always stand apart from them.

Looking at her sad little face, Bobby told Lem Billings, "Every time I see her, I want to go somewhere and cry."

"That John, he's a little rogue," remarked Bobby as he watched the boy scamper around the rollling lawn, "but Caroline doesn't let people get close to her."

If Caroline had vented her emotion in a torrent of tears, she might have recovered sooner. But she kept her sorrow locked tightly within her.

"I only cried twice," she told a classmate at the White House kindergarten Jackie had set up and which she continued to attend after the assassination. Classes met for two hours three times a week in the solarium on the third floor. (It was arguably the world's most exclusive preschool program, attended by only a dozen children of friends and aides of JFK. A teacher was hired, but mothers, including Jackie, took turns as helpers, soothing children who fell and hurt themselves and escorting pupils to the bathroom.)

By the end of January 1964, Jackie moved out of the Harriman house and into another home almost across the street, at 3017 N Street. She called the famous interior designer, William (Billy) Baldwin to help her decorate it.

Baldwin a slender, handsome man, agreed to come the next day from New York. Flying in a snowstorm, he arrived at the Harriman house and was greeted at the door by Jackie, who apologized profusely for asking him to travel in the dreadful weather.

She explained to Baldwin how she wanted her home to look. Baldwin had never before attempted a commission that was so emotionally charged. He glanced at Jackie as they walked. She appeared so young and vulnerable. "Losing someone one loves is a very private matter, and here she was forced to share her grief with the whole world," he said. "Her life had been absolutely shattered, her family uprooted, and I was faced with trying to make her feel at home somewhere." To Baldwin, the task seemed almost hopeless.

But Baldwin and Jackie went to work. Once, when he came to the house, he found her in the living room opening a crate filled with Greek and Roman artifacts. Jack Kennedy had developed an interest in these ancient ornaments and had begun a collection. Said Baldwin, "I had never seen anyone looking so bereft."

She was only thirty-four yet suddenly appeared to be much older: her eyes were red, hair uncombed, her face pinched and drawn. Jackie began opening more boxes filled with accessories. Within minutes she collapsed in tears, asking Baldwin between sobs, "Can anyone understand how it is to have lived in the White House and then, suddenly, to be living alone as the president's widow?"

The only person in Washington who could truly understand the depth of Jackie's anguish was Bobby Kennedy, because he, too, was wracked by grief and despair. Bobby frequently visited Jackie in Georgetown and afterward in New York, which eventually irked Ethel. Strains developed in their marriage. On one occasion in Washington, when they were en route to a friend's home for the evening, Bobby told Ethel to go on without him; he wanted to be with Jackie. They argued but Bobby insisted. Fuming, Ethel went on alone.

Jackie was forever grateful to Robert during those long months; Ethel, for her part, remained angry, particularly after rumors arose that Bobby and Jackie were becoming romantically attached. They were seen together in the back rooms of restaurants, heads together, whispering to one another. These stories were entirely untrue, but they persisted all through 1964 and the first half of 1965.

Jackie wept almost constantly all through that first year. "The poor woman was crying every time I saw her," said Kenneth P. O'Donnell, the tough special assistant to the president who was a member of his "Irish Mafia." "Each time I came in the room where she was she would throw her arms around me and cry on my shoulder. And she looked terrible."

The decorating of the N Street house was almost finished when Jackie realized she had made a terrible mistake. Each time she went out in Georgetown where she and Jack had spent happy years, each time she saw the buildings of the capital city, the White House, the Capitol, painful memories returned. Confused, emotionally torn, she told Billy Baldwin to stop all work. Her voice quavering, she said, "I cannot live in Washington any more. I'm moving to New York."

By autumn of 1964, she and the children were living temporarily in a suite at the Hotel Carlyle on Madison Avenue. A real-estate agent found the Fifth Avenue apartment, for which she paid $250,000 and where she still lives. Jean, Jack's sister, and her husband, Steven Smith, lived only a block away in an elegant duplex. Smith, the low-key but tough and shrewd brother-in-law, had been a powerful force behind many of the Kennedy campaigns, had kept a close watch on the expenditures and investments of the family and was its damage control expert. He died in 1991. Also living at number 969 Fifth Avenue, a block away, were her sister Lee and her husband, Stanislas Radziwill, known as "Stash," who had made a fortune in real estate and construction in England. McGeorge Bundy, a special JFK aide and his wife, who were good friends, lived in the building. And Patricia and Peter Lawford were at number 990 Fifth Avenue.

For all of the year 1964 Jackie was in a deep depression, said Ralph G. Martin. Martin quotes James Reed, a family friend, who visited her in March, "Jackie suddenly fell sobbing on my shoulder and couldn't stop for a long time." Usually Jackie had planned her days but now, said Martin, "her life was very disorganized and she was breaking appointments." During this period she needed pills to get to sleep and sedatives and antidepressants during the day.

The once-chic and elegant Jackie looked like a younger version of her Aunt Beale—"crazy Aunt Edith." Edith Bouvier Beale, who was fifty-nine in 1964, lived in a once-imposing twenty-eight-room mansion on Apoquogue Road in East Hampton with her spinster daughter, Edith ("Little Edie"), then thirty-six. The elder Edith's mind had disintegrated after her husband left her. Both were gathering an increasing reputation for eccentricity.*

Making matters worse for Jackie, she could not mourn alone. The spotlight that had shone upon her during the White House years followed her with even higher wattage into private life. Each time she left her apartment, each time she went to church, paid a visit to her sister Lee, went to the hairdresser, she saw photographers. Gossip columnists couldn't get enough of her, every move was chronicled and dissected.

Watching his old friend's wife tormented inwardly and hounded outwardly, Lem Billings cried out, "For Christ's sake, why the hell don't they leave her alone? Don't they know she's human?"

Once settled in the New York apartment, Caroline's spirits began to brighten. Jackie's instincts had been

---

* By early 1972, county authorities threatened to have the Beale house condemned as unfit for human habitation because of the cats, raccoons, and other wildlife with which the Beales had surrounded themselves, and the lack of sanitary facilities. That year, Jackie and her sister Lee helped clean up the house at a cost of $30,000. Aristotle Onassis, then Jackie's husband, also contributed $50,000 but insisted that his gift remain unpublicized.

good. Doris Kearns Goodwin, a friend who had written extensively about the Kennedy family, said, "Jackie understood the importance of creating a family apart from the larger Kennedy family. She recognized that the children would get strength from the grandparents and cousins, aunts and uncles, but it was growing up with a feeling of belonging to their own small family that would give them the most stability."

In New York, Caroline's large, almost square, bedroom had an oversize canopy bed and a large couch on the wall facing the park. Hanging on the off-white wall above the couch were more than two dozen framed photographs of Caroline and her father, including the one taken when she was four years old and interrupted a press conference attired in bathrobe and slippers. She was carrying her mother's high-heeled shoes, which she slipped on as her father gently escorted her from the premises.

Pictures of horses, another Caroline passion, and large, beautifully illustrated books about them, were also part of the décor.

Caroline, then eight, awoke each school day at seven fifteen and had a scrambled egg or waffle breakfast with John and her governess. By eight-twenty, wearing the red leotard, gray flannel jumper, and gray blazer required of Junior School students, she walked six blocks to the Convent of the Sacred Heart. The school on 91st Street is housed in a great stone mansion built by the financier Otto Kahn, and is modeled after an Italian palazzo in Florence.

An excellent student, Caroline received uniformly high grades for which she worked hard, doing more than two hours of homework each day. History was her favorite subject and she took an active part in the school's current events forum.

Jackie wanted Caroline to have a normal social life and worried that she was being excluded from parties by parents timid about appearing pushy. Several times when she learned parties were being planned, she called to ask that Caroline be included. "After all, Caroline's only a little girl," she pointed out. After that the invitations came.

A close friend, who had observed Caroline often, said, "She is a grown-up little girl." In public, she was beautifully mannered but reserved and somewhat shy. In private, however, she had many moments of ebullience, knew all the latest dance steps favored by preteens, and chatted gaily with her classmates, especially her best friend, Mary Nelson, with whom she had frequent sleepover dates, mostly in the Kennedy apartment.

She began to talk about her father casually. At home, Caroline and John chatted about Jack Kennedy with their mother, telling about the games he played with them, where they went, what they did.

Once, when the dessert at dinner was chocolate, Caroline observed: "Daddy used to like this."

Healing had started.

The Kennedy meals were served in the family dining room at a round table overlooking Central Park. Most evenings, Jackie dined with her children that first year. When she began going out, the children were joined by their governess. When Jackie had dinner parties, at which she served haute cuisine dishes, she tried to introduce Caroline to what she called "grownup food." Her teaching took—to a point—as this story will illustrate:

To celebrate the beginning of Christmas recess in 1967, Caroline, then nine, and six of her classmates were taken to lunch at La Caravelle, one of the country's most distinguished French restaurants, often patronized by Mrs. Kennedy. The youngsters, each dressed in school uniform, were accompanied by the mother of one of the girls. The group, seated at a table in the center of the room, acted like little girls anywhere—the meal was punctuated by laughter, giggling, and frequent trips to the ladies' room.

Caroline, handed a menu, scanned it carefully, finally deciding upon her order: artichokes vinaigrette. The dish, a gourmet specialty, is one of Jackie's favorites. But the rest of Caroline's order was pure JFK—steak and french fries.

On the first anniversary of the assassination, Jackie confessed her continuing grief in an emotional tribute to her late husband published in *Look* magazine.

"I don't think there is any consolation," she wrote.

> What was lost cannot be replaced.
> I should have known that it was asking too much to dream that I might have grown old with him and seen our children grow up together.
> Now I think that I should have known that he was magic all along. I did know it. I should have guessed it could not last . . .

Jack, she wrote, would have preferred to be a man, not the legend he became. But she was consoled by the thought that he did not share the suffering of those who loved him. "I think for him—at least he will never know what sadness might have lain ahead . . . His high noon kept all the freshness of the morning—and he died then, never knowing disillusionment."

In the spring of 1965, Lee Radziwill told Jackie she was hosting a dance at her duplex apartment. Would she come? "It's just a teeny, tiny dance for less than a hundred," Lee pleaded, adding that all the guests would be old friends, like the Leonard Bernsteins, Pierre Salinger, Ethel and Bobby.

Jackie went. About 1 A.M., some of the guests began leaving; by four most had gone. But Jackie remained, still dancing and enjoying herself hugely.

In the fall, she gave a party herself at The Sign of the Dove, a restaurant on Third Avenue. Here, too, she had a wonderful time.

Her new life had begun.

PART THREE

∽

Out of the Abyss

9

A Greek Bearing Gifts

She was only thirty-seven in 1965 when the mourning period ended, and even more attractive than when she was first lady. Gossip columnists reported every shred of information, true or not, they could uncover or were told; even that she wore undergarments embroidered with her initials. Headline writers altered her job description from first lady to world's most eligible widow. Newspapers conducted polls on whether she would remarry. The psychologist Dr. Joyce Brothers, who analyzes human behavior for mass audiences, asserted that if Jackie would ever take another husband "she would probably lose her place in the nation's heart."

But Jackie never considered herself an icon. She did not want to be enshrined forever in the hearts of a country grieving for a lost prince. She saw herself not as an idol, but as a woman.

Feminism was dawning. Betty Friedan's book, *The Feminine Mystique,* was raising the consciousness of women all over America, and eventually the world. Jackie's conversion to feminism was beginning to surface. It would bloom fully in later years.

Looking back, the likelihood of a second marriage was surely plausible. Jackie herself was quite aware that one day she might remarry. She offered a clue one evening when she listened with growing exasperation to a leading statesman expound on the tremendous loss the country had suffered with the death of John Kennedy. Afterward she burst into tears, not because of the statesman's eulogy but because of her own future. "For God's sake," she exclaimed, "the way the man talked you'd think I never even existed. Maybe we should import the Indian custom of women throwing themselves on their husband's funeral pyres!"

She flew all over the globe to the glittering salons of Paris, London, and New York as frantically as Ethel, Bobby's widow, threw herself into nonstop activity at Hickory Hill.* Jackie went to plays, the ballet, and opera, gave more parties and accepted more invitations. Both women were seeking to submerge the past by plunging full-tilt into the present.

At social functions, she was never without an escort, among them Mike Nichols, the film director; the lyricist Alan J. Lerner; writer George Plimpton; composer and conductor Leonard Bernstein; actor Anthony Quinn; then astronaut and later senator John Glenn; historian Arthur Schlesinger, Jr.; former Defense Secretary Robert J. MacNamara; and Adlai Stevenson, who was U.N. ambassador in Kennedy's administration.

All except two were the usual "safe escorts," men who were available to accompany her to engagements but with whom there could be no romantic alliance for one reason or another. (Adlai Stevenson once was so carried away

* Kennedys, even in-laws, appear to handle crises identically. Two weeks after the assassination, Bobby organized a touch football game on the grounds of the Palm Beach mansion. Close friends and associates from the Department of Justice had been asked to visit. "It was the roughest, wildest game I have ever seen," Pierre Salinger declared. "Everybody was trying to get the anger out of their systems. Bobby was absolutely relentless. He attacked the man with the ball like a tiger, slamming, bruising, and crushing, and so did everyone else. One guy broke a leg, and you couldn't count the bloodied noses. It was murder."

that he put his arm around her waist and then raised it to her breast. Jackie quickly pulled away, astonished, and said sharply: "Why Adlai!" Stevenson, reddening, withdrew his wandering hand.) In the five years following the assassination of Jack Kennedy, Jackie had one mini-romance and another that could be called "serious."

The first was with a British diplomat, Sir William David Ormsby-Gore. Ormsby-Gore, a year younger than Kennedy, had served as ambassador to the United States for four years during part of the Kennedy and Johnson administrations. A patrician later elevated to the peerage as Lord Harlech, Ormsby-Gore had ties to the Kennedys that dated back to the 1930s, when Joseph Kennedy served as America's ambassador to Britain. And a cousin, the marquess of Hartington, had married John Kennedy's younger sister, Kathleen, in 1944. (The marquess was killed in action four months later in Normandy during World War II, and Kathleen died in an air crash in France in May 1948.)

Oxford-educated Harlech, a widower, and Jackie went on journeys together to Ireland, Cambodia, and Thailand in 1967, and the media predicted an imminent announcement of an engagement. None came, and the romance, indeed if it existed at all, faded.*

The slender, debonair Roswell Gilpatric, undersecretary of welfare in Kennedy's administration, was a more likely suitor even though he was already married, but estranged from his wife, Madelin. Gilpatric and Jackie began dating in 1967, when Gilpatric was sixty-one. They traveled together to the Yucatan Peninsula in Mexico, accompanied by a few reporters. Years later, a number of letters surfaced that clearly showed that Gilpatric was more than a casual escort. He had confidently believed the letters were safely locked in the vault of Cravath,

---

* Lord Harlech was killed in a car crash on January 26, 1985, while returning to his family estate in North Wales.

Swaine & Moore, the Manhattan law firm where he was a senior partner. But in early February 1970, letters to him by Jackie between 1963 and 1970 were auctioned off by Charles Hamilton, who collects and sells autographs. He had obtained them from a young lawyer who worked for Gilpatric's firm.

One of the letters, written on June 13, 1963, while President Kennedy was in California, told how Jackie had felt about a trip they had made to Maryland six days before: "Dear Ros," she had written, "I loved my day in Maryland so much. It made me happy for one whole week. It is only Thursday today. But I know the spell will carry over until tomorrow."

When Gilpatric discovered that this and other letters were being auctioned, he checked and learned that they were no longer in the vault. "They have obviously been purloined by someone with larceny in his heart," he said.

While Jackie and Gilpatric remained friends, she did not later inform him of her plans to marry Aristotle Onassis. In the last of four letters that were auctioned off, she explained in a "Dearest Ros" note why she had not let him know. "I would have told you before I left," she wrote, "but then everything happened so much more quickly than I'd planned." This letter, written during her honeymoon with Ari, closed with "I hope you know all you were and are and will ever be to me. With all my love, Jackie."

Few understood why Jackie married Aristotle Onassis, the Greek shipping billionaire. There were numerous theories: she needed and wanted money to support her grand lifestyle. She wanted lifelong security for her children. She sought a father figure. (She was forty, Onassis sixty-two.)

When she married Onassis on October 20, 1968, world reaction was instantaneous—and uniformly negative. The Stockholm newspaper *Expressen,* lamented: JACKIE, HOW

COULD YOU? The *Long Island Press* said unkindly: WHY DID JACKIE MARRY ONASSIS? THERE ARE WELL OVER A BILLION REASONS. A columnist for *L'Espresso,* an Italian newspaper, wrote: "Onassis, a grizzled satrap with liver-colored skin, a fleshy nose, a wide horsy grin—*that's* the lady's new husband." A former member of the Kennedy administration said: "The marriage is ridiculous, preposterous, ludicrous, absurd, grotesque, rococo, and positively stinks."

Who was this "golden Greek," the short, homely man who dressed in ill-fitting clothes, but who captured the most sought-after woman in the world?

A refugee from war with the Turks, Aristotle Socrates Onassis fled to Argentina in 1923 with sixty dollars to begin a career unique in world history. He was born in the ancient city of Smyrna (now called Izmir) to Socrates and Penelope Onassis, Greek natives who had moved to the coastal city because it was closer to the Grecian mainland, and offered better prospects for employment.* Smyrna had been a pawn of war since ancient times. In 1919 it was seized by the Greeks from the Ottoman Turks but in 1922 Kemal Ataturk, known as the founder of modern Turkey, launched an offensive that ultimately destroyed Smyrna. Socrates Onassis, imprisoned by the Turks, pleaded with his son, then sixteen, to leave the war-torn area before he, too, was captured and jailed.

The U.S. vice counsel, John L. Parker, a friend of Socrates, got young Aristotle aboard an American destroyer packed with hundreds of other refugees. On September 21, 1923, Onassis ambled down the gangplank in Buenos Aires to start his new life.

The squat, dark-eyed boy who had walked virtually penniless from the crowded refugee ship was to become a

---

* Onassis's Argentina passport puts his birthdate at 1900, but he explained later that he deliberately added six years to his age to help him find a job.

legend before he turned fifty. He amassed a fortune variously estimated at five hundred million to one billion dollars, owned lavish homes and apartments on three continents, controlled more than one hundred ships, each of which was worth many millions, lived like a medieval lord on his own private island estate in the Ionian Sea, sailed aboard a luxury yacht, made love to some of the world's most beautiful and talented women (including Greta Garbo), ran an international airline, owned a casino at Monte Carlo in Monaco, took on governments in conflicts over oil and fishing, talked daily to the most influential men on the globe (including heads of state), wed the daughter of the man who was then the richest in Greece, lived openly with one of the world's best-known opera singers, and married the widow of a president of the United States.

Once asked his formula for success, Onassis came up with this program: work twenty hours a day; be willing to take risks; lend an ear to "important" gossip, and offer tempting bait to get what you want.

He used the rules to amass his fleet, which was larger than most countries' navies and employed more than three thousand men. Most of the vessels belonged to a separate corporation registered in Panama and flew the Liberian flag.

A bachelor until he was thirty-nine, Onassis married Athena (Tina) Livanos, the beautiful seventeen-year-old daughter of Stavros Livanos, a rival shipping tycoon, on December 28, 1946. A son, Alexander, was born on April 30, 1948, and a daughter, Christina, on December 11, 1950.

At first the marriage seemed ideal, but in 1959, Tina sued for divorce. Originally the suit, filed in New York State, charged that Onassis had committed adultery. Later Tina dropped the proceedings and was granted an uncontested divorce in 1960 in Alabama. There was considerable speculation in the world press that Onassis's long-time relationship with opera star Maria Callas had been the prime cause of the breakup.

Jackie had known Onassis since 1959, when she was thirty, when she and Jack were invited to a cocktail party aboard Ari's 325-foot yacht, the *Christina*, moored off Monte Carlo in the Mediterranean. The Kennedys were visiting Jack's father. He had rented a villa on the French Riviera. Onassis's wife, Tina, planned to have as many celebrated guests as she could gather for the party because Winston Churchill would attend. Onassis suggested she ask John Kennedy and his young wife because he knew that the senator had high regard for the former British prime minister.

Jack Kennedy and Churchill talked politics while Ari escorted Jackie around the ship. She was enchanted. "It's unbelievable," she told a friend later. "The whole thing is right out of the *Arabian Nights.*"

Two years later, when Jackie, then first lady, arrived in Greece for a five-day visit, she and Ari met again at the villa of Markos Nomikos, another wealthy shipowner. Ari invited her for a cruise on the *Christina* but Jackie gave a noncommital answer. Two years later, she was again invited, and this time, distraught at the death of her second son, Patrick, she accepted. Ari had called Lee Radziwill, who was in Greece, offering to put the yacht at Jackie's disposal for as long as she wished.

The first five days, it was Jackie's ship. Ari made every arrangement for her comfort; adding extra crewmen, hiring a dance band, employing two hairdressers, and stocking the ship with food and wine. He also took great care to have chaperons aboard, among them Lee Radziwill and Franklin D. Roosevelt, Jr., then undersecretary of commerce.

Onassis was aboard but did not attend the dinner party Jackie gave the first night, nor even appear until the *Christina* neared the island of Lesbos in the Aegean. He volunteered to be her guide around the island and later on Crete, where he showed her the Minoan ruins.

Jackie was entranced, but back home the president was growing increasingly angry as stories began appearing in the press about the luxurious cruise. His patience snapped when Rep. Oliver Bolton, an Ohio Republican, pointed out in a speech in Congress that the undersecretary of commerce was aboard. Bolton did not pull his punches: a high-ranking official of the Department of Commerce, he said, would surely wield influence with the Maritime Administration. No need to spell out the importance of the Maritime Administration to Onassis's shipping business.

The speech hit a political nerve in Jack Kennedy, who knew Bolton was right. He called Jackie and ordered her home. She came, but only after a magnificent shipboard party at which she received a diamond-and-ruby necklace as a parting gift from the billionaire Greek.

After the murder of Jack Kennedy, Onassis appeared at the White House to express his condolences, then withdrew. When Jackie moved to New York, he telephoned her and asked her to dinner, where he remained silent for most of the evening as she spoke and cried. His was a broad shoulder on which to weep.

Ari never told his children, Alexander and Christina, that he was courting Jackie, and it is possible that Jackie herself was unaware she was being wooed. One evening in Paris, he invited her to dinner at his penthouse apartment on Avenue Foch, and even gave strict orders to his house servants, Helen and George, to disappear after they had prepared the food. He didn't want them to know whom he was entertaining. The table was elegantly set with the finest crystal and china. Then Ari went into the kitchen and brought out and served the food himself with a gallant flourish.

He was a charming companion, and Jackie accepted more and more invitations to the theater, ballet, and dinner. One day he took her to a small Greek restaurant in Greenwich Village, where he danced and broke dishes, Greek-fashion, as Jackie laughingly encouraged him.

In the spring of 1968, Jackie accepted Ari's invitation for a second cruise on the *Christina,* this time in the Caribbean. Said one woman passenger:

> I looked out my stateroom porthole—I was very, very lucky, for I had a magnificent view. It was early in the morning when Jackie arrived, but I could tell she knew that everyone was looking at her. She was like an actress who's performing in the center of the stage and has studied her part backward and forward. She had on a *tant soit peau* [ever so simple] brown, collarless jacket and matching skirt that was four inches above the knee—I wore mine at half an inch longer, but never Jackie! *Non!* I could tell that the suit was designed by Valentino. He, Givenchy, and Balenciaga design most of her clothes.

Jackie had just returned from Paris and before she boarded, reporters asked her what she had bought there. Jackie replied: a Givenchy and a Balenciaga. When reporters asked where they were, Jackie, with her pixie sense of humor, replied: "They are aboard the ship, designing dresses."

The passenger said it was on that cruise that Ari asked Jackie to marry him.

By then she had recovered enough emotional balance to be able to think the crucial question of her future to its logical conclusions. There were obstacles, she told him. Yes, she liked him very much, wanted, in fact, to be with him as his wife, but . . .

There could be religious problems. Would she be excommunicated from the Church if she married a divorced man? What about the children, Caroline and John? How would they react to a stepfather? Wasn't it better for the children to feel that they "belonged" to a closely knit family like the Kennedys? And how about Bobby? She loved Bobby, owed him nothing less than her sanity, but he was strongly opposed to the marriage, telling Jackie it would not only hurt the family but his own chances of winning the Democratic nomination. Could she flout Bobby, to whom she owed so much?

Jackie and Ari talked hour after hour, but the question remained unresolved.

The murder of Bobby Kennedy on June 4, 1968, as he was on the verge of winning the Democratic nomination for president, plunged Jackie into a new emotional crisis that once again threatened her sanity.

She flew to Los Angeles, where Bobby had been shot in the Ambassador Hotel, arriving in a confused, disoriented state. The shooting of Bobby in the hotel pantry became mixed up in her mind with the tragedy in Dallas five years earlier. She rambled disjointedly, making little sense. She talked of Jack Kennedy as though he were still alive, and she was still first lady.

In Greece, when Onassis heard about the murder of Robert Kennedy, he ordered one of his jets to fly him at once to Los Angeles. He found Jackie in a state of profound emotional disorientation. Frank Brady, Onassis's biographer, wrote: "She was in a state of panic and disbelief, occasionally lapsing into dialogue that indicated she was confusing both assassinations."'

Onassis never left her side. He flew back to New York with her and attended Bobby's funeral in St. Patrick's Cathedral.

Jackie finally made up her mind. She would marry Aristotle Onassis. In late summer of 1968, she told the Kennedy family. She braced for a torrent of objections, and they came.

Look, they said, at the man's background. It was, at

best, shady.* Onassis, they pointed out, had been arrested by U.S. marshals in February of 1954 on charges that he had illegally purchased surplus ships from the United States government, which under the law could only be bought by American corporations. (Acquiring the ships had been easy enough; Onassis had set up dummy corporations under American names and ownership, bought the vessels, and added them to his fleet.)

After lunching at the Colony Restaurant in Manhattan that February, Onassis had been placed under arrest by officers who, considering his wealth and reputation, had politely waited for him to finish before taking him into custody. At the office of the U.S. Attorney in Foley Square, Onassis had been freed on his promise to appear in a few days before the Washington district attorney. He had arrived on time, had the charges read to him, and had been released after being mugged and fingerprinted. The case, which involved civil and criminal charges, dragged on for two years. Finally, the government had dropped the criminal charges and agreed to settle the $20 million civil suit it had brought against Onassis for $7 million. He had paid, and the case was closed.

"It was not money," said Kenny O'Donnell. "It never was money." Still, Jackie had inherited only $70,000 in cash from John Kennedy, and an annual income of $200,000 from a trust fund he had set up, his home at the Kennedy compound, and some personal effects. It is quite obvious that Jackie factored money into her decision, though it did not play a major role.

Emotional security for herself, and safety for her children, were the overriding reasons she had accepted the proposal. Aristotle Onassis was safe harbor.

She cried out in despair after the murder of Bobby

---

* The contradiction did not seem to trouble any of them, considering that the patriarch, Old Joe Kennedy, had used shady and even illicit means to accumulate his fortune.

Kennedy, "I hate this country. I despise America, and I don't want my children to live here any more. If they're killing Kennedys, my kids are number-one targets. I want to get out of this country!"

She had given voice to the impelling reason for marrying Aristotle Onassis: the death of Bobby Kennedy, her devoted friend, counselor, and support.

Kenny O'Donnell told me, "Bobby had played father to her children and was her refuge, her sanctuary. Whenever she felt emotionally unstable, she called him and he was there." However, one after the other, the men on whom she relied were snatched away by death.

Joe McCarthy, the Kennedy biographer who wrote *Johnny, We Hardly Knew Ye,* with Kenny and Dave Powers, told me: "I have no doubt that Bobby's murder threw her over the edge and that she ran to Onassis for protection against a hostile world."

There has been much speculation about a 173-clause prenuptial contract that Ari drew up and Jackie signed. It was first reported by a former steward on the *Christina,* Christian Cafarakis, in a book published by William Morrow in 1978, *The Fabulous Onassis: His Life and Loves.* Cafarakis and coauthor Jacques Harvey said the contract specified that they would sleep in separate bedrooms, that if they should separate Ari would pay Jackie $10 million for every year they had been married up to that time, that if she left him within five years he would pay her $20 million and that if he died while they were still wed, she would receive $100 million.

However, the so-called contract was not made public then nor has it been since, and considerable doubt has been expressed by Kennedy and Onassis historians about whether it existed at all.

What has been accepted by most is that Onassis paid Jackie a kind of reverse dowry, $3 million on their marriage, that he set up a $1 million trust fund for Caroline and John to be paid while they were still minors, and that if Jackie and Ari were divorced, he would pay her an annual sum of $100,000 for the rest of her life.

As a light rain dimpled the Ionian Sea, Jackie and Ari were married on October 20, 1968, in a candlelit ceremony inside a tiny chapel set in a cypress grove on the isle of Skorpios. The small dot of land lies two miles east of the sleepy fishing village of Nidri on the island of Lefkas off the western coast of Greece.

Onassis had bought the little island, for which he paid $100,000, for privacy. "I don't want anybody to watch me pee," he had said. It does not appear on any map of Greece and the surrounding islands in the Ionian and Aegean seas, perhaps because it is too small or, as many Greeks believe, because Onassis paid the Greek government not to permit cartographers to publish its location.

The island of Skorpios resembles a scorpion, one part short and thick, another long and slender, with little spits of land jutting out into the sea like a scorpion's pincers. On the island, Onassis had carved six miles of road, much of it from solid rock, and built several chalets to house guests. He had his own house constructed on the highest point. Skorpios, however, has no water, so every morning ships arrived to put fresh water into an elaborate pump system. Finally, a berth was needed for the *Christina*. At considerable cost, Onassis had the sea dredged and two harbors built, one for his yacht, the other for the floating palaces of the wealthy guests he invited. To insure additional privacy, Ari also purchased the small neighboring island of Sparti, about a mile away, which lay between Skorpios and Nidri.

Despite a force of 150 tough security guards Ari had hired and despite the fleet of patrolling Greek naval motorboats, newsmen managed to storm the island and engage in a short but furious battle with the guards. The media was undeterred by Jackie's personal plea to be allowed to marry in privacy. "We know you understand that even though people may be well known," she had said, "they still hold in their hearts the emotions of a simple person for the moments that are the most important of those we know on earth—birth, marriage, and death." A compromise was reached: a small pool of newspeople was permitted inside the chapel to watch the ceremony.

Only twenty-one guests* crowded into the Chapel of the Little Mother of God as Jackie, in a two-piece long-sleeved beige Valentino creation of chiffon and lace, and Ari, in a double-breasted dark blue business suit and red tie, exchanged vows in a Greek Orthodox ceremony. Flanking the couple were Caroline and John, each carrying a slender white candle. After the marriage prayer was chanted by gold-robed, black-bearded, Archimandrite Polykarpos Athanassion of the Church of Kapnikara in Athens, and attendants placed wreaths of white flowers on the heads of the bridal couple, who walked three times around the altar in a ritual dance. They were pronounced husband and wife at 5:27 P.M.

After the ceremony, which lasted forty-five minutes, the wedding party emerged from the chapel. The wind began to howl and the rain turned to a drenching downpour for which none of the guests were prepared. Still, they all made it to the *Christina* where, despite the dreadful weather, the reception went on as scheduled. It lasted all night, with bouzouki music, dancing girls imported from shore, endless bottles of champagne, banks of flow-

---

* The bride's relatives: Caroline and John; Mr. and Mrs. Hugh Auchincloss; Pat Lawford and Jean Smith; Prince and Princess Stanislas Radziwill and their two children. The bridegroom's relatives and friends: Alexander and Christina; Mrs. Artemis Garofalides, Ari's sister, who served as sponsor; Mrs. Yerasimos Patronicolous, his half-sister, and her husband; Mrs. Panos Drakos, his niece, and her husband; Mr. and Mrs. Nicholas Kokims, friend and business associates; John Georgakis, managing director of Olympic Airways, and his wife.

ers and, of course, enough food to feed a fleet's complement of sailors.

Guests and the media, too, wondered what Ari's wedding present to his new wife might be. Facetious suggestions came from all over: the Taj Mahal, perhaps, or the entire Boston Pops Symphony Orchestra, the Empire State Building, the De Beers diamond mines. Or the New York Stock Exchange, the S.S. *Queen Elizabeth,* or maybe Windsor Castle. When Jackie came into the ship's lounge for the wedding dinner, she was wearing his gift, a ring with a huge ruby set in a circlet of diamonds. She also wore matching earrings. The guests were speechless, all but eleven-year-old Caroline, who squealed: "Mummy, mummy, they're so pretty!" Jackie took off the ring and, as Onassis watched apprehensively, the little girl strutted around the lounge giving the guests a closer look.

Both Onassis children objected strongly to the marriage.

Christina was an attractive young woman, five feet five inches tall and just beginning to show the stockiness of figure that would soon turn into obesity. But at eighteen she possessed an oval, pretty face and a small nose, sculptured by plastic surgery. She hated the idea of losing her father to another woman. Christina adored him and was his *chrysomous,* "golden girl." The quintessential poor little rich girl, Christina had everything any little girl could wish for—the costliest playthings, the finest clothes, the best places to live, including a grand Paris penthouse apartment and magnificent villa in Glyfada, a fashionable Athens suburb. But rarely did she have her father, who traveled on business almost constantly. Her mother, Tina, and Ari had divorced in 1960, and on October 14, 1974, Tina was found dead in her Paris apartment. An autopsy found she had died of natural causes.

A close friend of the family told the following story, which illustrates Ari's notions of parenting and Christina's reaction:

One day, Ari and I were in his Monte Carlo office discussing business. Without warning, he jumped up from his desk and said that he wanted to buy Christina a present. He told me that it wasn't her birthday, but he had just remembered that he had promised to go home that evening, and he had to leave for Argentina instead. So he had his chauffeur drive us to a toy store. He wasn't looking for an ordinary present like you and I might buy for our daughters, but something extra-special. He asked for the most expensive item they had. The saleslady brought out a dainty ballerina doll that, when wound, danced to the tune of the Sugar Plum Fairy. It cost hundreds of dollars. He had it flown especially to Christina, who was in Paris.

He flew to Argentina—and Christina received her breathtakingly lovely doll. It was handed to her by a servant who took it from a messenger at the door.

Alexander, a strange, moody young man, was even more bitterly opposed to the marriage than was his sister, telling their father bluntly that he would not come to the ceremony. Ari pleaded, then struck a bargain with his son. An ardent flier, Alexander would fly almost daily, terrifying his father by his recklessness. And, almost daily, Onassis and Alexander would have shouting arguments about his flying. The son finally said that if Aristotle would stop nagging him about his piloting, he would attend the wedding. Ari was forced into an agreement.

The young man came, but the pool of media representatives noted that he waited outside the chapel until all the guests had gone in, then entered with obvious reluctance. Prior to the ceremony, Alexander had made his feelings known. "I didn't need a stepmother," he had said, "but my father needed a wife." He also told a friend that his father had done some "pretty weird things," asking, "Do you suppose he's getting senile?"

Alexander needled Jackie throughout the seven-year marriage. He would pointedly refuse most invitations to Skorpios and the Paris apartment. One evening, during one of the few dinners he had with Jackie on the island, the talk turned to the newest bit of gossip: a pretty young actress had married a much older, but extremely rich, Greek industrialist. Alexander faced Jackie and said loudly enough for all the guests to hear: "You don't think that's so bad, do you? To marry for money?" A shocked silence followed. After a moment, Jackie, who pretended she hadn't heard the cutting remark, resumed her conversation with the guests.

The effect on Caroline and John was markedly different than it was on Christina and Alexander. Caroline, not yet eleven, was dazed and uncomprehending; John, two years younger, took to Ari at once.

Caroline still called him "Mr. Onassis" the day he married her mother. It was a year before she could bring herself to call him "Daddy." Her bewilderment as she stood silently at the altar of the tiny church was evident. She emerged unsmiling beside Jackie after the ceremony and sat round-eyed and grave-faced on her mother's lap in a yellow gold cart as her new father drove them to his floating palace. John, as always, enjoyed himself hugely.

Ari told John that they were *filaracos*—buddies—and spent many hours taking him sailing, fishing, and waterskiing. After a fishing trip, Ari would pull in at a pier and the two would sit beneath shade trees while Ari spun tales about the pirates who once inhabited the area and the treasures that lay beneath the water of the Aegean.

John learned to speak fractured Greek. When Onassis took him to Nikos Kominates's tavern on Nidri one day after a fishing trip, John said, "*Thela na fao on the* Christina"—"I want to eat on the *Christina*." Onassis guffawed. Said Nikos, "He liked Ari a lot. Ari liked him a lot."

Sharp criticism also came from the Vatican.

Stories appeared that the Roman Catholic Church had granted special dispensation for Jackie, a Catholic, to wed Ari, a member of the Greek Orthodox Church, and a divorced man. However, in Rome, the Rt. Rev. Monsignor Fausto Vallainc, then director of the Vatican's press office, denied there had been an agreement, as published by the Athens newspaper *Ethnos*, for the Church to recognize the marriage.

Monsignor Vallainc told reporters: "There has been no such accord. When Mrs. Kennedy married Mr. Onassis, she knew what she was doing; that is that she was acting against the law of the Roman Catholic Church."

The weekly publication of the Vatican, *L'Osservatore della Domenica*, stated that while a marriage to a divorced man was not cause for excommunication, or a formal expulsion from the Church, it was "in effect, a renunciation of her faith." While the publication did not name Jackie specifically, there was no doubt the comments were directed at her. According to the Associated Press, the Vatican publication repeated and expanded upon what Monsignor Vallainc had said a few days earlier.

The newspaper wrote, "Contracting a marriage with a divorced man already linked by a previous marriage, implies for the Catholic party [Jackie] the assumption of an attitude which is, in effect, a renunciation of her faith." According to canon law, the publication said, Jackie must be considered a "public sinner," meaning that she was denied the sacraments, including a church burial and communion, although attending mass is permitted. However, the publication added that Jackie could change her status later by "penitence and redemption."

* * *

During her marriage to Onassis, Jackie became aware that she had changed. In an extraordinary interview, one of the few times she breached the wall of privacy she had built around herself, she replied in detail to a question by an Iranian woman reporter when she and Ari were visiting Tehran.

The reporter, Maryam Kharazmi of the English-language newspaper *Kayham International,* asked her: "Are you the same sort of person today [May 25, 1972] as you were when you were the wife of President John F. Kennedy?"

Jackie replied:

"Why do people always try to see me through the different names I have had at different times? People often forget that I was Jacqueline Bouvier before being Mrs. Kennedy or Mrs. Onassis. Throughout my life I have always tried to remain true to myself. This I will continue to do as long as I live.

"I am a woman above everything else. I love children and I think seeing one's children grow up is the most delightful thing any woman can think about.

"I have been through a lot and I have suffered a great deal, as you know. But I have had lots of happy moments as well.

"I have come to the conclusion that we must not expect too much from life. We must give to life at least as much as we receive from it.

"Every moment one lives is different from the other, the good, the bad, the hardship, the joy, the tragedy, love and happiness are all interwoven into one single indescribable whole that is called life."

Discussing her own experience as a journalist, Jackie said:

"My job was to ask a single question from six or seven different people each day and then photograph them while they talked," she explained. "Often it was difficult to get anything. It taught me not to expect too much and not to take things for granted . . .

"I get afraid of reporters when they come to me in a crowd," she explained. "I don't like crowds because I don't like impersonal masses. They remind me of swarms of locusts.

"The truth of the matter is that I am a very shy person. People take my diffidence for arrogance and my withdrawal from publicity as a sign, supposedly, that I am looking down on the rest of mankind."

10

The Truth About *That* Marriage

The celebrated marriage is now recalled as a terrible failure. It is also commonly believed that Jackie was never in love with Onassis, nor he with her.

Neither is true.

For the first two or three years, the marriage was a good one because, essentially, each met the other's deepest emotional needs. Ari gave Jackie the security and stability she wanted in her troubled life. And before six months had passed, she—and Caroline too—came to love him.

She showed her feelings by her actions and her words. Gushing like a schoolgirl describing her rapture over an older boy, she told a friend at the Grand Bretagne Hotel in Constitution Square in Athens, "It's a delightful feeling to be in love."

On his part, Ari was as much in love with her as his personality and character would allow. He confessed to his friends, "I love that woman. I truly love her." Jackie gave him the emotional satisfaction of having won what he yearned for most, a crown jewel. He demonstrated his affection in the only way he knew how, by showering Jackie with gifts and attention.

Jackie and Ari had a great deal in common. According to Pearl Buck, who had close ties to friends of both, "He loved beauty, she loved art, and he had the money to indulge her tastes . . . And he loves children. He has a natural ability to communicate with them. And he loves her with maturity and compassion."

Ari said soon after the marriage: "[Jackie] is like a bird. She wants the protection of the nest, yet she wants, as well, the freedom to fly. I offer her both."

"He is a wise and kind man," Pearl Buck said. Charlotte Ford Niarchos, the divorced wife of Stavros Niarchos, another wealthy shipping tycoon, described Onassis as a "marvelous father, with tremendous charm and personality, extremely bright, polite and well-mannered, very attractive and very masculine."

Just after the marriage, the *Chicago Daily News* published the comments of a New Yorker, who was not identified but who knew Onassis well. "He pays absolutely mad, dedicated, constant court when he is attracted to a woman, literally sweeping her off her feet. He is known for the sheer, driving force of his personal passions as well as his business maneuvers."

It is little wonder that such a man could get a woman, even Jacqueline, to fall in love with him.

He had demonstrated the "driving force" of his passions in the late 1950s after he met Maria Callas, the opera star, who was then married to Giovanni Battista, a Milan businessman. Battista was thirty years older than the twenty-five-year-old Callas when they were married on April 21, 1949.

Onassis planned his campaign to possess Callas as carefully as Bismarck devising a battle plan. Central to his strategy was the *Christina*. He invited Marie and her husband for a cruise; his wife, Tina, of course, would be along.

But neither Tina nor Battista impeded Onassis. His target was Maria, whom he wooed ardently—and successfully. Just two months after the cruise, the opera star succumbed completely. "Maria had totally fallen in love for the first time. Onassis swept her off her feet," said Callas's longtime friend, Helen Rochas of the French perfume company.

Callas rationalized the affair by invoking fate. "I was not a home breaker," she said afterward, "nor was he. Tina was going to leave anyway. I had to follow my destiny."

By 1967, Ari had begun to tire of Callas. She summed up the reason perfectly in this bitter remark: "Aristotle is obsessed by famous women. He was obsessed with me because I was famous. Jackie is even more famous."

On the day Ari married Jackie, Maria was in Paris attending the premiere of the movie version of the Georges Feydeau farce *A Flea in His Ear.* She smiled and waved as she entered the theater, and afterward she was radiant at a party noting the seventy-fifth anniversary of Maxim's restaurant. Said Arianna Stassinopoulos, "It was one of the most convincing performances of her career. Only someone who had looked closely into her huge dark eyes could have seen the anguish that dimmed their light."

Surprisingly, for a sophisticated man who understood the capriciousness of love, that men can be, and often are, unfaithful, and that women could also cheat on their husbands, Aristotle Onassis was capable of extreme jealousy. He was tormented by what some psychiatrists have called the "Othello syndrome." He wanted to know all he could about Jackie's romantic attachments after the death of Jack Kennedy.

Said one of Jackie's friends, who was a frequent guest at their parties, "This was a man of the world, but at times he would act like a jealous, heartsick husband as he tried to pump me about Lord Harlech and some of the other men he thought Jackie had favored." Not once, however, did he ask Jackie. He knew better.

Onassis tried hard to make his marriage to Jackie work, and in the first years he succeeded. A solicitous husband, he catered to her whims and wishes. He did everything he could to make her happy; most important to Jackie was the attention he paid to her children.

Once, while both were reading on the deck of the *Christina,* Jackie suddenly rose from her chair, walked over to him, and kissed him. Surprised, he asked: "What's that for?"

"That's because of last night," she said. Ari had stayed up all night long because young John had a stomachache. "I just thought about it," Jackie said, and she kissed him again. Ari grinned.

A minute later he rose, went to her, and kissed her—passionately.

"What's *that* for?" she asked.

"I just remembered," he said, "that a couple of months ago I was ill and you stayed up with me." They both laughed and kissed again.

He was the most considerate of husbands. At the Grande Bretagne Hotel, she said to her friend, "His constant attention and ingenuity are wonderful. Last Thursday morning, for example, he told me I looked quite pale and needed a bit of a change. He suggested we fly to Paris and have dinner at Maxim's.

"He's always doing things like that. He notices things others fail to see. He has such a brilliant mind and can pick up things and completely analyze them and be right."

And then came the frank, artless admission that she was in love.

His generosity was boundless. On her fortieth birthday, he presented her with roses and a diamond necklace and bracelet valued at more than a million dollars. He hosted a birthday party that evening at an open-air night spot near Piraeus, attended by daughter Christina, a number of relatives, and a few close friends. Said Lee Guthrie: "They sat close together all evening—or rather, well into the morning. Ari had his arm around her and they whispered together and kissed each other like two high-school kids in the throes of first love."

"He made a tremendous effort to be a good father," Lem Billings told me. At the start, he explained to Caroline and John that while he could never replace their father, he would be honored to be their friend and protector.

Although his work took him all over the world, he made a valiant effort. He brought them gifts, was unfailingly cordial to their friends, and would take them fishing, sailing, and water-skiing on their trips to Skorpios. Once he learned Caroline had her heart set on a special horse. He told Jackie to buy it for her, then cut short a multimillion-dollar deal to fly to America so that he could be present when she received it.

In the end, he won Caroline over. After his death in 1975, she confided to a boyfriend, Juan Cameron, then a student at Middlesex Academy in Massachusetts, "I didn't see him that much, but I really did love him."

The billing and cooing lasted only two years.

Jackie, who had recovered emotionally, began traveling with increasing frequency, and Onassis, exercising the right he felt he had as a Greek man, sought other women. Indeed, not long after his marriage to Jackie, Ari was back in the life of Maria Callas, a fact which, by his code, did not mean he was any the less in love with his new wife. "He knew his prey well," observed Arianna Stassinopoulos. While the marriage to Jackie presented an obstacle, he believed he could win Callas over once again.

And he was right.

He sent Callas flowers and gifts, and a little more than two months after his marriage to Jackie, had Christmas dinner with Maria—not alone, of course, but with friends of both.

At the start, Ari had said that Jackie "can do exactly as she pleases—visit international fashion shows and travel and go out with friends to the theater or any place. And I, of course, will do exactly as I please. I never question her and she never questions me."

It was a bold statement, and perhaps Onassis truly meant it, but Jackie overdid it and, for Ari, disenchantment set in. While Jackie hardly spent $20 million on her honeymoon, as Fred Sparks claimed in a sensational book published in 1970, she did manage to spend about $1.5 million on clothes, travel, gifts, and—her special passion—redecorating the Skorpios house. Said Stassinopoulos: "There was something compulsive, almost manic, about Jackie's lavish spending. And the more he [Onassis] felt used by Jackie, the more he felt loved by Maria."

As tragedy stalked the Kennedys, it did no less for Onassis. On January 22, 1973, his beloved son Alexander, who had exacted the pledge from his father not to "nag" him about his flying, was killed in an air crash shortly after he took off from Athens Airport in a twin-engine amphibian Piaggio. Alexander was not flying the plane. It was piloted by Donald McCusker, forty-eight, an American. The flight was to test McCusker's ability to supervise a fleet of air taxis that Alexander had hoped to organize. Ari, in New York at the time, rushed to the Athens hospital where they found that Alexander, his face smashed beyond recognition, could survive only as a living vegetable. Next day, mercifully for him, Alexander died of a brain hemorrhage.

Onassis was devastated. The two patriarchs, Joe Kennedy and Aristotle Onassis, who reveled in the making of money by crushing others, were crushed themselves by the deaths of their sons. Joe Kennedy shut himself in his room at the Big House on Cape Cod after his eldest son was killed in an air crash over the English Channel during World War II, listening for hours to symphonic music. Aristotle Onassis wept for days, canceled all appointments, and never again regained his zest for life, for love, and for the acquisition of more and more wealth. He would walk the streets of Athens, find a café, and sit for hours drinking the national aperitif, which turns milky when mixed with water and carries a mighty punch.

One day several friends, on their way to a dinner party, spotted him at a café near the Acropolis. Stopping, one told the others he would see them at their destination. "I sat down next to him," the friend said. "At first he was silent, which wasn't like him. After a while he began to talk. He talked about his boy. Slowly, softly, he spoke about Alexander, how much he loved him, how he missed him. He said that, other than Christina, he was all alone now. Jackie, he said, just refused to understand him. For an hour he continued to speak in that same sad way. Then, I offered to take him home, but he said all he wanted was a taxi. I was pleased to see that he walked out in a straight manner, without weaving or wobbling. He didn't seem drunk any more."

By 1973, the five-year-old marriage was unraveling rapidly.

Unable to talk to Jackie about the problems that weighed heavily on him, Onassis confided his innermost thoughts and feelings to Maria Callas. Maria listened patiently as he paced the floor of his Paris penthouse apartment, raging about Jackie's indifference, complaining about her excessive spending and her hard outer crust.

While he had returned to his own mistress without a twinge of guilt, he became suspicious of Jackie. Late in 1974, he engaged the flamboyant lawyer, Roy Cohn, to see if his mistrust was justified. He also hired a private investigator to search for evidence of infidelity. Said Stassinopoulos: "His body had turned against itself, and Onassis turned viciously against the woman whom he now irrationally considered the source of his accumulating woes."

The double standard of demanding fidelity on the part of his wife, while failing to impose the stricture on himsclf, never occurred to Ari. Declared Prince Michael of Greece: "Cheating on your wife is a must in Greece. Adultery is a national sport. For the most part, men dislike the confinement of their homes. They enjoy trailing from one café to another most of the night. It's a very Greek trait, very much part of Onassis."

Cohn told me that no evidence of any infidelity on Jackie's part was ever uncovered, and that it was quite possible that the decline in Ari's health had created a paranoia that led him to think she had been unfaithful.

That year, 1974, Onassis had been diagnosed as suffering from myasthenia gravis, a muscle-wasting disease that causes abnormal fatigue. Often the most affected muscles involve the eyes. Onassis had to use tape on his eyelids to keep them from shutting.

Although he wore dark glasses, the media soon discovered his illness. Despite treatment with cortisone, which made him increasingly irritable, his condition did not improve. In the fall of 1974, he was admitted to a New York hospital where doctors said nothing more could be done for him. A few months later, now white-haired, pale, and drawn, he was flown to Paris aboard a specially equipped Olympic Airways jet, then admitted to the American Hospital in Neuilly-sur-Seine, on the outskirts of Paris.

On February 8, 1975, doctors found stones in his gall bladder and performed surgery at once. But in his weakened condition, Onassis contracted pneumonia and spent five weeks at the hospital.

By this time, the hostility between Jackie and Ari's daughter, Christina, had escalated to the point where neither spoke to the other. Both would visit Onassis at his hospital room, number 217 of the Eisenhower wing, and sit at opposite sides of his bed, ignoring each other. Ari talked to his daughter in Greek and to Jackie in French.

On March 10, doctors told Jackie she could safely leave for the United States for a few days because Onassis appeared to be making progress in his fight against pneumonia. Caroline, who had taken a job in the Visual Arts Department at the Metropolitan Museum of Art, had prepared a television documentary Jackie was anxious to see.

Jackie boarded an Olympic jet and arrived in New York on Thursday evening, March 13. Next morning she phoned the American Hospital and was told that Onassis was in stable condition. Later that night, however, he went into a sharp decline and died on Saturday, March 15, of bronchial pneumonia which, according to Dr. Mercedes Mercadier, had resisted all antibiotics. At his death, Ari was sixty-nine.

Three days later, Jackie, who had flown to Paris and remained secluded in the Avenue Foch apartment, buried her second husband; accompanied this time, too, by Caroline and John. Onassis was buried on Skorpios, next to his beloved son Alexander.

The death of Onassis began an ugly series of lawsuits that eventually made Jackie a wealthy woman.

When she married him, she had insisted on a cash payment of $3 million, which actually amounted to a reverse dowry. In return, she gave up all claims to his estate.

In his will, Onassis—to everyone's surprise because he had never exhibited a social conscience while he was alive —left half of his estate for the establishment of a foundation that would distribute funds for public welfare organizations, mostly in Greece.

The bequest was due to Jackie's influence. Until he married Jackie, said Pearl Buck, who quoted a report in a small Vermont newspaper, Onassis "had not believed in charity." People, he felt, should take care of themselves. "Now, under the influence of this strong, beautiful woman, he is changing the image he has built for himself through the years. He is giving large sums of money to help unfortunate persons, especially children," Ms. Buck said.

Jackie had imbued the acquisitive Greek with Kennedy-style liberalism.

As for Jackie, his instructions were specific: He bequeathed to her $250,000 annually in tax free funds, specifying that the amount should be adjusted for inflation every three years. Of this sum, $50,000 in tax-free funds would go for the support of Caroline and John until they reached twenty-one, when the money would revert to Jackie.

He added this provision: If Jackie contested the will, every effort must be made to battle the suit in court, the costs to be borne by his estate.

Jackie did contest the will. Christina countered with an offer to raise the annual payment to eight million, which was refused by Jackie's attorneys. A year of legal haggling followed, which ended when Christina, weary of the battling and wanting to be rid of her much-despised former stepmother, finally instructed her attorneys to arrange a settlement.

Jackie received $20 million, plus $6 million more for taxes. In return, she promised never again to visit Skorpios and gave up all rights to the yacht *Christina*.

The Greek tragedy, which began in 1968, approached its climax two and one-half years after Onassis died. Maria Callas, who had come to rely more and more on tranquilizing drugs and sleeping pills, became increasingly depressed. A rich woman with a fortune estimated in excess of $10 million, she had no desire to spend any of it; she wanted only to remain in her suite in a Paris hotel and mourn her lost love, whom she considered in her heart to be her late husband.

She said in a bizarre statement, "All of a sudden, I am a widow." Ari's death, said Stassinopoulos, had struck her "a mortal blow."

In the spring of 1977, she went to Skorpios for one of her many visits to the grave of Aristotle Onassis, where she knelt and prayed for hours. Five months later, on

September 16, she died of a heart attack in her Paris apartment.

Costa Gravas, Ari's trusted aide who became head of all Onassis's business enterprises, said she had died of a broken heart. "Life for her was not worth living after he was gone," he declared.

Eleven years later, on November 19, 1989, the tragedy was finally played out.

As in the plays of Sophocles, life brought only death and despair. Man, Sophocles believed, was a divine creature but also helpless, a plaything of the gods, who manipulated him at their whim and, when they wished, decided his fate.

Onassis, his wife Tina, his son Alexander, his mistress Maria Callas—all had died.

And now, Christina.

She had grown enormously fat. She had gone through four marriages and, eight years before, had attempted to end her life with an overdose of sleeping pills. Christina was only thirty-eight years old when she died of pulmonary edema in Argentina while visiting friends in a Buenos Aires suburb.

She was buried on the island of Skorpios next to her father and brother. Jackie issued a statement of sorrow but did not attend the funeral in the tiny chapel where, in 1968, she had married Onassis.

11

⌒

Jackie's Children—
Caroline

In contrast to Onassis's children, whose tragically short-
ened lives were, in the main, unhappy, Jackie's daughter and son are happy and productive.

Caroline, thirty-seven in 1994, is an attorney, a graduate of Columbia University's School of Law, mother of
three young children, and coauthor with Ellen Alderman,
a law-school classmate, of a best-selling book. John, two
years younger, also a lawyer, served for three years as an
assistant prosecutor in the office of Manhattan district
attorney Robert N. Morgenthau, resigning in mid-1993 to
pursue other interests, which, at the time, he did not
specify.

Unlike the children of Robert and Ethel Kennedy, neither got into any trouble more serious than receiving traffic tickets. One of Bobby's children died of an overdose
and several others have had drug problems. Both Teddy
Kennedy, Jr., and his younger brother, Patrick, have admitted they had problems with alcohol. In June of 1992,
Ted, Jr., at the age of thirty-one, voluntarily entered the
Institute for Living in Connecticut for alcohol depen-
dency, remaining there for three weeks. Patrick said that
at the age of nineteen he had checked into a rehab center
in Spofford Hall, in Spofford, New Hampshire, for treatment of a drug habit, which he said he had overcome.

And, as a teenager, Ted's daughter Kara had experimented with hashish and run away from home a number of times.

Jackie's excellent parenting kept her children on the right path.

In 1970, she decided Caroline should transfer to the Brearley School in Manhattan where, she felt, she would be exposed to a broader spectrum of people than in a religious school. Ever watchful of her children's privacy, teachers and staff at Brearley, and at Collegiate, where John was a student, had to promise in writing not to discuss the Kennedy children with outsiders.

She tried, too, to shield her children from the press, particularly from the free-lance photographers whose modus operandi was to follow celebrities and snap their pictures without permission. A persistent offender was Ron Galella, who sought pictures not only of Jackie but of Caroline and John, too.

Once she had an Onassis employee grab his camera. Another time she had him arrested. Finally, she sued Galella, charging he was harassing her and invading her privacy and that of her children. Galella countersued. Jackie, he said, was interfering with his right to earn a living. Onassis, who had tried to persuade Jackie not to sue because it would result in bad publicity for her and increased importance for Galella, could not get her to drop the case. Privately he asked Galella if an out-of-court settlement could be reached. When the photographer demanded $100,000, Onassis backed off.

Jackie won the suit, the court ruling that Galella could not come closer than a fifty-yard radius of her and her children. However, her attorneys' bill was more than $200,000.

Brearley had the reputation of being "hard to get into," but Caroline passed the entrance examinations with high marks and entered the eighth grade. Her courses there included English, history, Latin, algebra, physical science, music, art, and French. The school, whose students were children of the social elite, was progressive and stressed initiative and independence.

When Caroline neared the age of fifteen, Jackie felt she was ready for boarding school, where she would have a greater measure of freedom and achieve more independence than would be possible at home. After much searching she selected Concord Academy, then a fifty-one-year-old girls' school on a thirty-two-acre campus in Concord, Massachusetts, a short drive from Boston.

Concord was a town out of yesterday, with its nineteenth-century homes, quiet elm-shaded streets, and Walden Pond and the Old North Bridge a short distance away. Concord Academy had grown accustomed to having the children of the rich and famous studying there.

That summer, while Caroline vacationed in Skorpios and learned the art of bullfighting in Spain, community leaders, aware of her mother's almost frantic efforts to shield Caroline from the public, made plans to provide a normal setting. A few weeks before her arrival a special plea was made on her behalf by the weekly newspaper *Concord Journal*.

In a leading editorial, A LITTLE GIRL IS COMING TO VISIT, the newspaper said of Caroline: "As the daughter of Camelot's prince and his ethereal princess, she was marked for mass adulation too early in life. Events not of her making or choosing have crept up and around her to make her a sometimes frightened child denied the pleasures of childhood in an American town, the heritage guaranteed by the country her father headed to millions of kids." The editorial continued: "Please treat her as you would any other Concord kid. Ignore her as you do your neighbor's kids, except for the occasional circumstance when a cheery word or two might be indicated. . . . Remember, she's only a kid."

Caroline, in the ninth grade, shared a small room, about fifteen feet square, in one of the school's seven

Jacqueline Bouvier, the daughter of John Vernou Bouvier III and
Janet Auchincloss, was born into elegance and reared in privilege.
An avid horsewoman all her life, she is seen here in riding togs as
she entered her teens. She is flanked by her father (*left*) and grandfather, John Vernou Bouvier, Jr. Photo was taken at her parents'
home in East Hampton, L.I. (JOHN F. KENNEDY LIBRARY)

The new president, the new first lady, and the first daughter pose on the lawn of the Kennedy compound. (JOHN F. KENNEDY LIBRARY)

Christmas 1962—Still in their nightclothes, Caroline and John Jr. examine their Christmas stockings in the White House. (JOHN F. KENNEDY LIBRARY)

The Kennedy family leaves St. Matthew's Cathedral. Jackie, holding the hands of Caroline, six, and John, three, is followed by Robert Kennedy and Jean Kennedy Smith. Peter Lawford is in the back. (WHITE HOUSE PHOTO)

The flag-draped coffin is taken from the Capitol to St. Matthew's Cathedral for the funeral mass. (JOHN F. KENNEDY LIBRARY)

On May 27, 1967, Caroline Kennedy christened the aircraft carrier U.S.S. *John F. Kennedy*. Grinning at the splash of champagne are Jackie and John Jr. (U.S. NAVY PHOTOGRAPH)

Jackie and Maurice Tempelsman, a diamond merchant who is her longtime escort, attend the theater in New York City. (ALBERT FERREIRA/DMI)

Tempelsman and Jackie walking in New York City the day after she was released from New York Hospital in April 1994. (© BILL DAVILA)

Jackie and John Jr. leave the JFK Library after a meeting, passing in the hall a picture of the late president. (JOHN F. KENNEDY LIBRARY)

JACKIE—A PORTFOLIO OF HER MOODS.

Laughing (at thirty)
(JOHN F. KENNEDY LIBRARY)

Mysterious (at thirty-one)
(JOHN F. KENNEDY LIBRARY)

Glamorous (at fifty-seven)
(BOSTON HERALD)

Happy (at fifty-seven)
(BOSTON HERALD)

At sixty-something, her countenance, though serene, often mirrored the tragedies of the past. Yet she did not dwell on them. She greeted the future smilingly. (BOSTON HERALD)

dormitories. The dorms are actually former residences that lined Main Street at the turn of the century. There are no private baths.

Two "house parents" were permanent residents in Caroline's dorm, as in all of the others, to exercise overall supervision. There was a bare minimum of rules and regulations, though, the academy taking the view that the young people should have the maximum amount of personal freedom.

The students were not campus-bound on weekends but free to select their own activities, visit in the homes of day students, participate if they wished in community programs, and even to work and study in Boston. All students were permitted to wear what they pleased to class and meals. Caroline, along with her classmates, would appear in dungarees, slacks, or shorts most of the time.

Classes were small, averaging twelve to fourteen students to a teacher, and the total enrollment came to only 265, about a third of whom were day students, and fifty were boys. (Concord, following a tide running strong in many schools and colleges, became coed in 1971).

Her friends and classmates told many stories about Caroline's unpredictability. One day, she stared at her image in the mirror over the dresser in her dormitory room. "My face," she announced, "is too symmetrical." Whereupon she picked up a razor and methodically shaved off one eyebrow.

She was famous for her practical jokes. On one occasion she poured bubble bath into the tank of a drinking water fountain; on another, she added chocolate laxative to some brownies she and a friend were baking for a school bake sale.

One spring morning Caroline and a friend managed to lock themselves out of their dormitory at 7 A.M. On a whim, they had gone outside. To their shock, the door clicked shut behind them. They shrugged and, in slippers and robes, began walking the short distance to the town center for breakfast. On the way, a policeman in a squad car picked them up and returned them to school, arousing the occupants of the dorm. The officer firmly told Caroline and friend not to go wandering around Concord in the future in nightclothes.

She played hide and seek—literally—with the Secret Service agents who guarded her night and day until she was sixteen. They lost her frequently or, rather she lost *them*. Once she slipped away to Boston in a car to hear her uncle, Senator Ted Kennedy, speak. The agents, who thought she was in her dormitory, were amazed and chagrined to learn by radio that she was seventeen miles away. Another time, she boarded a bus but left it at once through a rear door without being observed. The agents followed the bus while Caroline went her own way.

Throughout her growing-up years, and even now, Caroline has been acutely sensitive to charges, which have surfaced over the decades in the media, that she is snobbish and arrogant, taking advantage of her celebrity to obtain favored treatment.

Juan Cameron, a student at Middlesex Academy a mile away, who dated Caroline and saw her almost daily, told me in 1973: "She needs constant assurances that people like her. It means an awful lot to her not to be thought arrogant. I never saw any signs that she was." Juan, who comes from Washington, was introduced in the fall of 1974 by Ethel Kennedy's son Michael, Juan's best friend.

Once Caroline and several classmates were gabbing earnestly in a Concord ice cream shop. They had finished their sodas but the conversation was so fascinating they wouldn't leave. Two boys asked for the table and Caroline replied: "Can't you see we're talking?" One of the youths thereupon said loudly: "Who the f—— does she think she is?"

Caroline rose and left the shop in tears.

Her attachment to the memory of her father has always been deep. Her dormitory room at Concord, like her room in New York, was filled with photographs of him. And while most people shied from mentioning her father for fear of saddening her, she and Juan discussed him often.

"Her father was supreme to her," Cameron said. "He's on top of her list of all the men she ever talks about. She says he was the best president the country ever had."

In the summer of her first year at Concord, Caroline's interest in public causes had her ringing doorbells in Concord on behalf of John Kerry, and she enjoyed the experience hugely. Kerry was the antiwar candidate for Congress who bore a resemblance in appearance, voice, and political ideology to her father, the late president. She also journeyed to New Hampshire in early fall to join groups of young people campaigning for Senator George McGovern, the Democratic presidential candidate. There was a poignant moment in October when, attired strikingly in a jet-black pants suit, Caroline, not yet sixteen, made her first political appearance since the assassination, in Boston, where her father had begun his climb to fame. She accompanied Ted Kennedy and her Aunt Joan to a McGovern fund-raising affair and received a tumultuous welcome.

The following summer she spent six weeks in the hill country of eastern Tennessee with a film crew, helping to make a documentary about the lives and work of coal miners. Arriving without fanfare in mid-June, in the rugged Appalachian area around the tiny town of Clairfield, just below the Kentucky border, she worked hard helping to interview miners, assisting in the camerawork and film processing. The documentary was a government project, made under the Federation of Communities in Service program.

During her stay in Appalachia, Caroline lived with a family in Clairfield. In faded, patched jeans, she blended inconspicuously into the film crew and, for that matter, into the population. One woman was quoted by the

Knoxville *News-Sentinel* as saying: "You would never know she's the daughter of the late president and so rich. She goes up and down these mountains just like us other hillbillies."

When Caroline was sixteen, Jackie took her and John to a cavernous building in Waltham, Massachusetts, where all the Kennedy memorabilia was stored until the presidential library was built. Dave Powers, the Kennedy aide who was named library curator, a position he still holds, said he had to fight back tears that day.

"It was a remarkable experience," he told me. "She was barely six years old when she last saw all those things. Yet, ten years later, they were all vividly in her mind."

Powers said Caroline recognized at once the rocking chair that had stood in the Oval Office near the fireplace. She remembered the huge whale's tooth JFK had kept on his desk as a paperweight, and she swooped down upon the mounted coconut shell on which he had scratched out a message for help when his PT boat was cut in half by a Japanese destroyer in World War II.

John, only three when the president was slain, did not remember any of it, so Caroline explained as they wandered through the aisles: This was Daddy's desk, that was on the wall over the fireplace, this stood on the floor right near the door . . .

Her passion for horses, begun in childhood and flaming throughout most of her adolescence, had dimmed. It was supplanted at age seventeen by a new excitement—flying.

Early in 1974, Caroline had told her mother that she wanted to take flying lessons. Jackie called an old friend, Frank Comerford, who runs the Comerford Flight School at Hanscom Field a few miles east of Concord. Mr. Comerford was John Kennedy's pilot in short hops he made during his campaigns for the House and Senate in the 1950s.

The arrangements made, Caroline would go up in a red-and-white Cessna 150 single-engine, two-seater airplane, with chief flight instructor Laurie Cannon at her side. She would soar over the historic town, above the celebrated Old North Bridge where "the embattled farmers stood and fired the shot heard round the world" in the first battle of the Revolutionary War. "She did fine," says Mr. Cannon, "with no trouble, just the usual ups and downs." Caroline took fifteen lessons, at thirty dollars per hour, and was almost ready for solo flying when she stopped. She explained that work was piling up at school and she was too busy.

Skiing and tennis have been favorite sports for years, but in 1975 Caroline had taken to jogging in the countryside, field hockey and lacrosse. She was first-string defense for the Concord girls' lacrosse team and performed credibly, though the team lost more games than it won.

In her senior year, Caroline applied to only one college—Radcliffe, the woman's division of Harvard University, which three generations of Kennedys, her grandfather, father, three uncles, and several cousins had attended. She was accepted, but decided to put off college in favor of a year's study at the London art auction house, Sotheby's. The course of study would include visits to galleries and museums in England and on the continent, attending lectures and learning to appraise the value of works of art.

In London in 1975, Caroline had a brief but wild fling with the trendy, wealthy British set. Invited to the best places by Britain's young bluebloods, Caroline partied until dawn.

Word reached Jackie, who warned her daughter by transatlantic telephone to wind down. Rose, reading news accounts of Caroline's "wild life in London," called Jackie a number of times, urging her to bring the young lady home at once. Even her uncle Ted Kennedy was enlisted to subdue her.

Caroline herself ended her frantic partying after she

got a big scare. A bomb exploded outside the home of the late M.P., Sir Hugh Fraser, where she was staying. No motive was ever discovered but police did not believe Caroline was the target. Still, it was enough to cool down her lifestyle.

At Radcliffe, Caroline roomed at Winthrop House, where her father and uncle Bobby had lived. Although she studied hard and made excellent grades, the live-it-up years continued. She attended parties frequently, chugged beer from cans at local taverns, and made a reputation as a "good fellow." On trips to New York, she was often seen at Studio 54, then the "in" disco, with a variety of boyfriends.

She developed an interest in journalism and spent a summer as an intern for the *Daily News* in New York. Her fame proved something of a drag. Once, while covering a minor story, she was chagrined to discover on returning to the office that pictures of her snapped by paparazzi had preceded her to the city room.

At college, mother-daughter battles intensified. Jackie, an apostle of all that is elegant and tasteful, railed against Caroline's sloppy room at Winthrop House in Cambridge, but to little avail. Nor could she convince Caroline to upgrade her wardrobe. Once, in what was obviously a show of defiance, Caroline appeared in an old plaid shirt, Levi's corduroys, and a sweater at a fundraising dinner for the Joseph P. Kennedy, Jr. Foundation in a Boston restaurant. All the other women wore afternoon dresses and the men wore three-piece suits. Jackie could only gasp.

But Jackie, though aghast at times, always held the reins loosely, never allowing a chasm to open that could not be bridged.

Caroline's attitude toward money was far closer to that of her father and her uncles than to her mother's. Jackie's habit of overspending had plagued both her marriages. John Kennedy had rarely carried money. Often Dave

Powers would have to put a bill in the collection plate for him. Bobby, too, often irritated his middle- and working-class teammates when they had to shell out for his share of late-night coffee and sandwiches.

Caroline's allowance and personal checking account were generous, but she spent little on herself. In the local Harvard Square eating places she was known as a poor tipper, exasperating waitresses.

A friend said, "It's not that she's cheap. She simply has little awareness of money. Some days she'd have a lot of it in her pockets, other days not enough. She doesn't calculate carefully."

Yet she could be very generous. She wrote large checks for charitable causes. On one occasion, a classmate told her about a male friend, a dropout from another school, who was drifting penniless around Harvard Square. Even though she didn't know the youth, Caroline gave him several large bills.

She often attended campus meetings and lectures on social issues, which provoked further discussion for hours with her friends. Once, in 1977, nearing the age of twenty, she was one of the thirty-five hundred shouting and chanting students who marched around the campus to protest against the Harvard Corporation's ownership of stock in American companies that did business in South Africa. It was the largest protest rally at Harvard since the Vietnam War.

Demonstrators bore lighted candles and torches as they marched and listened to speakers. Caroline, with candle held aloft, chanted with the others: "One, two, three, four, throw apartheid out the door. Five, six, seven, eight, don't support the racist state." The demonstration lasted until dawn and Caroline stayed until the end.

Jackie's lifelong influence has taken strong hold in one area—the arts. After her year at Sotheby's, Caroline's interest deepened and at Radcliffe she elected to major in fine arts, a concentration of historical courses in visual and environmental studies, classical architecture, humanities, anthropology, Afro-American studies, language, history, and philosophy.

But Jackie's attempt to mold her to a life of sophistication in the social set failed miserably. She wanted her daughter to be introduced to society at the age of eighteen in the traditional manner at a debutante ball. Jackie pleaded with Caroline, but her daughter adamantly refused. Jackie finally gave up and there was no coming-out party for Caroline.

There were, of course, romances for Caroline along the way, only one of them serious. In 1978, she met thirty-one-year-old Tom Carney, an author, Yale graduate, and Irish Catholic. Jackie gave him high marks and Caroline fell in love. Carney was invited frequently to the family compound on Cape Cod and visited Caroline in Cambridge on many occasions.

It ended in heartbreak for Caroline. In 1981, Carney married Maureen Lambrey, a young photographer.

Only a few months later Caroline met Edwin A. Schlossberg, from an Orthodox Jewish family, at a dinner party. Handsome, wealthy, and thirteen years her senior, Schlossberg, the son of a wealthy retired textile executive, has been described as a "Renaissance man." He has doctoral degrees in both science and literature from Columbia University and he is the founder of a firm that designs museum and educational exhibits. Four years later, in 1986, their engagement was announced.

Caroline had been on the verge of announcing the betrothal many times but had drawn back at the last minute. In the spring of 1986, Caroline made her decision to marry, and Jackie had an announcement sent to the society page of *The New York Times*. Her friends at Columbia gave Caroline a prenuptial shower in the school lounge and her former Metropolitan colleagues another in a

Central Park West apartment, where among the other gifts was a Jewish cookbook.

After graduating from college in 1979, Caroline had moved to a Manhattan apartment that she shared with three friends, a girl and two boys, on the top three floors of a narrow, 100-year-old building on West 84th Street. Her small bedroom, in sharp contrast to her earlier room on Fifth Avenue, had simple white shades and peeling paint on the walls, which she covered with pictures. Caroline's share of the rent was five hundred dollars per month.

She worked in the film and television division of the Metropolitan Museum of Art for six years and then resigned, after consulting with her mother, her uncle Ted, and Schlossberg.

"I'm bored with museum work," she said. "I felt I had nowhere to go."

She enrolled in the Columbia University School of Law, where she was as quiet and unobtrusive as she had been boisterous in her undergraduate days. Shy in the beginning, she made no friends. As her first year progressed and students became more accustomed to her presence, she appeared to be more confident and developed a small circle of acquaintances with whom she would have lunch and chat in the first-floor lounge.

At the start of the semester, like many in her class, she confessed to a friend, "I'm totally snowed under by the work."

In near panic, she sought help from her cousin Robert F. Kennedy, Jr. Bobby, who worked for a time as an assistant D.A., taught her the trick of reading and quickly digesting scores of cases.

Still, there were discouraging days. Once, after a class in a complex aspect of property law, she sighed to a classmate, "Why am I doing all this? Somehow, I think all I want to do is stay home and have babies."

As the semester ended she won a commendation for

her work in moot court, a mock trial all first-year students must argue before a jury of outside judges and lawyers.

As the school year drew to a close, it was evident that Caroline had love and marriage very much on her mind.

Said a classmate, "She constantly fingered the engagement ring Ed had given her, a wide gold band with a large submerged diamond." Observing her, other friends noted that a Mona Lisa-like smile played on her lips as she glanced at the fourth finger of her left hand.

Once, during a lecture on constitutional law, she was seen bending over a pad on the table in front of her, brow furrowed. But she was not taking notes. She was sketching her wedding gown, which she excitedly showed to a friend after the session.

She never lingered at school after classes, but rushed home to her tiny apartment for a few hours of study before dining nightly with Ed Schlossberg. Often she would meet him at his studio at 20 West 20th Street and then go to a quiet restaurant in Greenwich Village.

In April 1983, Caroline suffered yet another shock when her cousin David, to whom she had been especially close in her growing-up years, died of a drug overdose in a Palm Beach hotel.

When David Kennedy was a student at Harvard, Caroline had visited him frequently at the small apartment he shared with Juan Cameron on Ellsworth Street in Boston. David's worsening drug habit had forced him out of school.

On Wednesday morning, April 25, 1984, David's mother Ethel tried repeatedly to call him but got no reply. Alarm grew at the Kennedys' palatial winter home on North Ocean Boulevard, where Caroline was staying. In midmorning, she and a friend went to the Brazilian Court Hotel on Australia Avenue, where she rang David from the house phone. Still no response. The two then went to room 107, knocked on the door, and left when nobody answered. Neither knew that inside the room David was dead, his fully clothed body lying between two beds. Later, the autopsy report found cocaine, Demerol, and Melaril in his body, with puncture marks on his scrotum.

Choking back tears, Caroline, accompanied by her cousin, Sidney Lawford, and her aunt, Jean Smith, entered the morgue in the medical examiner's office. Attendants uncovered David's body. Holding one hand to her mouth, Caroline quickly glanced at his face, now in repose, the deepening lines of anxiety erased by death. She nodded briefly when asked if the youth on the slab was David Kennedy.

His death reportedly devastated Caroline. "She wept for days," a friend recalled.

Caroline and Ed Schlossberg were married on July 19 in Our Lady of Victory Roman Catholic Church, in Centerville, Massachusetts, near the Kennedy compound in Hyannis. The Reverend Donald A. McMillan, a Jesuit priest who conducted the ceremony, described it as "a traditional Catholic service without the Mass." Caroline was twenty-eight, Ed, forty-one. The differences in their ages was about the same as that of Jack Kennedy and Jacqueline Bouvier.

Rumors that Schlossberg had wanted a rabbi included in the ceremony were denied by Father McMillan. Schlossberg's father and mother, Alfred and Mae, attended the ceremony, but would not discuss the marriage, according to one news report, "because my son prefers that we don't." In a later interview with the *Jewish World,* a Long Island, New York, newspaper, the elder Schlossberg admitted that the marriage had been "upsetting" for his family and probably for the Kennedys as well.

"It's just as much of a trauma for the devoutly Catholic to see their family member marry a Jew, as it is for observant Jews," he said. "But people make accommodation to it."

More than four hundred persons, many veterans of the

Kennedy administration, such as speechwriter Ted Sorenson, former assistant attorney general Burke Marshall, and former ambassador to India Galbraith, attended the ceremony. "We all wept," one guest said.

Outside, more than two thousand persons cheered the arrival of the bride, who entered the church on the arm of her uncle, Ted Kennedy. She was astonishingly beautiful, wearing a gown by society designer Caroline Herrera.

The wedding reception, held on the grounds of the Kennedy compound, was watched by Rose Kennedy, Caroline's grandmother, from a wheelchair on the porch of her home.

John Jr., who had been asked by Ed to be the best man, toasted the couple. He said, "All of our lives, there's been just the three of us—Mommy, Caroline, and I [sic]. Now there's a fourth."

After a Hawaiian honeymoon, the pair returned to Manhattan and a marriage that Schlossberg himself later said "couldn't be better." Caroline moved out of her small East Side apartment. Ed left his Soho loft and they settled into a $2,500,000 apartment on the eleventh floor of a red brick and limestone building at 888 Park Avenue, not far from Jackie Onassis. There are only two apartments on the floor, insuring privacy. It is decorated with modern furniture Schlossberg has designed and artifacts he has collected on his travels.

Caroline continued her studies at Columbia; one summer she had an internship in the law firm of Paul, Weiss, Rifkind, Wharton and Garrison, where Ted Sorenson, her father's close friend, was a partner. Her salary came to $1,200 a week. Once a month she traveled to Boston for meetings of the board of trustees of the John Fitzgerald Kennedy Library, of which she was the youngest member. She was the Kennedy family's official representative on the Massachusetts Commission to select the artist who would create a statue of the late president to be erected outside the golden-domed State House on Beacon Street in Boston. The bronze statue, sculpted by Isabel McIlvain, was dedicated on May 24, 1990, the seventy-third anniversary of her father's birth. President Kennedy is shown in a characteristic pose—walking, elbows bent, left hand tucked in his jacket pocket.

After the honeymoon, Caroline confided to friends she would become a mother as soon as she could. Pregnant during her third and final year at law school, "she didn't miss a single day of classes," Ed Schlossberg said. Despite the snow and ice of a bitter January and February that kept other students who lived off-campus at home, Caroline always arrived on time.

Caroline graduated in May and one month later gave birth to her first child, a girl, on June 24, 1988. The baby was named Rose Kennedy Schlossberg after her maternal great-grandmother. Caroline and Ed brought Rose home and deposited her in the nursery they had started to build early in May.

Rose's room, not especially large, was an imaginative triumph. Ed and Caroline combined their skills—he as a museum exhibit designer, she as a former specialist at the Metropolitan Museum of Art—to produce, as Ed told me, a "fun décor." It had colorful, free-form wall hangings, ingeniously contrived cutouts and other child-friendly figures.

Throughout that summer and fall Caroline crammed for the law examinations in February, which she passed on her first try.

When Rose was five months old, and prone to hiccups as all babies are, Ed was inspired to write a children's story, which he called "Hiccup's Tale," about a family named Bloboreneo who lived in a mansion. The "smartest, most observant and littlest" Bloboreneo narrated the story of the Skebleens and their "awful ugly" enemies, the Grossttttuffferrsss, and how the latter stole all the Christmas trees in the whole world and how the intrepid and wily little Hiccup got them all back.

Most weekends the couple would pile Rose and her belongings into a car and drive to their summer home in the tiny hamlet of Chester, Massachusetts, about one hundred miles west of Boston. Before Rose was born, Caroline and Ed would relax from their work on the weekends, occasionally at Jackie's beachfront home in the Gay Head area of Martha's Vineyard, most often in Chester.

The Chester house is an oasis of beauty and privacy. About fifteen years ago, Ed found an old barn set on several acres in the Berkshire Hills and had it converted into a two-story rustic residence. Here he and Caroline would sit before a roaring fire in the winter, reading and studying while classical music tapes played, watching the spectacular colors of the changing foliage from a deck hewn from timbers, or walking through the woods.

Ed is more than a casual visitor to Chester. A community-minded resident, he works with the Citizens' Cooperating Group, a volunteer organization that paints the homes of residents who cannot afford to hire professionals; and serves on the Conservation Committee and the local library's board of trustees. In 1976, he served as chairman of the town's bicentennial committee.

The town, with fewer than a thousand inhabitants, ignored the handsome couple when they came to shop. Ed, a gourmet cook, would carefully select prime cuts of meat, the freshest vegetables, and uncommon seasonings at a local market.

Back home, he would prepare dinner, with Caroline as a not-too-helpful sous-chef. Caroline's culinary accomplishments are limited to opening cans and, in a pinch, cooking eggs. In the Concord Academy graduates' yearbook, she listed her ambition as "not to be a housewife."

One weekend when Rose was ten months old, the Schlossbergs took her to visit a barn near their Chester home. First they went to see the sheep, but they were big and scared Rose, so Caroline scooped her up and took her to another part of the barn.

Here Rose was introduced to Shirley, a long-eared, snub-nosed lamb with brown eyes, the same color as Rose's. Girl and lamb stared at each other with considerable interest.

On December 11, a freezing twenty-two-degree day in New York City, Caroline and Ed, shielding a bundled-up Rose, hurried up the steps of St. Thomas More Roman Catholic Church on East 86th Street, where the child was baptized in her mother's faith. Already at the century-old church were Jackie, Great-Uncle Ted Kennedy, Ethel Kennedy, John, the baby's uncle, and many Kennedy cousins. The baptism was performed by Father McMillan, who had married Caroline and Ed and had come from Centerville.

Caroline now has two other children, Tatiana Celia Kennedy Schlossberg, born on May 5, 1990, and John Bouvier Kennedy Schlossberg, who was born on January 19, 1993.

Caroline and Ed are raising their children much as Caroline and her brother John were brought up, Schlossberg told the author, with firmness on the one hand, yet at the same time allowing the child's personality to develop freely. Caroline's relationship with her mother, though at times rocky, has always been loving, and is now closer than ever.

All who know them agree that Jackie's parenting has been almost faultless. She devoted much time to Caroline and John despite her own busy life, taking them with her on extensive travels, seeing to it that male companions were around to act as father figures, being a mother and yet a companion at the same time. Caroline, well aware of the pitfalls into which children of celebrated persons can plunge, knows the role her mother played, and will follow the path she charted.

In 1991, Caroline entered the spotlight again to publicize a book written in collaboration with a Columbia classmate, Ellen Alderman. *In Our Defense: The Bill of Rights in Action,* landed on the bestseller list of *The New York Times* and both women appeared on television to talk about it.

Developed from an idea sparked by one of their courses, it analyzes the way ordinary people have used the protection afforded citizens by the first ten amendments to the Constitution, the Bill of Rights.

Caroline visited sacred Indian tribal grounds, as well as prisoners on death row to get their stories. The authors edited the book together in the Schlossberg apartment because Caroline "wanted to be around the children." It was published at the beginning of 1991 and reviewed very favorably.

The New York Times Book Review said on February 24, 1991, "[the authors] tell the stories of people who 'have used the Bill of Rights in their—and our—defense.' These people are presented not as faceless parties to lawsuits but as human beings with both good and bad traits . . . the authors provide insight into how the courts have wrestled with such rights as freedom of speech, freedom of the press and the right to an impartial jury, while showing how ordinary people have struggled with those same ideals." Wrote the influential *Library Journal* in January 1991, "Although the authors emphasize the human side of the Bill of Rights, rather than its judicial interpretation, their legal analysis is sound, and the extensive notes and bibliography provide direction for further research." On December 14, 1990, *Publishers Weekly,* the bible of the publishing industry, called it "a compelling case book" which presents its illustrations in "clear, impartial, jargon-free discussions . . ."

Does Caroline plan another book, a career in law, or—on the outer edge of possibility—a life in politics?

Said Ed Schlossberg, "She hasn't decided what she wants to do."

Thus Caroline Kennedy Schlossberg, famous daughter of a famous family, finds herself in a position no different than the dilemma faced by countless other well-educated young women, torn between pursuing a career track or a mommy track.

12

∽

Jackie's Children — John

The family never called him John-John. His father was Jack and he was John. In his growing-up years he resented being addressed by the childish nickname that he detested.

Upon meeting someone for the first time, he just sticks out his hand and says, "Hi, I'm John."

Dave Powers explains how the double name developed:

One day Jack was trying to get John's attention and he called his name, clapping his hands at the same time. When the child did not respond, Jack clapped again and called "John, John." Somebody in the press overheard and it was "John-John" after that.

After the double name got going, I asked the president: "What would the boy have been called by the media if you'd clapped your hands three times —"John-John-John?"

He startled the nation and the world when he made his brief speech at the Democratic National Convention where he introduced his uncle Ted, and the buzzing has not ceased. Suddenly, it seemed, the small boy had become a tall, husky, and appealingly shy young man, even handsomer than his illustrious father.

Soon he acquired another nickname. Six feet tall, with dark wavy hair, an athlete's physique, and a brilliant flashing smile like Jackie's, he was dubbed "the Hunk" by headline writers, and People Magazine decided in 1988 he was "the sexiest man alive."

When John left the White House that last day in 1963 with his mother and Caroline, he clutched in his hand the Presidential Medal of Freedom, which President Johnson had just awarded to John Fitzgerald Kennedy posthumously. It was accepted by Robert Kennedy for Jackie, who was still in mourning and viewed the proceedings from behind an Oriental screen. She later gave the medal to John.

In New York John was enrolled in Saint David's, an elementary Catholic school for boys that was located a few blocks from his home. Like Caroline, he was escorted to and from school by Secret Service men. His code name was Lark. Later, at about the same time that Jackie transferred Caroline to Brearley, she enrolled John at the Collegiate School on West 77th Street. At the time newspapers reported that the move was prompted by the school's wish to have him repeat the second grade. "He was described as restless, disruptive and inattentive." This was denied by Headmaster David Hume. A more likely reason was to give him a more secular education.

John was permitted to ride the Collegiate School bus, his Secret Service escorts following in an unmarked car. While he was at class they waited in the basement of the school, playing gin rummy until the end of the day, when they again followed his bus until he was deposited at the Fifth Avenue apartment.

Active and something of a cutup, John was popular at school and got average grades. The rambunctious child, then six, disrupted the wedding of Janet Auchincloss in Newport in 1966 by fighting with his cousins and trying to drive ponies through the reception tent with a stick. On Bailey's Beach near the Auchincloss estate, he would fling buckets of sand at the sunbathers, giving no warning but a cry of "Watch out!" a second before he spattered them.

John and Caroline returned to America and school shortly after attending their mother's wedding to Onassis in Greece.

In New York Jackie sent him to a top adolescent psychiatrist when she felt he could do better in school. She also switched schools again and enrolled him in Phillips Academy in Andover, Massachusetts, from which he graduated in 1979.

It was John's decision to attend Brown University in Providence, Rhode Island, instead of Harvard. He majored in history, receiving his degree in 1983. He took a number of courses and attended seminars dealing with aspects of the JFK years and, although he has no personal recollection of the White House days, he knows as much about the Kennedy administration as most New Frontiersman who worked in it.

Even as a young teenager he knew a great deal about his father. In the winter of 1975, he accompanied his Uncle Ted and Aunt Joan and some of his cousins on a skiing vacation in the Berkshire Mountains in Massachusetts. As he was leaving the hotel in the morning, he saw a photograph of John Kennedy on a wall. He stopped, a younger cousin beside him, and read aloud the words on a plaque beneath the picture: "Ask not what your country can do for you; ask what you can do for your country."

"That's his most famous quote," the fifteen-year-old John said, pride in his voice, then walked out to join the others.

His summers were spent productively. Before he went off to college he studied environmental issues on Mount Kenya in Africa with young people from the United States and Canada. The next summer John worked for an

African company owned by Maurice Tempelsman, who assigned one of his executives to accompany John on an extensive trip throughout the countries of southern Africa, where the firm had many mining and manufacturing interests.

The following year, again at Maurice Tempelsman's suggestion, John applied for, and obtained, a student internship at the Center for Democratic Policy, a liberal organization in Washington. Another summer he served as a Peace Corpsman in Guatemala, helping to rebuild the country following a disastrous earthquake. Later he spent six months working with desperately poor natives in India, at the same time taking courses at the University of Delhi on methods of increasing food production in underdeveloped regions.

At Brown he developed a keen interest in the theater and had roles in several campus productions, among them *Volpone, Short Eyes,* and *In the Boom Boom Room.* He turned down an offer to play young John Kennedy in a film.

In mid-summer of 1985, at twenty-four, he starred in a revival of a play called *Winners,* produced with the help of the Irish Arts Center in a tiny, seventy-five seat theater on West 51st Street in Manhattan. John played an Irish youth who meets a tragic fate with his pregnant girlfriend. The girlfriend was portrayed by Christina Haag, whom John had dated after graduation from Brown in 1982.

The play ran for only six performances before a selected audience. Jackie did not attend.

It has been widely reported that the theater, not law or politics, is John's real love. The truth is that performing is only a hobby and he never seriously considered a stage career. No theatrical experiences have occurred since.

Commented Sandy Boyer, head of the Irish Arts Center, "John is an extraordinary and very talented young actor, who could have a very successful stage and film career if he wanted it." But John apparently did not. "He didn't seem to have any burning theatrical ambition," Boyer added. "This play was just something he wanted to do with his friends." John himself laughingly said that *Winners* was "definitely not a professional acting debut by any means."

He doesn't like publicity and grants few interviews. One exception occurs when he and Caroline talk about their *Profiles in Courage* award.* When he graduated from Brown, he marched in the traditional processional along with his classmates, but he was almost completely surrounded by friends who sought to shield him from news photographers.

Another attempt by friends to protect him resulted in a brawl with photographers as guests left a joint birthday party for him (he was eighteen) and Caroline (she was twenty-one) arranged by Jackie at Le Club, a swank supper club. Met by a *National Enquirer* photographer as they left the party in the early hours of the morning, some of John's friends decided not to permit his picture to be taken. A melee ensued.

Lean and hard-bodied, he is an authentic "hunk," working out regularly at the Plus One Fitness Center near lower Broadway in Manhattan, a private medically oriented health club. He bicycles around town frequently, often in shorts and no top in summer, and is an excellent water-skier, tennis player, and swimmer. He hikes, climbs mountains, goes whitewater rafting and kayaking.

Jackie winces every time her son dons sweats and goes to Central Park opposite her Fifth Avenue apartment to play tackle football, without protective gear. Three years ago, John, who plays as hard as his father and Uncle

---

* The award is presented annually by the John F. Kennedy Library to the political figure who best exemplifies the theme of the late president's book—standing by one's principles on controversial issues, even though a career or more may be at stake.

Bobby ever did, broke a leg during a scrimmage and was on crutches for weeks.

He can be impulsive at times. Two years ago, his cousin Maria Shriver chartered a boat for a luncheon the day before her marriage to Schwarzenegger. After the lunch, while the yacht was still hundreds of yards from dock, John and a friend suddenly dove overboard and swam to shore.

In 1984, he and a friend lived in a West 86th Street apartment, which they subleased. Kennedy, though rich, was continually in arrears on his rent. That was a problem for the owner of the apartment. He also frequently forgot to take his keys along when he went out. To be admitted on those occasions, someone had to buzz him in. Said a resident, "John would ring everybody's bell until someone buzzed and he could open the door. He drove the super crazy." Not only that, John slept on a waterbed, which the coop board had ruled no occupant could have. The board was on the verge of evicting John and his friend when the apartment's owner returned to take over. Said the resident, "Somebody had clearly put their fist through the wall. The carpet looked like they'd had a cookout on it."

John Jr.'s first political interview was at the 1988 Democratic convention when NBC's Connie Chung corralled him after his speech. It revealed little in content but highlighted comparisons with his father and Uncle Bobby. The son was twenty-six and had no idea whether he even wanted a career in politics. At twenty-eight JFK was already planning a race for Congress, and at twenty-nine Bobby was chief counsel for a Senate subcommittee. The son was muscular, the father painfully thin, seemingly all hair and teeth. In 1993, nearing his thirty-fourth birthday, young John was still at sea about his future. At thirty-four, JFK was only one year away from his election to the Senate.

CHUNG: Tell me. That was your first time speaking before such a large audience wasn't it?

KENNEDY JR.: It was. I've done occasional campaign appearances with Teddy, but this was certainly the largest that I've ever seen.

CHUNG: And how did it feel?

KENNEDY JR.: It felt pretty good. Surprisingly.

CHUNG: Were you nervous at all?

KENNEDY JR.: Yes, right now. (laughter) But it happened, you know. It's over. I knew it would be over soon. That's all I thought about really.

CHUNG: Tell me why you decided to do it.

KENNEDY JR.: 'Cause Teddy asked. That's enough.

CHUNG: Now you're—what year in law school are you in at NYU?

KENNEDY JR.: I'm finishing my last year.

CHUNG: Do you think you might be interested in going into politics?

KENNEDY JR.: Well I'm completely busy and consumed by what I'm doing right now. And, obviously, I find public issues interesting and I can't help but find a convention like this interesting, but I'm just—you know, I'll see what happens and I'm happy doing what I'm doing.

CHUNG: One of your cousins, I think, Patrick, is a delegate from Rhode Island.

KENNEDY JR.: Yeah.

CHUNG: Would you consider doing that maybe four years from now? Becoming a delegate?

KENNEDY JR.: Gosh, I really can't think what I'm doing next year. What I'm doing in four years I really don't know. But I'll just have to see.

In 1986, at the age of twenty-six, he got his first paying job, in the New York City Office of Economic Development, a nonprofit organization. Jackie was a member of the board. That fall he entered New York University

School of Law, often biking to school in Greenwich Village from his apartment on the Upper West Side. Later, he moved to a penthouse loft in the downtown TriBeCa section.

When he showed up for work in the Office of Economic Development, more than one girl whispered: "Oh, God! He's gorgeous." All that day, women in the department made all sorts of excuses to come by and look at him. During his cousin Joe's campaign for Congress, John appeared at a rally in Somerville and auctioned off a basketball which had been autographed by the Boston Celtics. According to one newspaper account of the event, "women of all ages virtually swooned, some for real," when he showed up.

At the 1984 Democratic convention in San Francisco he chatted with Maria Cuomo, the New York governor's beautiful daughter, who was then unmarried. When he went off to get her a drink, she was taken aside by a rich contributor who said he admired Cuomo's keynote speech and wanted to donate millions to his campaign if he ran. "That's illegal!" Maria blurted out. When John returned with the drink and couldn't find her, he wandered off. That night, the governor jokingly chided Maria: "You just blew millions in contributions," he said.

"The hell with the millions," Maria replied. "I just blew my chance with John Kennedy!"

During one summer vacation he was working in the civil-rights division of the Justice Department. The next summer he was an associate at Manott, Phelps, Rothenberg & Phillips. Charles Manott had been Uncle Ted's roommate at law school.

At New York University John took his turn as a student lawyer in Brooklyn Municipal Court where Joseph A. Esquirol, Jr., the supervising judge, fearing that "every woman will leave her desk to come see him," cautioned his staff to "try not to drool until he's gone."

He was sworn in as an assistant district attorney in

Manhattan at a starting salary of $29,999 in August 1989. Riding the subway from his West Side apartment to the Manhattan Criminal Courts Building, he appeared relaxed, rolling his eyes when reporters rushed at him as he approached the office.

"I'm just starting my first day at work," he said, as he tried to make his way through the crowd. Later, after joining the sixty-eight other rookies at the swearing-in ceremony and a Chinatown lunch, he got a little annoyed with the press waiting outside the restaurant.

"Please, this is embarrassing," he told them. "I have to work with these people."

John stayed with the Manhattan District Attorney's Office for three years, the usual commitment for young lawyers. He prosecuted six cases and won them all. He failed the New York State Bar examination twice, passing on his third try. After his second failed attempt he gamely countered headlines shouting THE HUNK FLUNKS with a vow to try again to pass it in July.

"I'm clearly not a major legal genius," he said modestly.

After he announced he would leave his job, speculation followed that he would be offered a place in the Clinton administration.

What is ahead for John? Will he seek public office?

In 1990, when he and Caroline announced the Profiles in Courage Award, he sounded very much as though he was preparing for a political career.

"Those phrases, like 'public service,' 'a need to be involved in public issues'—ideas associated with [John Kennedy]—tend to lose their meaning when they are repeated over and over again," he said.

But all his life, my father felt deeply about politics, that in fact it was an honorable profession. I think probably his proudest legacy is that, during the time he was president and in the years after he died, people who normally wouldn't have chosen a political career or involved themselves in politics, suddenly had a new feeling about politics and public service. Therefore, they got involved and committed themselves.

Throughout my life, people have come up to me and said, "I got into government because of your father." I feel great pride in that. So, as my father tried to do in his book and in his life, we want to recognize and encourage not only excellence in public service but also rare courage: people who have sacrificed something, taken a position that is politically unpopular and stuck to it because it is the morally right thing to do . . .

My father believed deeply in the importance of politics and public service—that, in a democracy, it's one of the highest callings. So we want to encourage people to enter politics to serve their country. As many people as possible should be involved in political life—the more, the better. And when people don't care about the issues and decline to be involved, that can be a shame and a loss for the country.

Family members and close friends agree that there would indeed be powerful pressures tugging at young John.

On the one hand, his mother Jackie, who knows too well the sacrifices he must endure if he chooses public life, would not encourage him to seek political office. But, said former Senator George Smathers of Florida, his uncle, Senator Edward M. Kennedy of Massachusetts, would be delighted. Also, unseen but strongly felt, would be the pull to continue the work his father barely had time to begin: to improve the quality of life for Americans.

If John Jr. does decide to seek public office, according

to Washington experts, his future would not only be bright but unlimited. Senator Smathers said,

> He'd make a marvelous candidate. He's far and away the best-looking of all the Kennedy kids and has all the other attributes that can take him a long, long way—even to the White House.
>
> He is not a political animal like some of his cousins, but if he ever did get into the game [of politics] he'd be damned successful.
>
> John Jr. would probably come as close to making it to the White House as anyone I've seen of the Kennedys. The question is, how badly does he want it? There are lots of sacrifices ahead. Is he willing to make them?

John goes to extreme lengths to avoid public appearances. Asked to participate in a memorial service planned in Boston on the twenty-fifth anniversary of his father's death, he begged off. His campaign speeches on behalf of cousin Joe were always to small groups without the media present.

When he campaigned for his cousin Patrick, who was running for the Rhode Island state legislature in 1988, he was so shy voters could "almost feel that he wished he was back home, doing anything but campaigning," said a store owner in Providence. He would stick out a hand, mutter, "Hi. I'm John Kennedy. It would be great if you would vote for my cousin."

Wouldn't this retiring nature be a handicap in politics, where brashness can carry a candidate a long way? Dave Powers pointed out that John's father, too, was afflicted with extreme shyness at the start of his career. Recalled Thomas P. O'Neill III, former Massachusetts lieutenant governor and son of the late Speaker: "His father practically had to be pushed onto a platform." Bobby Kennedy was so shy his hands trembled on the podium.

Reports about his lovelife appear regularly—but all, so far, point to only one thing. Like his father, he likes girls. As one friend said, "The apple doesn't fall far from the tree. Girls come and go."

Some, however, have lasted longer than the others. He dated Sally Munro, who was a year ahead of him at Brown, for five years; Ashley Richardson, a swimsuit model; and was spotted smooching on the beach in the Hamptons on Long Island with actress Sarah Jessica Parker. Other reports have linked him with Madonna, with theatrical director Tony Kotite, and with actress Molly Ringwald. Most recently an on-again, off-again romance with the actress Daryl Hannah had newspersons trailing them as they traveled in this country, the Pacific, Hong Kong, and Vietnam. Reports of an impending marriage at the East Hampton home of Lee Radziwill caused a stakeout of the town by reporters and photographers.

In late summer, 1993, the story of the marriage had become the marital guessing game of the year, if not the decade. Tabloid newspapers gave it more space than the events unfolding in the world's troubled nations. Each turn of events was breathlessly awaited, just as moviegoers at the beginning of the century looked forward to new episodes of "The Perils of Pauline."

Every gossip columnist had an "exclusive": Jackie did not want John to marry Daryl because she lacked sufficient "class" and was trying to dissuade her son from a union; Daryl was too possessive and John, bridling at her jealousy, was seeking to end the relationship; Daryl was pregnant and John was in a dilemma; John had met someone new. These and other rumors flew like confetti, but nothing of substance was served up to the palpitating public by year's end.

As for Madonna, Jackie reportedly stared at the sex queen when John brought her home, said little to her while she was there, and berated her son for even entertaining the notion of an alliance with her. She ordered John to stay away from her, and he did.

John is a millionaire, thanks to a trust fund left by his father and the settlement his mother made with the Onassis estate.

As one goes in search of the essential John F. Kennedy, Jr., the same assessments of his character and personality are heard over and over: "Decent. Affable. Unpretentious. Sweet-natured. A down-to-earth, regular guy."

All this is tribute to Jackie. She has never allowed her own reputation to overshadow her children.

John once invited a few of his friends to the Fifth Avenue apartment. Jackie met them at the door, shook hands with each, and introduced herself. "Hello," she said. "Please come in. I'm John's mother."

PART FOUR

New Horizons

13

∞

Close-up

Jackie's Manhattan apartment is at 1040 Fifth Avenue, on the corner of 85th Street, facing Central Park and diagonally across from the Metropolitan Museum of Art.

Visitors enter through an ornate, black wrought-iron covered door into a small foyer with French doors that open into the large main lobby. One passes a table holding a huge vase filled with seasonal flowers, a large crystal chandelier hangs overhead. To the left are the elevators, to the right a fireplace with a carved mirror framed in brass above. The floors are diamond shaped black and white marble tile.

In 1964, she bought the cooperative apartment for $200,000. Since then, its value had skyrocketed to more than $4 million, but when the recession began and prices skidded, the value slipped to the high $3 millions.

The elevator stops at the fourteenth floor and visitors step into an entrance foyer before her door. Hers is the only residence on the floor. The foyer opens into a vast rectangular gallery, with fourteen rooms radiating outward and around it. The living room, forty feet long, its windows facing Central Park, leads into a somewhat smaller library. There are five bedrooms, three servants' rooms, a kitchen, and a butler's pantry.

A staff of five maintains the apartment. Marta, her

sixtyish housekeeper and general overseer, has been with Jackie for decades and is so much a part of the family that she has attended the graduation of Caroline and John Jr. from prep school, college, and law school. Jackie also employs a maid, a cook, and two part-time housemen who also double as servers at cocktail and dinner parties.

Not unlike many women who become tired of the décor they have lived with for years, Jackie has redecorated the apartment several times. When she moved in, she chose dark, heavy, and formal furniture, in the style of Louis XIV. A visitor at the time told me: "She 'dresses' her apartment as she does herself—with quiet understatement but in exquisite taste."

In the early 1990s, she switched to French country, a casual yet elegant style intended to give the appearance of a home in rural France, but one owned by sophisticated, wealthy people. The tables and chairs are made out of carved, light-colored fruitwoods, such as peach, apple, and cherry. Harmonizing with the woods are fabrics in small patterns which impart both elegance and a cheerful hospitality. She has done away with strong, intense colors. The walls are whitewashed to simulate stone used in farmhouses and the floors are terra-cotta tile.

Her dinner parties are far less frequent than they were in the seventies and eighties. They are small affairs, with no more than ten or twelve guests, sometimes as few as eight, seated at a round table in the dining room which can be enlarged by inserting leaves. While she underwent treatment for cancer, she had even fewer dinner parties but did not eliminate them completely.

Her guests, seated on straight-backed chairs, are old friends and their wives, whose conversation is lively and stimulating. Former Secretary of State Henry Kissinger is there often; Robert S. McNamara, defense secretary in JFK's cabinet; historian Arthur Schlesinger, Jr., and Ambassador John Kenneth Galbraith are asked frequently. Candace Bergen, George Plimpton, the Roger Mudds, and Barbara Walters have been guests. When he was alive, Rudolph Nureyev, the great Russian dancer, was a favorite visitor.

There are new friends, too, at times: authors, singers, ballet dancers, editors, are all in her circle.

She serves mostly French-style food with light sauces, but when John Jr. and his friends come, or she has invited guests with appetites she knows are lusty, she will offer meat dishes. Then, most of the time, she will do her own shopping at Lobel's Prime Meats on Madison Avenue and 83rd Street, an exclusive establishment patronized by many celebrities, including designers Calvin Klein, former football star Joe Namath, and director Mike Nichols.

Evan Lobel, the proprietor, said, "Jackie comes in about once a month. Usually she buys veal or baby rack of lamb, her real favorite, sometimes steak. She's always very gracious, very polite, but," he adds, "don't cross her." If there are other customers in the store, Jackie waits for her turn, never demanding preferential treatment. Lobel added, "She wouldn't get it anyway."

The food is prepared in Jackie's all-white kitchen, which is twenty-four feet square and hasn't been redone in twenty years. The stove and other appliances are years old.

Jackie has not abandoned an early love of painting. An artist's drawing table stands in front of one window in the living room. When the drapes are open, the morning sun shines in brilliantly. From time to time, she will sit there, adjust the tabletop for the proper tilt, and sketch.

There are many photographs in the apartment, nearly all of them remembrances of Camelot. There are pictures of a wide-grinning John Kennedy alone, of John and Jackie at Hyannis Port in happy times, family photos with Caroline and John. The pictures rest on the piano and bookshelves in the dining room, on the end tables in the living room, and are hung in the bedroom.

In the entire apartment, there is only one photograph of her second husband, the late Aristotle Socrates Onassis. It is in her bedroom.

Despite her illness, Jackie tries to maintain her usual routine, awakening about 8 A.M., needing between eight and nine hours of sleep to function efficiently. Breakfast is light—usually orange juice, toast, and tea.

She leaves for work as a senior editor at Doubleday & Co. between nine and nine-thirty, carrying a briefcase stuffed with manuscripts, occasionally hopping into a waiting cab called from her apartment but most often driven in a chauffeured four-door greenish-blue BMW 325.

Sometimes she skips lunch or slides onto a stool of a hamburger shop near her office, has a plain burger on half a bun and coffee. When she goes out to a fancy restaurant with an agent or author she orders mostly seafood (red snapper is a favorite) or other fresh fish, always broiled, and passes up dishes swimming in rich sauces. She eats only a portion of the food she does order and sips wine, champagne, and on occasion a daiquiri. Her favorite restaurant for lunch is Mortimer's on Lexington Avenue at 75th Street, where she comes so frequently that the management holds one of its best tables for her just in case. In midafternoon, she will usually have a small container of yogurt. At home she will snack on thin wheat crackers or fresh strawberries, all low in calories. But like everyone else, she backslides. Riding in a cab in Battery Park, she asked the driver, who had recognized her, to hop out and get her a hot dog—"with everything."

Jackie goes to the office three or four days a week, returning in midafternoon, her briefcase bulging even more than when she left.

To help her cope with her tragedies, Jackie began the study of yoga, a mystical system in Hindu philosophy that teaches the diversion of the five senses from the outside world and calls for the mastery of a number of physical and mental disciplines. One of the simplest is meditation, an exercise intended to calm anxiety by ridding the mind of the accumulated tensions of the day.

Jackie began meditating daily in 1967, and she still does. Wherever she is, she closes the door of her office or home, draws the curtains, puts out the lights, assumes the lotus position, and begins the process of mind-clearing. (Beginners simply sit on the floor cross-legged and seek to work up to the full lotus position, twisting both legs above the thighs, close to the abdomen. When meditating, yoga instructors advise subjects to concentrate on a peaceful, quiet scene, perhaps a beach or a green valley, breathing rhythmically and slowly, and consciously keeping other thoughts from intruding into the image.)

Residents of the Upper East Side have seen her so frequently around the neighborhood that they rarely take much notice anymore. "She's a 'regular,' " said a woman walking her dog on Madison Avenue, "just like the rest of us."

Here, then, are some snapshots of Jackie in the neighborhood before her illness struck.

• Window-shopping at Village Designer Shoes between 86th and 87th Streets on Madison Avenue, she sees a pair of shoes she likes, enters and leaves disappointed. They don't have her 10½ size.

• In T-shirt and jeans, wearing sunglasses, she goes into The Gap on 86th and Madison, and buys blue, gray, and white sweatpants, noting someone will come to pick them up.

• At Alexander Brothers, florists off 86th Street, she buys several dozen red peonies.

• She often food shops at Gristede's, a supermarket nearby, loading a cart with boxed cereal, crackers, fresh fruit, and cheese (she favors Swiss and Italian Fontina).

• She browses through an antiques shop, likes a small bench, and asks the price. "Three hundred dollars," she is told. "My God, you're expensive," she says and doesn't buy it.

Salespersons like Phyllis at The Gap, say she is "always gracious and charming, very reserved, a delightful customer." They also note that she is alone most of the time as she wanders around. "She doesn't seem to have any women friends to shop with," another clothing saleslady remarked. "Usually women come by twos, but Jackie is by herself."

How does she look now, at sixty-five-plus?

In the early 1980s, she began showing signs of aging. Lines, like spokes of a tiny wheel, radiated outward from her large brown eyes. A half-inch beneath each lower lid there were now two deep parallel folds. Her forehead was clear but the cheeks, perpetually tanned by a tropical or summer sun, or burned by the winds on a ski slope, had lost their smoothness of earlier years. Tiny pores were visible and the cheeks had a weathered look about them. Two diagonal lines from the nostrils to the corners of her mouth had deepened perceptively.

But the skin on her neck was still taut with no sign of looseness or sag. Nor was there yet any indication of the double chin that comes when the fat beneath the skin of the face starts to sag.

As early as 1969, when she turned forty, Jackie, inspecting her face carefully, noticed some early signs of aging and consulted Dr. Henry Lax. Should she have a facelift? Dr. Lax said, no, not yet.

It wasn't until ten years later that Dr. Lax told her that she could have minor cosmetic surgery, if she wished, around the eyes but nothing so drastic as a full facelift.

"At this stage in your life," Dr. Lax said, "a facelift is too radical and too apparent." So Jackie had her eyes "done."

Another decade later, in 1979, she finally underwent a complete facelift. It was performed by Dr. Michael Hogan at New York Hospital in Manhattan. After five weeks of healing, she looked forty again.

But if her face is early baby-boomer, her hands are golden-ager. Plastic surgery can do nothing for them. Jackie's hands are small, with long slender fingers, the tips of which are cigarette-yellowed. She smokes incessantly, though never in range of a camera. The backs of the hands are prominently veined, the skin thin, with brown and yellow blotches of varying sizes, the so-called liver spots common to many persons as they reach the half-century mark. Recently she began wearing white or ivory gloves at social events to cover her hands. (She is such a trend-setter that when photographs of Jackie in white gloves began to appear, glove manufacturers were surprised to notice a bounce in their business. Women were following her again.)

Jackie's hairdresser is Thomas Morrissey on Madison Avenue between 66th and 67th Streets, where Morrissey himself attends to her in a private room as Margaret does her manicure and pedicure. Until 1993, she had twice-a-week facials at Nardi's salon on Lexington Avenue and 57th Street, where she was given treatments with a face cream, the formula for which was given to her by Queen Elizabeth II of England. The cream contains lanolin and vitamins. Jackie also had her hair colored. Everyone who sees her around town had noted that her hair, once dark brown, is now a light brown, with blond streaks.

She has always been committed to exercise. Before the cancer was diagnosed, she worked out several times a week at the Vertical Club on 60th Street alongside other celebrities who usually took little notice of her. She skied in winter, water skied in summer at her palatial home at

Gay Head on Martha's Vineyard, and played excellent tennis. She is also an expert horsewoman, driving to New Jersey in the fall to compete for trophies at the Essex Hunt Club near Peapack, and she keeps two horses in the Virginia fox-hunting county near Upperville, where she would compete in the Piedmont Hunt's weekend races.

As a result of all this physical activity, she developed the body of dancer, with hard muscles beneath the smooth skin of her thighs and forearms. Her weight varies between 123 and 133 pounds, nearly perfect for her five-foot, seven and one-half inches. She can wear bikini bathing suits; she has no flab or "cellulite," dimpled flesh that often forms on the upper arms or thighs of women.

During daytime hours, Jackie wears very little makeup, just a touch of rust-colored lip gloss, but no eye shadow or eyeliner, said author Shaun Considine. When jogging, she doesn't warm up by stretching, doing knee bends, or running in place, Considine said, but gets right to it. And, he adds wonderingly, even in warm weather she never perspires. Nor does her nose run when it's cold.

Despite an active social, civic, and business life, Jackie is alone more often than anyone might imagine. Several evenings a week, she will settle down with a manuscript to edit, or a book too long set aside. If she likes what she reads, she may even telephone the author to tell him how absorbing she thinks it is.

A film buff, Jackie will check a newspaper to see what is showing at a nearby cinema. If she thinks she'll like the movie and hasn't seen it, she will go—by herself. Aware that she would attract considerable attention if she stood on a box-office line, she will send her maid to buy a ticket then, at the last minute, will appear and slip inside, leaving just as the movie ends. Until it closed, she went many times to the Trans-Lux movie theater on Madison Avenue, a block from her apartment house. By Thursday afternoon, at the latest Friday morning, she is off in a chartered plane to Gay Head in warm weather, to Aspen or the Caribbean in winter, always accompanied by Maurice Tempelsman.

Let us now look closely at this man, the third most important in the life of Jacqueline Onassis.

14

Her Mysterious Significant Other

He is a reclusive diamond merchant whose wealth is estimated in the hundreds of millions and about whom most people, including business associates, know very little. He has been Jackie's close friend since the late 1970s, and her "significant other" since the late 1980s.

Maurice Tempelsman shares her apartment in Manhattan and is with her constantly, at dinner parties, important social and theatrical events, even at family functions such as weddings and graduations.

In New York, he receives his personal mail at Jackie's Fifth Avenue apartment. *Star* magazine proved this with a clever stunt. An editor at the tabloid assigned a reporter to hand the doorman at the Fifth Avenue apartment house a letter addressed to Tempelsman.

The doorman took it but said Tempelsman had just gone out. Tempelsman would get the letter on his return, he said. Had Tempelsman possibly returned unnoticed? the reporter asked. The doorman wasn't sure, so he called Jackie's apartment. There was no reply.

After Onassis died, other men had entered Jackie's life. In the year after the mourning period ended, she dated a total of fifteen men, among them George S. McGovern, a former senator from South Dakota and presidential candidate; Henry Platt, president of Tiffany & Co., and Frank Sinatra.

At forty-seven, her weight had not changed because she exercised as much as before and still ate sparingly. It was at this time in her life that she had, as Nancy Tuckerman said, her "nip there and a tuck there" at the hands of a plastic surgeon, which eliminated the folds beneath her eyes.

As they had been following Kennedy's death, most of her dates were "safe" men who escorted her to functions. William Walton, for example, was never a serious romantic interest though she dated him often. Walton, a former journalist who had become an artist, was New York State coordinator during JFK's presidential campaign. U.S. Senator Charles Mathias, Jr., a Maryland Republican, was "safe"; so were the publishing executives, designers, and museum officials escorting her. She was seen in the company of Michael Cacoyannis, who had directed *Zorba the Greek,* starring Anthony Quinn. Many reports circulated that Cacoyannis was her latest romance. In truth, he was a friend she had known since her marriage to Onassis, and nothing more.

Pete Hamill, the husky, handsome New York journalist, was more than a date but less than a serious candidate. Hamill, who had been involved with actress Shirley Maclaine for a long time, ended his relationship with Maclaine and began dating Jackie frequently.

For a time, it was serious enough. Jackie seemed captivated by the brilliant Hamill, five years her junior, by his newspaperman toughness and charming ways, and by the battles he waged in print against social injustices.

There was even gossip for a while that they might marry, but it was unlikely that the elegant Jackie could wed or even maintain for long an interest in the Brooklyn-born Hamill. They broke up after eight months.

A few dates were not casual ones. In 1976, she was attracted to Felix Rohatyn, the financier and internationally known partner in the banking firm of Lazard Frères. At the time, Rohatyn was involved with a New York photographer named Helene Gaillet, who was, in the inelegant but accurate phrase, "dumped" by him. Helene denounced Jackie furiously.

"She runs through men like she runs through clothes," she said. "I thought she was my friend. I've even been her house guest on Skorpios. But men get bowled over by her." Helene said Jackie sought to attract men because of her insecurity, and she was probably right. "She covers her insecurity by buying clothes and everything else," Helene added.

Then came Maurice Tempelsman.

Tempelsman keeps such a low profile that even though he has been called America's premier diamond merchant and one of the world's most important businessmen, his name does not appear in the current *Who's Who in America*, which carries a fifteen-line entry on Jackie.

No movie or television casting director would ever choose him for the romantic role he is now playing in Jackie's mature years.

An inch taller than Jackie (he is five feet, eight inches), he is a year younger, sixty-four in 1994, weighing 180 pounds, balding, pudgy-faced and constantly fighting a losing battle against increasing girth. In bathing attire, his ample stomach protrudes in a rubber-tire roll over the top of his trunks. He has tried to diminish the paunch by dieting and exercise, especially after he suffered a mild heart attack in 1985. Failing that, he tries to make the pot-belly less apparent by wearing dark, usually double-breasted suits. With his moon face and wide, thin lips, which often break into a pleasant smile, he looks more like a kindly uncle than the man who won the world's most sought-after woman.

Jackie cares deeply about Maurice. She visited him every day at Lenox Hill Hospital, on Manhattan's East Side, after his heart attack, hovering anxiously over him, asking nurses and doctors innumerable questions about his condition. He remained hospitalized for two weeks, then went to Jackie's apartment to recuperate. Ever since, he walks from the Fifth Avenue apartment to his office at 44th Street. Often, he will stride through Central Park.

One of Tempelsman's colleagues in the diamond trade, who does a good deal of business with him, told me, "They hold hands in the theater, sit with their heads together at corner tables in restaurants, and kiss each other between courses."

Tempelsman is steeped in culture. His knowledge of art and archaeology, music and dance, films and literature is extensive; he knows and loves good food and wine. He has traveled to every civilized country on the globe, and to many that are not. He is a witty, charming conversationalist, at home—as she is—in the playgrounds and drawing rooms of the rich and famous.

Since his company, Leon Tempelsman & Son, Inc., is not publicly traded, he is not constrained to open his books to anyone. "Only Tempelsman himself knows what he is worth," said Holman Jenkins, Jr., a business journalist for *Insight,* a newsweekly magazine, who was granted a rare interview in 1991. He is rich enough, Jenkins said, to pay people hundreds of thousands of dollars a year just to hang around in steamy African capitals on what he calls "watch missions," waiting for something to turn up.

He is the controlling shareholder in the world's largest maker of diamond jewels, Lazare Kaplan International, and owned the American Coldset Corporation, makers of drilling bits for mining operations, which he sold in 1982. According to Jenkins, diamond traders believe, but are not sure, that he has an "inside track" to the De Beers Consolidated Mines, which control the diamond industry in South Africa.

Tempelsman's entire fortune, as well as his personal interests, have been centered around Africa: seeking new sources for diamonds; creating a diamond-cutting and -polishing factory in the Republic of Botswana, directly north of South Africa; arranging a deal with the government of Angola to the northwest, to market their diamonds. He has also formed joint ventures with Standard Oil of Indiana, Mitsui of Japan, Union Carbide of the U.S., and the French Atomic Energy Commission.

"Always the philosopher," Jenkins said, "he likens Africa's postcolonial ordeal to that of the Israelites, who had to spend forty years in the wilderness to purge themselves of their colonial mentality. Tempelsman has devoted a lifetime to trying to prove that it's possible to do business with Africa. He isn't about to give up now."

"Tempelsman keeps himself well-insulated in his office," says a man who does business with him. "He is very secretive in a trade noted for people who shun publicity. Yet he is a close friend of persons in very high places in this country and abroad. He is on friendly personal terms with ministers and heads of state, and frequently is seen at functions attended by persons on the highest levels."

He has served, with virtually no fanfare, on several presidential commissions, including the President's Commission for the Observance of Human Rights, the Citizens' Advisory Board of Youth Opportunities, and the President's Council at the Center for International Studies at New York University.

The world's most important power brokers accept him as one of their number. When about fifty men and women met at the St. Regis Hotel in New York to set investment policy in Zaire, he was asked to sit alongside representatives of such giants as Chase Manhattan Bank, Irving Trust, Lazard Frères, General Motors, American Express, Texaco, and Mobil. Tempelsman, wary lest the publicity crack the low profile he wanted to maintain, did not go himself, but sent two senior aides.

Unlike Onassis, who sought to boost his own importance by putting Jackie on display, thus showing the world that he had captured the celebrated lady, Tempelsman is careful to stay out of range of the ubiquitous cameras in public. When Jackie attended a graduation of one of her children, or Caroline's marriage, Maurice was there but made sure he was seated a row or two behind her and several seats away, so that photographers could not snap them together.

In the summer, Tempelsman docks his palatial yacht at Jackie's mansion in Gay Head on Martha's Vineyard and they go by boat to waterfront restaurants, leaving the same way.

In August of 1993, he dodged the media when President Clinton and his family, vacationing on Martha's Vineyard, were invited by Jackie for a cruise. Jackie was hostess, Tempelsman the host. He greeted the president, Mrs. Clinton, and their daughter Chelsea when they boarded his seventy-foot yacht, the *Relemar,* at Menemsha Harbor, then went below.*

A page-one photo of the sailing party in *The New York Times* on August 25 showed all the guests—the Clintons; Ted Kennedy and his new wife, Victoria; Jackie, Caroline and her husband Ed Schlossberg; and Washington lawyer Vernon E. Jordan. The host was belowdecks until the vessel sailed out into the Atlantic for a five-hour cruise and was out of sight of photographers.

The romance began quietly. They were together frequently during the late 1970s and early 1980s, dating sometimes three times weekly and speaking often on the telephone. They attended the ballet and theater, went to museums and, during the 1980 presidential primary campaign, he was her escort at several fund-raising events for her brother-in-law, Massachusetts Senator Edward M.

* The vessel's name combines the first syllables in the names of his three grown children, Rena, Leon and Marcee.

Kennedy, who was seeking to wrest the Democratic nomination from the incumbent president, Jimmy Carter.

In 1984, Tempelsman made his first, and only, comment on his relationship with Jackie. He authorized a spokesman to tell me: "They dine together in top-of-the-line restaurants, such as Quo Vadis, Le Cote Basque, and Lutèce. They are good friends and enjoy each other's company. And they have gone on vacation trips together."

From other sources, I learned that the couple had sailed on Tempelsman's yacht along the eastern seacoast a number of times. Once they took a leisurely hundred-mile cruise from Savannah, Georgia, to Hilton Head Island off South Carolina.

"Maurice Tempelsman did not pop into Mrs. Onassis's life suddenly or recently," one of his friends asserted. He has been a friend of the family since Jack Kennedy's presidency. Tempelsman was one of the eleven hundred specially invited guests aboard the Robert F. Kennedy funeral train on its eight-hour journey to Washington from New York on June 8, 1968. Even then, although a world leader in the diamond industry, Tempelsman was so little known that he was not selected by Jean Stein and George Plimpton for interviews in their book *American Journey,* which consisted of recollections of RFK by prominent guests aboard the train and from onlookers along the tracks.

"They remained friends all along," the colleague says, "all through her marriage to Onassis. After he died in 1975, the relationship took a new turn. It ripened and strengthened as they saw each other more often and saw more in each other."

They were, indeed, together a great deal. When Prince Radziwill, her sister Lee's divorced husband, died in 1979, Tempelsman accompanied Jackie to London for the funeral. He never left her side.

Tempelsman's friend continues, "Is it the kind of

starry-eyed romantic love that bowls people over and leaves them breathless? Only they know, of course, but if I could hazard a guess I would say that it is not likely. But I am convinced it is a deep and genuine love of two mature people."

The "deep and genuine love" is complicated by one key fact: Maurice Tempelsman is a married man. Nor has there been any indication that he will seek a divorce.

In 1949, at the age of twenty, he married a seventeen-year-old girl named Lily, an Orthodox Jew. For years they lived together in a fourteen-room duplex apartment in the Normandie, at 86th Street and Riverside Drive in Manhattan, raising their three children. Leon now works with his father. All three children are married and have families of their own.

The marriage soured about 1975 after Maurice met Jackie. From then on, Lily and Maurice led separate lives, rarely seeing one another. "How was that possible?" I asked one of Tempelsman's colleagues. "After all, they lived in the same apartment." He answered dryly: "So? It's not a studio."

In July 1981, when reports of Jackie's involvement with Tempelsman began to surface, I spoke to Lily. To my knowledge it is the first and only time she has ever talked with a journalist.

She spoke in a well-modulated voice that retained a hint of a foreign accent. Lily, too, was born in Belgium, although she met Maurice in America, where they were married.

At no point during the brief conversation was Jackie's name mentioned, although we both, of course, knew she was the subject of my questions.

"I'm sure you have heard the rumors about Mr. Tempelsman," I began.

"Yes," Mrs. Tempelsman replied in a cautious tone.

"Is everything all right with your marriage?"

A slight pause. "Private lives," Mrs. Tempelsman answered slowly, "should not be made public."

"But when a matter involves a person of international prominence, there is, unfortunately perhaps, a legitimate public interest."

Her voice hardened. "Then maybe she should answer your questions."

"Are things all right with you and Mr. Tempelsman," I persisted, "or are they not all right?"

She answered, "You want to know whether we are married. Factual information. I will give you the fact that we are married and living together."

"How do you feel about all these stories that are being published about your husband and the other woman? Are you angry about them? Do they bother you?"

Mrs. Tempelsman refused to make further comment, and the interview ended.

Two years later, Tempelsman moved out of the apartment into a hotel suite.

While Lily Tempelsman is understandably furious at the woman who appropriated her husband, she and Maurice have remained on friendly terms. Even after he left, they went to dinner together, sometimes in the neighborhood, and on nice days he would escort her home.

In one of life's ironies, Lily Tempelsman works part time as a marriage counselor at the Jewish Board of Guardians.

Maurice Tempelsman's career is as much a rags-to-riches story as that of Aristotle Onassis. Like Onassis, his family was driven from its homeland by an invading army. When the Nazis overran the Low Countries in 1940, he and his family fled from their home in Belgium to the United States.

Maurice was then eleven years old. His father, Leon, opened a small diamond-trading business in New York City while the boy attended city schools and commuted by subway to New York University. He dropped out after two years and took over his father's business, building it to its present stature.

The offices of Leon Tempelsman & Son are disappointingly ordinary. Any middle-size law firm has more opulent quarters. They occupy the entire twentieth floor at 529 Fifth Avenue at 44th Street, with the entrance between Fifth and Madison Avenues. Step off the elevator into a narrow hall with beige floor tiles and four paintings of ships on the beige walls. Glass doors open into a waiting room with a beige couch and two blue-upholstered side chairs. Usually the waiting room is empty; people do not enter and leave often. Another large painting of a ship hangs over the couch, two smaller ones to the right of the entranceway. A receptionist sits behind a glass partition and, as in many offices, buzzes visitors with appointments into the warren of other offices.

Jackie visits there occasionally, though not often, mostly in the early or late afternoon hours.

In the past few years, Tempelsman has shifted his business from dealing in industrial diamonds to gem-quality stones. "You can't go to Tempelsman and buy a one- or two-carat ring for your fiancée,"said a colleague, "but if you're in the market for a gem that will cost you $100,000 and up, the company will do business with you."

In 1986, Tempelsman made a move that startled the industry. He and his son Leon launched a $4.5 million advertising campaign to offer, for the first time, brand-name diamonds. Leon said, "A diamond purchase is one of the largest a person makes, and for many of them it's a blind purchase. So we provide name recognition, similar on the low end to a Perdue chicken or on the higher end to a Rolls-Roycc."

When Tempelsman and his son had bought a controlling interest in publicly traded Lazare Kaplan International, Inc., Maurice boosted sales by publishing ads with the slogan: "The Lazare diamond—Setting the standard for brilliance," and imprinting a special Lazare logo and identification number on each gem.

Said a spokesperson for the Lazare Kaplan company: "The campaign, which is still going on, has been successful. It is one of the cornerstones of our business strategy."

The 1993 Dun & Bradstreet's *Million Dollar Directory of America's Leading Public and Private Companies* lists the sales of Lazare Kaplan at $133 million, a fourfold increase over 1992. The company, said Dun & Bradstreet, employs 197 persons and is listed as a subsidiary of Leon Tempelsman & Son. Ward's *1992 Business Directory of U.S. Private and Public Companies* lists the company's sales as $35 million.

As Onassis did, Tempelsman provides not only an anchor of stability but reassurance, wisdom, and, above all else, kindness. "Maurice," says an associate, "is cool and distant if you do not know him, but to his friends he is extraordinarily kind. He is quite a rarity in the business world, a man of gentleness and sweetness."

Maurice possesses a deft, quiet wit, and says a friend, is "an absolute charmer who is enormously magnetic and a thoroughly delightful companion."

In the early years of their romance, Tempelsman visited Jackie often on summer weekends at Hyannis Port, where she still maintained Kennedy's home on the compound. They spent much time in and around the rambling white house and in Jackie's eighteen-foot open-hull speedboat, the *Seacraft*, which she kept moored at the dock. Tempelsman, in bathing trunks, sat at the wheel of the trim little boat, guiding it across the blue-gray waters of Nantucket Sound, as Jackie glided behind on water-skis. She was generally unrecognized because all that people on passing craft could see was a trim figure in a bikini, a bathing cap pulled low over her head and, when the weather was cool, wearing a sweatshirt.

As for Tempelsman, virtually nobody recognized him. He was just a middle-aged man in bathing attire, not obviously well-off, at the wheel of a speedboat on the Sound.

Jackie admires a strong dominating man. She held the patriarch, Joe Kennedy, in high esteem because he was strong in business dealings and strong with his family. At first, Jackie rebelled from Joe's autocratic rule, and his attempt to rule her. She once told a friend: "The Ambassador acts like a general and all the rest of the family, including the in-laws, are privates. There are no ranks in between." But they came to respect each other, she for his strength, he for her feistiness, and they became extremely fond of one another.

Jack Kennedy lacked his father's forceful personality but he was a domineering husband who tolerated her ways to a point, but told her what to do—and she did it. Onassis had been a protector and a man who showed tender, sentimental feelings at the same time he exuded energy and strength.

Now, in Maurice Tempelsman, she has found a "gently" domineering man. Tempelsman is authoritative with Jackie in a quiet way. At home, he is the man of the house, acting as a husband would, and Jackie likes it that way. When they have dinner parties, he helps her arrange the menu and discusses seating arrangements with her. He will often disagree with her suggestions, and Jackie will not say no.

At times, he will go into the kitchen to show the chef how to prepare a special French sauce.

In the early 1980s, some of his colleagues were sure they were on the verge of marriage. "It is hard to say when it will happen," one diamond merchant told me, "but it would not surprise me if it is quite soon. As for wives who say, 'I'll never divorce him'—well, we've heard that before, haven't we?"

But now the same colleagues admit they were wrong. "Why does she need another husband?" one said.

"She's an enormously wealthy woman and, while she enjoys the company of Maurice, she has what she wants—his daily companionship, his affection, and his considerable help in financial matters, at which he is little short of a genius." A woman journalist who has covered Jackie for decades, and has requested anonymity, added: "Certainly she's not going to start another family. There isn't a single good reason for her to marry again."

Moreover, if Tempelsman and his wife are ever divorced, a marriage to Jackie would involve religious complexities which, in Jackie's case, are already somewhat murky.

After she wed Onassis, the Vatican issued a statement that she would be considered to be living in a state of mortal sin, for which only confession and penance could atone. It is not known whether Jackie expiated the sin, but according to Stephen Birmingham, she still continued to receive the Sacraments of the church.

Since the Catholic Church does not recognize divorce, Jackie would not be free to marry Tempelsman in the Church. If she should marry outside the Church, and since Tempelsman would still be considered married to Lily, Jackie could not receive the Sacraments, but would not be excommunicated.

Making it clear that he was not referring to any particular persons but speaking only in general terms, a priest at the Archdiocese of New York explained that a church tribunal could be asked to evaluate the marriage of a divorced person to see if circumstances existed under which it could be "declared null." Then, if a marriage is thus nullified, it is considered never to have existed and the new marriage is recognized. If Tempelsman were to wed in the Church, experts said that, considering his age, he would not be asked to receive Catholic instruction beforehand. "That is generally required only of young men and women," said one priest.

15

Working Woman

If Robert Kennedy's death drove Jackie to marry Aristotle Onassis, his life was the inspiration for the change in her thinking and her goals as she neared fifty. She took her cue from Bobby's example.

Jackie knew about Bobby Kennedy's startling metamorphosis from a self-confessed social-problems illiterate to the Kennedy who felt the deepest, cared the most, and fought the hardest for humanity; that he had crusaded tirelessly against the suffering of children, the elderly, and others bypassed by social and economic progress.

Historians have called his radical transformation the most astonishing ideological reversal of a major public figure in this century. "She knew all about Bobby," said Kenny O'Donnell, "because she had the deepest respect for the guy. She would often speak of him in terms you would reserve for a great teacher." Jackie once said of Bobby, "He's the one I'd put my hand in the fire for."

She knew that Bobby had held a sick child in the Mississippi Delta and wept that he had gone miles out of his way to spend hours to talk to youngsters in deprived areas. At the time, she may not have been able to share fully the emotions he felt, but she came to revere him for the courage of his stands.

Back in 1964, though he himself was in deep mourning

over the loss of his brother, Bobby understood what Jackie had to do. During the long and frequent conversations they had, the talks that irritated Ethel and gave rise to rumors of a romantic interest in Jackie, he counseled her about her future. Interviews with close associates disclosed that Bobby had told Jackie she had arrived at a crossroad in her life.

In essence, he told her that it was a big world out there, beyond her ability to view it at the time but filled with many things that could capture her interest. For the sake of Caroline and John, he told her, she could not live in the past but must look ahead. "I can't tell you the words he used," said O'Donnell, "but that about sums up the gist of what he was trying to tell her."

Jackie listened but did not take his advice at the time. Unable to think in terms of new goals because of her state of mind, she fled a year later into her world of pleasure seeking. Then, after the murder of Bobby, she hid on Skorpios for security.

In 1975, once more a widow, she recalled the talks with Bobby, his remarkable turnaround and, clear-minded now, planned her own future.

By the fall of 1975, Onassis had been dead six months and the legal battle over his estate was still in the courts. Jackie was only forty-six, with several decades of productive life ahead of her. What would she do with them?

The decision was difficult. Already she had reached pinnacles granted to few other women. Her children were in their teens—Caroline would soon be eighteen, John fifteen—and had little need for her full-time attention. Fashion and social affairs had now come to bore her.

She received many offers.

Run for the Senate from New York opposing the Republican incumbent, James Buckley, suggested Dorothy Schiff, publisher of the *New York Post*. Mrs. Schiff presented her case forcefully at a luncheon in the executive offices of the newspaper, but Jackie declined with thanks. Mayor Edward I. Koch of New York offered her a $62,000-a-year job as the city's commissioner of cultural affairs, but she turned it down. Fashion houses asked her to be a spokesperson or to create a collection of her own. Many thought she should be offered, and should accept, a post as ambassador to France, where she was adored and would burnish America's image. Others believed she should coast on her accomplishments; after all, her courage and dignity had helped the country emerge from its own trauma following the assassination. But Jackie would not pursue any of them.

Then Letitia (Tish) Baldridge, her six-foot-tall, blond, outspoken social secretary during the White House years, with whom she had remained friendly, came up with the idea that led to a major change in her life. Tish had established a public relations firm in New York, which was prospering.

One afternoon in her apartment Jackie talked about the problem in the forefront of her mind. What would she do with her life? Tish suggested she should work in publishing.

Jackie became increasingly interested as Tish went on to explain why: Jackie loved books, had been a lifelong reader, was almost at expert level in her knowledge of the performing, graphic, and visual arts, was fluent in several languages and—perhaps most important—had close personal relationships with many individuals whom she could induce to write books.

Jackie was excited at the prospect. Within a few days, Tish got in touch with Thomas Guinzburg, a founder of the *Paris Review,* and who was then president of a small, elite, but financially troubled publishing house, Viking Press. He offered her a job. She accepted.

It was a good marriage. Jackie needed a new outlet for her creative talents and Guinzburg needed a star attraction for his ailing firm.

When the appointment was announced, the opinion in the small, closely knit publishing business was that Guinzburg had made an inspired public relations move. Jackie had no illusions. She was perfectly aware that she was being hired for her "contacts" with noted personages whom she might persuade to write books. Guinzburg was blunt: "In publishing these days it's not what you know but whom you know."

She created a furor when she showed up for work at Viking's offices on the sixteenth floor at 625 Madison Avenue. Hordes of reporters and paparrazi milled around the lobby near the elevators as she walked in. Said Helen Markel, a magazine editor and writer, "It was like a Hollywood opening." The Viking staff, mostly young women, pretended to be blasé but, Tom Guinzburg noted, they were wearing clothes to work that they normally wore after work.

Becky Singleton, only four years out of Georgia State University, gasped when she was told she would be Jackie's editorial assistant. "Wow!" she said. That first day Becky discovered to her horror that she had a run in her pantyhose. The standard temporary fix is to apply fingernail polish to stop further spread. "I was so nervous," Becky said, "that I shellacked my entire hip. I could barely get myself unstuck that night."

Jackie eventually became an excellent editor. "But in the beginning she was as green as any young journalism school graduate who wanted a career in publishing, only more than twenty years older," said a former colleague. "She was bright, learned fast but bumbled and fumbled a lot until she got the hang of what she was supposed to do."

She was paid $200 a week and given a sparsely furnished, long, narrow office, with a desk, chair, typewriter, window, and some Viking books on the shelves. She came in each morning about ten, publishing fashion, discussed the day's business with Becky, would perhaps have a conference with an author, and would attend editorial meetings. Her door was always open and staff members would wander in and out to discuss ongoing projects; just as likely, she would pop into their offices for brief discussions.

She would scribble short memos to Becky, or type them herself; Becky, in turn, would carefully shred them to prevent the memos from becoming part of Jackie trivia in some auctioneer's collection. Said Becky, "Not a scrap of paper was ever left in the wastebaskets."

But Jackie's experience at Viking was an unhappy one. After so many years as a queen, she could not adjust to being a subject. Neither could the editors adjust to a queen. When she offered suggestions at editorial meetings, they were received politely but coldly; few were acted upon. One editor said: "There was no way Jackie could ingratiate herself with the company. She was resented at the beginning and her presence became a nagging insult to the professionals in the company. Jackie felt this keenly, and it must have hurt her."

She lasted only two years. In the summer of 1977, Guinzburg informed her that the firm planned to publish a novel by British author Jeffrey Archer, a former Member of Parliament, called *Shall We Tell the President?* The novel, set five years hence in 1983, dealt with a plot to assassinate the president of the United States, Edward Kennedy, Jackie's former brother-in-law.

The book was harshly reviewed by some critics. One, John Leonard of *The New York Times*, wrote a particularly nasty criticism pointed directly at Jackie: "There is a word for such a book," he said. "The word is trash. Anybody associated with its publication should be ashamed of herself." The *Boston Globe* quoted Tom Guinzburg as saying that she "didn't indicate any distress or anger when I told her we bought the book in England several months ago."

Jackie winced at the clear implication that she was connected with its publication. In mid-October, 1977, she sent a hand-written letter of resignation to Tom Guinzburg, followed by a statement to the media:

"Last spring, when told of the [Archer] book, I tried to separate my lives as a Viking employee and a Kennedy relative. But this fall, when it was suggested that I had something to do with acquiring the book and that I was not distressed, I felt I had to resign."

How should one interpret the resignation? As evidence that she was a Kennedy and would stand by them whenever shafts were leveled at the family? Doubtful, in view of the slow estrangement from most of the family that had already begun and would accelerate as the year passed. Or did she grasp at a convenient way of getting out of a situation that was bad and rapidly becoming worse?

The resignation was impulsive, evidence that Jackie had learned nothing from her previous unhappy experience with another book she had not read, William Manchester's masterful account of the Kennedy assassination, *Death of a President.* In 1964, she had asked Manchester to write the authorized account of the events in Dallas. She and Robert Kennedy had been impressed by a brief book he had written earlier, *Portrait of a President.*

Manchester worked twelve to fifteen hours daily in an office at the National Archives Building in Washington to complete his manuscript. Jackie herself had given him five lengthy interviews between April and August 1964. Moreover, Bobby had prepared the contract between the Kennedys and the author. Despite all this, Jackie demanded that the book be suppressed because the serialization rights had been sold to *Look* magazine for $665,000. "I thought that it [the book] would be bound in black and put away on dark library shelves," she said. She enlisted Bobby, who reluctantly tried to persuade Harper & Row, the book's publisher, to abrogate the agreement with *Look.* He also wired Evan Thomas, who edited the book for Harper, telling him the book should neither be serialized nor published—this despite a telegram he had sent to Manchester on July 28, 1966, saying: "Members of the Kennedy family will place no obstacle in the way of publication."

Jackie's insistence, accompanied by a temper tantrum of formidable intensity, made him change his mind. Jackie fought the case in court, and eventually a settlement was reached, under which some personal details (which had been leaked to the press anyway) would be deleted. Manchester, physically and emotionally drained after his intensive effort, commented bitterly in *Look* on the suppression attempt: "It was as though the First and Fourteenth Amendments had been struck from the Constitution."

Jackie was severely criticized then, and again ten years later. The syndicated columnist Liz Smith called Jackie's behavior over the Archer book "short sighted," adding: "Jackie knew *all along* [Smith's emphasis] that Viking was publishing this book. She could have read it right from the beginning and made a quiet decision *then* to take a stand. . . . Even if Jackie had felt she didn't want to stay with Viking because of the book, she could have resigned some months back on some other pretext."

Once an editor leaves a job, particularly from the bottom rung of the editorial ladder, it's not easy to find another in the small publishing business, where competition for positions is strong.

But Jackie had no trouble. In the spring of 1978, she accepted a job at Doubleday & Company as an acquisitions editor—one whose chief responsibility is to acquire books for the house. Knowing the boss, particularly one who would occasionally escort an editor in search of work on dates, helps a great deal. Jackie had gone out with the chief executive officer at Doubleday, John Sargent, one of her "safes," and talk in publishing circles was that Sargent, apparently recognizing a good opportunity when it came his way, put out the word to his staff to hire her. This, of course, was never made public but, as Stephen Birmingham pointed out, "unlikely things have a way of happening when Jackie is concerned."

Jackie's second attempt at publishing was a good deal more successful than her experience at Viking. Her colleagues were more congenial and she made an extraordinary effort to blend seamlessly into the workplace. She came to work earlier than she had at Viking and made a point of going to the Xerox machine to do her own copying. She dialed her own phone calls, got her own midafternoon coffee, and even lunched occasionally in the company cafeteria on the thirty-eighth floor. She dressed simply in tweed skirts in muted colors with unadorned silk blouses and wore low-heeled or flat shoes.

It worked. After she had been at Doubleday only a few weeks, her colleagues, especially the younger assistants, were puzzled by the stories they had heard through the publishing world grapevine about Jackie's "arrogance" and "haughtiness." They saw none of that in their day-to-day contact with her.

When I interviewed company employees in 1978, I heard comments such as these: "She's great, just great . . . a very pleasant person . . ." "smiles at you, says hello and chats . . ." "a wonderful, wonderful person. I just can't say enough." At the same time, despite the effort she was making to be friendly, women particularly were self-conscious when they found themselves near her. They tried not to stare but, as one editorial assistant said, "It's hard not to steal a peek. After all, she's *Jackie.*"

She worked hard at being a team player. When the company had a picnic in Central Park, she showed up, dressed in slacks and a sweater, and drank beer with the others. When Betty Prashker had a Christmas party at her home on Central Park West, Jackie came, mixed with everyone, and sang carols.

At Doubleday, as at Viking, she received no special treatment and requested none. Since 1978, she has had three offices—the first at the company's brick-and-glass building on Park Avenue and 46th Street, the second at 666 Fifth Avenue, the third and most recent at 1540 Broadway at 44th Street. The building faces the Marriott Marquis Hotel in Times Square and is next door to the Lyceum Theatre, which houses Tony Randall's National Actors Theatre.

None of the offices was in the least imposing. Her first was about a dozen feet square, white-painted, with no name on its wood-and-glass door. The second was little different, and the present one, on the eighteenth floor, is boxy, sparsely furnished with a decent-looking desk, two chairs for visitors in front, and walls lined with books, but no couch. Her assistant, a young man, sits outside in a cubicle. She has a direct telephone line.

Years before, when she began her editing career, she would present projects at editorial meetings that appealed strongly to her but had limited appeal to general readers—books about minor figures in the art, dance, and entertainment world who fascinated her and books about aesthetics and social history that would probably be sent back promptly by bookstores if they were ordered at all.

She has since absorbed a lesson: companies have to make money. Publishing had long since been transformed from being a genteel occupation indulged in by literary types to a highly competitive business. Her baptism into commercialism came about after a number of experiences at editorial meetings at which most of her suggestions were shot down, some politely, some with acerbity. "Jackie," one editor said to her, "that book might sell seven copies, but only if you bought six of them yourself."

It wasn't long before Jackie learned to distinguish between books she likes and those she likes that would also capture the interest of other readers. Only a year after she joined Doubleday, she acquired her first novel, *Call the Darkness Light,* by Nancy L. Zaroulis, which became a best seller after publication in August 1979.

The subject of the book gives clear evidence that Jackie's consciousness about the emancipation of women had been raised. The novel, on which Zaroulis, a Boston author, had worked five years, dealt with the plight of the women mill hands in the great textile factories of Lowell, Massachusetts, in the 1940s when Irish, French-Canadian, and other immigrants were imported to work at the looms. While they labored long hours in dreary factories, stifling in summer and freezing in winter, it was the first time, Zaroulis pointed out, that women were given an opportunity to earn money without losing their respectability.

The theme had considerable appeal to Jackie, who pushed hard for the book, won acceptance for it, and, publishing executives agreed, was mainly responsible for its success, which included a $550,000 paperback sale to New American Library, serial rights to *Family Circle* magazine for a large sum, and a number of foreign sales, including one for six figures in England.

Still, Jackie was not cutting her ties with the world of haute couture, stardust, and art. While she was working on the Zaroulis book, she was editing a volume of entrancing floral pictures by the photographer Eugene Atget, called *Atget's Gardens,* and on eight other editorial projects.

In addition to her three half-days a week at the office, she spends many hours at home on her manuscripts. One Doubleday assistant who worked with her said, "She's no nine-to-five person, that's for sure. She vacations a lot and whenever she pleases. Practically all of September she is away and she takes lots of weekends in summer that extend into the early part of the week. She also takes plenty of time for skiing in winter. I never saw her work a full day, like the rest of us."

Jackie has been promoted to senior editor and is paid

$50,000 a year. On average she edits between ten and twelve books a year, about the same workload as any senior editor for a major house. Many of her early contributions to Doubleday were large, coffee-table volumes, such as a book about Russian culture and Russian fairy tales, neither of which were very profitable, but she soon switched to "book books," mostly novels and nonfiction, though not exclusively in the artistic and entertainment fields.

For an editor, shepherding a book onto the best-seller lists is like hitting a home run with bases loaded. Jackie has done it several times.

In 1988, Michael Jackson's *Moonwalk,* the name of a dance step originated by Cab Calloway and popularized by Jackson, was published and leaped to the top of the lists in three weeks. Jackie had prepared carefully. In a telephone call to Jackson, she had suggested that they meet in Los Angeles to discuss the possibility of having the entertainer write a book about his life. Impressed at being called by Jackie Onassis, Jackson agreed to see her.

Her meeting with Jackson went extremely well. She had caught him at a vulnerable time. He wanted to explain, in fullest detail, his true self because, he felt, he was completely misunderstood. Just a few weeks before he had said: "Most people do not know me. That is why they write things which most [sic] is not true. I cry very often because it hurts . . . Animals strike not from malice but because they want to live. It is the same with those who criticize. They desire our blood not our pain. I've been bleeding for a long time now."

They liked each other at once. Jackie was nothing like the boisterous show business people Jackson feared. Her quiet demeanor and extraordinarily good taste appealed strongly to him. Before long a contract calling for an advance payment of $450,000 was drawn.

At Doubleday, she has veto power—unwritten but

powerful nonetheless—over books that deal disparagingly with the Kennedy family. In 1988, author James Spada's biography of Peter Lawford, who had married Jack's sister Patricia, was turned down by Doubleday, reportedly out of respect for Jackie's feelings. Spada's book said unequivocally that Lawford had been a go-between for Jack and Marilyn Monroe. But in the convoluted business of publication, the book was immediately taken over by Bantam Books, which was then owned by the German media giant, Bertelsmann, which also owned Doubleday.

Among her other best sellers were *Dancing On My Grave* in 1986 by the brilliant and controversial ballerina Gelsey Kirkland, an autobiography in which the dancer disclosed her drug addiction, anorexia, and suicidal despair; *Joseph Campbell and the Power of Myth* by Bill D. Moyers, the television commentator and one-time aide to Bobby's arch foe, Lyndon B. Johnson; and the 1992 biography by Edward Radzinsky, *The Last Tsar: The Life and Death of Nicholas II.*

While cherishing her own privacy, Jackie apparently had no qualms about asking other celebrities to write "tell all" autobiographies.

She prevailed upon Gelsey Kirkland to reveal every detail of her past. She worked hard to get Mia Farrow to tell her side of the bitter dispute with Woody Allen in which, among other charges, she accused the actor, filmmaker and writer of molesting his eight-year-old adopted daughter, Dylan.*

In 1993, there was a published report that Jackie had offered $2 million to Camilla Parker-Bowles, with whom Prince Charles of England has had a long-running affair,

---

* Late in September, 1993, the Connecticut State Attorney, Frank Naco, said he was dropping the molestation case after a thirteen-month investigation even though there was "probable cause" to believe that Allen had molested the child. Naco, obviously, was trying to please both sides. Allen was infuriated, saying the investigation "reeks of sleaze."

to "tell all." This followed a widely published story of a taped telephone conversation in which the Prince of Wales told Camilla that he wanted to return "as a tampon and live forever in your knickers." Jackie has tried hard to get Parker-Bowles to write a book about her relationship with Charles.

If Camilla accepts the offer, and some observers say there is a chance she might, what is one to think about Jackie, who circles the wagons when her own privacy is concerned?

In the spring of 1993, when she agreed to give one of her very rare interviews to John Baker, executive editor of *Publishers Weekly,* she set down the list of rules that had to be rigidly observed.*

Baker told me he abided by all her dicta, including submission of quotes. "She made only one change," he said, "a minor grammatical correction."

How did she look? "Much better than one would expect," he said. "Approaching sixty-five, she would seem to be in her mid-fifties, perhaps even younger."

John Baker calls her a "thorough professional." She does not do "line editing"; she does not correct a manuscript for sentence structure, spelling, facts, and other details, he said. Rather, Baker pointed out, Jackie is a "conceptual editor, suggesting changes she feels should be made in the overall concept of a book. She may, for example, tell an author that a passage he or she has written required elaboration for fuller understanding; or she might say the author belabors a point too much and needs to compress it."

Baker added, "She also pays considerable attention to detail, the paper on which it would be printed, the typeface to be used, and especially the illustrations."

In his article, Baker quoted Jackie as saying,

* See page 8.

I'm drawn to books that are out of our regular experience. Books of other cultures, ancient histories. I'm interested in the arts in general, especially the creative process. I'm fascinated by hearing artists talk of their craft. To me, a wonderful book is one that takes me on a journey into something I didn't know before.

I want my books to look as beautiful as possible. Perhaps it's a reaction against the time when Doubleday books used to be quite bad.

Could she imagine having her own imprint, that is, publishing books under her own name? No, she said. "One of the things I like about publishing is that you don't promote the editor—you promote the book and author." She had no "profound thoughts," she said, "on the current state of the publishing industry." But, she added, "I'm always optimistic that people will buy good books."

Jackie's personal anguish, which has led her to seek emotional relief through twice-weekly psychiatry sessions and the discipline of yoga, also led her directly to her most recent success—persuading Bill Moyers to turn a popular television series he had made for public broadcasting into a book. Moyers, an ordained Baptist minister, had long been interested in the effect of the psyche on the soma—how thoughts and emotions can hurt or heal the body. Jackie canceled appointments in order to watch the series and she taped the segments when she could not.

The inspiration for the series, Moyers said, was Norman Cousins,* the well-known author and editor, who coped with a life-threatening illness with laughter—he

---

* In 1964, Cousins was stricken with a serious collagen illness. Collagen, a protein, binds the body's tissues together. Wrote Cousins in *Anatomy of an Illness,* "In a sense, I was coming unstuck."

belly-laughed his way through old Marx Brothers, Charlie Chaplin, Jerry Lewis, and other slapstick films in the hospital—and was cured. Moyers said his own explorations of the link between the mind and the body led to the TV series. Given only one chance in five hundred, Cousins lived another twenty-five years.

What interested Jackie most was an interview Moyers conducted with Jon Kabat-Zinn, founder of the Stress Reduction Clinic at the University of Massachusetts Medical Center, on meditation, which could help patients find relief from stress-related disorders and chronic pain. "It may turn out," Kabat-Zinn said, "that the deep psychological relaxation that accompanies meditation is, in itself, healing." He added, "Meditation can calm the mind and help patients develop strategies and resources for making sensible adaptive choices under pressure, feeling better about their bodies, and feeling re-engaged in life."

Jackie called Moyers and told him that his series interviews with leading authorities in the still partly explored area of mind-body connection, could be turned into a book that could help countless other people. Moyers demurred. The talks, he told her, were merely talks; he didn't see how they could be translated into book.

Jackie told him he was wrong. She herself couldn't tear herself away and neither, she was convinced, could others. And, it turned out, he was wrong and she was right. The book, *Healing and the Mind,* was published in mid-1993 and rested securely on the best-seller lists for months. By the end of the year, it had sold more than half a million copies.

She is a perfect illustration in this stage of her life of the modern woman who challenges the prevailing views in our society that older women are in decline. Jackie never believed this for one moment. She could have served as a role model for Betty Friedan, whose newest book, *The*

Fountain of Age, published in the fall of 1993, explores the reality of the new years of human life open to women who are no longer young. "It's a different stage of life," says Ms. Friedan, "and if you are going to pretend it is youth you are going to miss it. You are going to miss the surprises, the possibilities and the evolution we are just beginning to know . . . because there are no guideposts and there are no signs."

In one of the few glimpses she has allowed into her private life and thoughts, Jackie explained why she wanted and *had* to work.

It came about this way:

She had become friendly with Gloria Steinem, the well-known feminist leader and one of the editors of *Ms.* magazine. Steinem told Jackie that the publication was planning a special issue on "Why Women Work." More than ever before in American history women were spreading out into occupations nobody ever dreamed they would, or could, handle successfully, and the issue would be especially timely.

Ms. Steinem told Jackie that an article by her in which she explained why she, certainly a woman who did not need to work, chose to engage in a paid, productive occupation, would be an inspiration to millions of women, in and out of the workplace.

The talk with Ms. Steinem struck a chord in Jackie. As she had told Tish Baldridge in the late 1970s, she was reassessing her goals. It was plain she could never become an "ordinary" woman: she was a "legend," as journalists called her, too firmly placed on a pedestal from which the public would not allow her to descend. But she had made a great discovery: the life of a goddess could not give her access to the real world like other women of the new generation.

There was ambivalence in her attitude.

Jackie would still court public attention given her as the Most Famous Woman in the World (as Steinem called her). But she also wanted personal fulfillment. "With the exception of Robert Kennedy," Steinem said, "no one ever mentioned that she might simply lead her own life. With feminist hindsight, it's clear that neither I nor anyone I interviewed [about Jackie] was paying her the honor of considering her as a separate human being she was or would have been whether or not she had become the wife of a president."

At home, Jackie wrote down her thoughts in longhand, had them typed at her office, and sent the manuscript to Gloria Steinem. The fourteen-hundred-word article was published in the March 1979 issue.

Jackie wrote, "What has been said for many women of my generation is that they weren't supposed to work if they had families. There they were, with the highest education, and what were they to do when the children were grown—watch the raindrops coming down the windowpane? Leave their fine minds unexercised? Of course women should work if they want to. You have to be doing something you enjoy. That is a definition of happiness: 'complete use of one's faculties along lines leading to excellence in a life affording them scope.' It applies to women as well as to men. We can't all reach it, but we can try to reach it to some degree."

While working people may not always love the work they do, often tolerating and even despising their jobs, they nonetheless have high regard for the work ethic. Jackie told this story: One day the taxi driver who drove her to her office said to her incredulously, "Lady, you work and you don't *have* to?" When she answered yes, he turned around and said with a broad smile, "I think that's great!"

16

Jackie and the Kennedys

In her mature years, Jackie has all but divorced herself from the Kennedy family. Reverence to the memory of Jack is her sole emotional connection with the clan, to which she no longer feels any obligation.

Once she did and she was drawn into their political ambitions, but those days are gone. She cares little about what any of them does or aims to do in politics. Said a close friend: "I can no more imagine Jacqueline campaigning for a Kennedy any more than I can imagine her suiting up as an astronaut."

She still owns a house inside the compound but, said her nephew Anthony Shriver, son of Eunice and Sargent Shriver, when Jackie was a no-show at his wedding in July of 1993, "She never comes to the Cape at all." Young Shriver, twenty-seven, wed Aline Mojica, twenty-eight, at the Big House, Rose and Joe's original home on the compound.

Jackie never attends Thanksgiving and Christmas dinners, cherished family traditions at the compound. Dozens of Kennedys come from all over the country and Europe to be there. Joan Kennedy was present at the two functions before her divorce from Ted and even afterward, until Ted married Victoria Reggie in 1992. Caroline and John are nearly always there. Family members commented on Jackie's absence at one time but they don't any more. Nobody expects her.

And she wasn't present at the one-hundredth birthday celebration for Rose Kennedy on Mother's Day, July 16, 1990, held a week before her actual birthday. It was the biggest family party since the election of John Kennedy. Kennedys and Kennedy friends came from all over to attend.

The guests, 370 of them, were seated at small tables under a huge tent set up on the great lawn in front of the Big House, overlooking Nantucket Sound. Many wept at a special movie, which showed scenes of her life, narrated by Ted. At the party, the Joseph P. Kennedy Foundation, which supports research in mental retardation, presented awards for outstanding leadership, service, and research. The singer Maureen McGovern performed a medley of Rose's favorite Irish melodies, among them "The Rose of Tralee," and, of course, she sang "Happy Birthday."

Four of Rose's surviving children were present. Most of the twenty-eight grandchildren and twenty-two great-grandchildren were there. Caroline attended but John had a good excuse—he was boning up in New York for his bar examination. Rose, though confined to a wheelchair, had a grand time. "I'm like old wine," she said, "they don't bring me out very often but I'm well preserved."

But Jackie was not there, even though she was only a short distance away. She was on Martha's Vineyard helping Carly Simon promote her new book.

Her absence from the centennial of the clan matriarch was an affront to the family that won't be forgotten, or forgiven, by them.

Despite her fondness for Ted Kennedy, she sent another strong signal on October 10, 1993, that she was separating herself from the clan: she was a glaring absentee from the wedding of Teddy Jr.

Scores of journalists and photographers converged on

Block Island, a dot of land twelve miles south of Rhode Island and accessible by an hour's ferry ride from Point Judith. Young Teddy, thirty-two, married Dr. Katherine Gershman, thirty-four, a New Haven psychiatrist and assistant professor of psychiatry at Yale Medical School. Teddy is enrolled at the University of Connecticut School of Law. He has a master's degree in forestry and environmental studies from Yale, where he met his bride.

John Jr. was at the ceremony, escorting Daryl Hannah; Bobby Jr. was there; Rep. Joe Kennedy and his fiancée, Beth Kelly, were there; Dr. William Kennedy Smith, Jean's son, who was acquitted in December 1991, in the sensational Palm Beach rape case, attended.

But Jackie did not. "She had conflicting obligations" was the official excuse given by Melody Miller, the senator's deputy press secretary.

Nor did she attend the wedding of Joe Jr. and Beth Kelly two weeks later, on October 24, in Boston. It was a small affair with only family members present, plus a few invited guests, including Father Jean-Bertrand Aristide, the exiled president of Haiti. But Jackie did not appear.

She visits Jack's grave, and then Bobby's, in Arlington National Cemetery several times a year, but never with any other Kennedy family member. She either goes alone, most frequently at dusk, or with Caroline and John.

Said Luella Hennessey Donavan, the Kennedy family's longtime nurse: "Jackie is a wonderful woman who contributed so much to the family and its heritage, but I always felt that she was an outsider."

Jackie would grimace every time she had to go to the Cape or the Kennedy mansion in Palm Beach. There was always too much go-go activity for her taste, too many sports, too much emphasis on the physical and too little on the cultural.

She and Rose irritated each other. Rose felt that Jackie, as first lady, was too regal, too aloof, and Jackie resented her mother-in-law for interfering too much in her personal life. Rose would dispense unsolicited advice to her and everyone else in the family. Notes and telephone calls went out regularly on everything from personal grooming to the way they were bringing up their children. Bobby was once instructed to get his hair cut; he did. When Ted Kennedy said he might "get my ass shot off one day," a note arrived swiftly admonishing him not to use "that word." She sent reminders to everyone about upcoming Catholic observances and once she told Eunice to ask her daughter Maria to cover up more at the beach. Her breasts were showing too much in her two-piece bathing suit, Rose said.

Jackie, an independent woman from the start, never accepted this kind of interference in her life. She would mimic Rose's flat Bostonian accent to an audience of one, her secretary Mary Barelli Gallagher. Rose, no fool, became aware of Jackie's feelings toward her and seldom visited the White House when she was there.

Jackie hated football, the family's passion. When she was drawn—pulled would be more accurate—into her first game, she asked: "If I get the ball, which way do I run?" The men stared at each other.

She was a spectator most of the time, when she couldn't think of an excuse not to be there at all. Not even a spectator really, because she would drag over a lawn chair and read while they played.* She gave up completely when she was dragooned into a game and broke an ankle trying to catch the ball. Thereafter she was neither participant nor observer.

---

* One day, the president made a spectacular catch. Beaming, he jogged over to his wife and said, "Hey, Jackie, did you see that?" She had not and offered no compliment. Bobby, hurt that his brother received no acknowledgment from his wife for his brilliant performance, whispered to her, "It would help if you could say something nice. It would mean a lot to him." Jackie put her book down and made a great show of applauding the feats of the players.

Jackie tried to fit in but within a few months discovered she neither could nor ever would. Accustomed to a genteel atmosphere at dinner, with muted conversation, she was startled and then repelled by the confusion at Kennedy meals. It reminded her of the films and stories she had seen and heard about the court of King Henry VIII of England, where great quantities of food were passed around, everyone grabbed, and bedlam ensued. The din of loud voices, often rising to bellows as disagreements over political matters escalated, offended her sensibilities.

She never understood the Kennedy women, who were not of her world of quiet sophistication, and they, in turn, never accepted her. They were clam chowder, she was lobster bisque. They yelled, she talked quietly. And before her marriage to Jack was three months old they—all except Ted's wife, Joan—were referring to her as "the debutante." They mimicked her put-on whispery voice, going into gales of laughter as they derided her; they mocked her clumsiness on the athletic fields and what they called her "Marie Antoinette" taste in furnishing her home.

Ethel, Bobby's wife and later widow, was the ringleader of the anti-Jackie contingent among the Kennedy women. Jackie took an almost instant dislike to her, which deepened as the years passed, and Ethel has always despised Jackie. When she heard that Jackie preferred to have her name prounounced "Jack-leen," Ethel said cuttingly: "Like in queen?" Relayed to Jackie, the putdown prompted a retort that Ethel was a "country bumpkin" and "a little Catholic schoolgirl." Jackie grimaced at what she felt was a mishmash of decorating styles at Ethel's Hickory Hill home, saying she was "the type who would put a slipcover on a Louis Quinze sofa and then spell it Luie Cans." After watching Ethel and Eunice running and tumbling on the lawn during a touch football game with the other clan members, she said contemptuously:

"They're a bunch of gorillas falling over one another," and went back to her home.

According to a story, at Hyannis Port one summer weekend, family members went sailing on Nantucket Sound. Everyone was dressed in old clothes and windbreakers, but Jackie and her sister Lee were in fashionable sailing attire straight out of *Vogue* magazine. At lunchtime, sandwiches were distributed to the clansmen and women from a hamper and beer from a cooler was passed around. On a signal from Ethel, a white-coated steward appeared, bearing a tray of cold crab and white wine, which he solemnly served to Jackie and Lee.*

Jackie's dislike of Ethel intensified when she led the Kennedy outcry against her marriage to Onassis. When Jackie returned to America several months after the wedding on Skorpios, she met Ethel for lunch at La Caravelle, an elegant Manhattan restaurant. Diners at nearby tables heard Ethel ask scornfully, "Well, have you had enough of your Greek supertycoon?"

---

* While the story has never been authenticated, it bears Ethel's prankster imprint. She would spend hours, even days, concocting practical jokes. Her most famous one—which backfired loudly—took place in 1957 when she sent an announcement to the newspapers that labor leader Dave Beck and his son Dave Jr. and their wives would attend a party in her parent's Greenwich home, honoring Bobby and Ethel. Newspersons showed up in hordes because at the time Bobby, as chief counsel for the Senate Labor Rackets Committee, was making headlines investigating the senior Beck, president of the International Brotherhood of Teamsters, on charges of embezzling union funds.

The Associated Press sent out a story attributing this astonishing quote to the elder Beck: "Although our policies differ, socially we get along famously." Ethel compounded the joke by having one of the couples present pose as Mr. and Mrs. Beck. Ethel's prank blew up in her face when the AP bureau in Seattle found that Beck Sr. was at his home there. Ethel was berated by E.R. McCullough, managing editor of the Stamford *Advocate*, in a front-page editorial that included this note to readers: "If you have any thoughts on adult delinquency, please let me know."

Jackie was infuriated. "I won't sit here and listen to you talking that way about one of the sweetest men on earth!".

Replied Ethel, "You've hurt the family, all this publicity about your almost obscene big spending . . . It's disgraceful. Why don't you walk out on him?"

Jackie summoned a waiter and asked for a check. "I'm going to walk out on you," she told Ethel, and did.

They saw each other infrequently after that. When Jackie returned to New York after the funeral of Onassis on Skorpios, Ethel telephoned to offer condolences. "Tell her I'm indisposed," Jackie said to her housekeeper. Yet less than an hour later she was seen walking in the early spring sunshine in Central Park.

Jackie had once been close to Joan because she realized she, too, was having trouble adjusting to her role as a political wife and fitting in with the Kennedys. They had many intimate conversations about the problems Joan had, but there was little Jackie could do when Joan began slipping into alcoholism. After Joan's divorce, Jackie called to offer supportive advice, but they drifted apart and now rarely communicate with each other.

The only living Kennedy for whom Jackie always had high regard is Ted, whom she sees fairly often and talks to frequently by telephone.

Kenny O'Donnell told me: "I suspect Jackie admires the guy's approach to life, doing what he pleases, when he pleases, and the hell with the consequences. She likes his good nature, his basic kindness, and, most particularly, the way he is carrying on the liberalism of Jack and Bobby. Not least, she likes the guy because of his concern about her and her welfare, financial and otherwise."

In earlier years, Jackie was wary of the third generation of Kennedys, especially the children of Ethel and Bobby. "She found the behavior of most of Ethel's brood all but intolerable," said Richard Burke, Ted Kennedy's former top administrative aide. She knew that David Kennedy "was completely immersed in drugs and that Bobby Jr.

was part of a destructive triangle that included Christopher Lawford and Lem Billings," Burke said. (Bobby Jr. has since become a respected environmentalist attorney, teacher, and activist, and the others have grown up too.)

During their growing-up years, Jackie was particularly careful to keep Caroline and John apart from their cousins. This protection, said author Harrison Rainie, "helped make their lives more stable."

Jackie shows up only at a few weddings of the younger cousins. She and her children were present when Victoria Lawford, daughter of Patricia and the late Peter Lawford, married Washington lawyer Robert Beebe Pender at Pat's Southampton estate on Long Island in June of 1987. And she attended the wedding of Maria Shriver and film star Arnold Schwarzenegger the year before in Hyannis.

As a sign of her estrangement from the family, nobody —especially not the young cousins and their families—is allowed to enter the home she still maintains within the compound without her express permission. Only one hundred yards from the Main House, it was willed to her by Jack. She hires a young girl to act as a "house watcher." Her chief duty is to warn off trespassing Kennedys. Aware of her attitude, the cousins do not venture near the house.

Caroline has adopted her mother's aloofness from the cousins. She is close only to Maria Shriver and to Courtney, Ethel's daughter. She and her husband, Ed Schlossberg, are not among the "Kennedy Kids" who flock to the newest "in" restaurants and the trendiest discos. When Kerry, another of Ethel's daughters, graduated from Boston University in 1988, forty of the sixty guests went to the Capiteau Restaurant in Manhattan, and later went to Nell's disco. Caroline and Ed were at the party, but afterward had a quiet dinner at home.

Once a year, in summer, Jackie makes a gesture to embrace the clan, but everyone in the family knows it's a halfhearted one. She invites them for a weekend at Gay

Head. The older members came years ago but now fewer and fewer attend. Ted and Joan were regular visitors even after their divorce, but now Joan has stopped coming and even Ted's visits are rare. Ethel is never there; neither are Eunice, Jean, or Patricia.

The young Kennedy cousins and their children are the only ones who can be counted on to be present. "Hey, it's a nice place, good food, and we can have some fun," one of the cousins told me. They apparently don't mind that, while Aunt Jackie allows them free range of her property and its amenities, she remains secluded from them.

17

Ĉ

A Woman of Independent Means

In chapter 4, we visited Jackie's magnificent apartment in New York. Come now to the place she loves best of her four houses, her vacation retreat on Martha's Vineyard, a triangular island separated from Cape Cod by only a few nautical miles. The Vineyard is only twenty-one miles long and ten miles in breadth at its widest point.

When Jackie was ten years old, she wrote this quatrain:

> When I go down by the sandy shore
> I can think of nothing I want more
> Than to live by the booming blue sea
> As the seagulls flutter round about me.

Forty-three years later, at fifty-three, she fulfilled that dream. Touring the island, she found exactly what she wanted on its southwestern tip, in Gay Head, one of the six towns on the island. It is a 365-acre tract of land, low-lying like the rest of the island, thick with tangled underbrush and stunted oak trees. Deer roamed wild on the property, blueberry bushes were everywhere. Venturing through the vegetation, she reached a beach where Vineyard Sound met the Atlantic Ocean. The scene was the "booming blue sea" of her childhood fantasy and even seagulls swooped around the shoreline.

She bought the property in 1978 for a reported $1.15 million from the Hornblower family of the Hornblower & Weeks-Hemphill Hayes stock exchange firm. When the islanders learned of her intention to build a vacation home there, anxiety ran high among the inhabitants, the locals as well as the many celebrities who had homes there. They feared it would become an outpost of the Kennedy compound in Hyannis Port, with visitors trooping in and out constantly, security guards everywhere, hordes of tourists and, worse, the media, who would no doubt set up observation posts for photo ops.

For two years, residents saw lumber and other building materials being trucked onto the property. Albert Fischer III, the caretaker, refused to comment on Jackie's design plans and other employees engaged in the construction could not be pumped for information. Finally in 1980, the secret emerged. Community-wide angst subsided when it became known that Jackie was not planning a Camelot castle but nothing more than one large, thirty-one-hundred-square-foot saltbox, a form of architecture quite in keeping with other homes on the island, and a smaller nine-hundred-square-foot guesthouse alongside.

The interiors, however, were Jackie-style opulent.

Jackie insisted on only the finest materials. When white oak flooring was delivered, at a cost of $14,000, it was wrapped in burlap to prevent dents; a ton of imported teak from Burma for the sun decks was trucked in, also carefully wrapped. She wanted, and got, windows made as colonial Americans created them, with wooden pegs instead of screws and nails. She wanted, and got, towel racks in the six bathrooms that were heated and toilets that flushed hot water. Most kitchens have four-burner stoves; Jackie's has sixteen.

She did not trust moving vans to deliver her furniture and accessories. She enlisted the help of an old friend,

Mrs. Paul (Bunny) Mellon of the Mellon financial family to fly in her private jet beds, bric-a-brac, paintings, couches, chairs, tables, and everything else Jackie had selected to fill nineteen rooms. Bunny, who would do anything for Jackie, readily complied. (When Jackie moved into her Manhattan apartment, Bunny gave her a $17,000 bed, which Jackie sent back. Bunny was so hurt she wept.)

Privacy is guaranteed. From the entrance a long winding road leads to the houses, which are entirely hidden by the trees and dense shrubbery. When the media descends, reporters, TV crews, and photographers camp outside, unable to see a thing. Most of the time they leave without a glimpse of Jackie or anyone else.

The cost of the hideaway, exclusive of the furnishings, has been estimated at about $3 million—in 1980 dollars.

"Ironically," *People* magazine commented the following year, "Jackie's choice of location may insure her more privacy than even money can buy. Some islanders cherish Gay Head's seclusion even more than she—they cultivate marijuana in its dark woods."

In Edgartown, largest of the island's six towns, Richard Reston,* editor of the venerable *Vineyard Gazette*, one of the oldest community newspapers in the country, told me: "There were some occasional bumps and hiccups at the beginning, but on the whole Jackie's presence has not been disruptive up here. She has been a good and quiet neighbor and the islanders by and large have accepted her."

Mrs. Onassis has not been reclusive. She is seen fairly frequently at various points on the island, at the theater, at local restaurants, or walking and shopping in town centers, sometimes accompanied by Maurice Tempelsman,

---

* Richard Reston is the son of James Reston, the former editor and later columnist of *The New York Times*. The elder Reston bought the *Vineyard Gazette* in 1968 from Henry Bettle Hough.

sometimes alone. "Most people here tend to leave celebrities to their privacy—there are so many here," said Dick Reston, "the residents are quite accustomed to seeing them in their midst." Walter Cronkite, Billy Joel, Beverly Sills, Carly Simon, Katherine Graham, Jules Feiffer, Mike Wallace, Spike Lee, Robert McNamara, and Vernon Jordan are just a few they are likely to see at an adjoining table in a restaurant or the aisles of the A&P.

The first of the "bumps" was minor, another far more serious.

When plans for the house were disclosed, neighbors registered loud complaints: the plans called for a thirty-four-foot high central chimney to heat the huge master bedroom, many feet higher than was permitted under the zoning codes. Architect Hugh N. Jacobsen, who designed the saltboxes, seeking a variance, defended the up-thrusting chimney, saying, "My client wants an upstairs fireplace because she likes to sleep on the second floor."

Jacobsen argued that the surrounding trees would effectively screen the chimney from public view. The zoning board agreed, so, finally, did the neighbors, and Jackie won a variance. But she had to yield on another zoning violation. The silo-style wings of the two-bedroom guesthouse were three feet too high and the board was adamant on this. They were lowered.

Paradox piles upon paradox.

Bobby, the Kennedy Jackie admired most, whose counsel and example she followed in reshaping her life, loved and befriended Indians. During his presidential campaign, Robert Kennedy would spend considerable time with Indians on reservations. Fred Dutton, a top campaign aide, urged him to stop wasting precious time. He pointed out that while Indians are entitled to vote, few of them do. "Knock off the Injuns," Dutton said, adding that after he was elected he could do as much as he wanted for them but now he needed votes. Bobby, his voice hoarse from his many speeches, scribbled a note to him. "Those of you who are running my campaign don't love Indians as much as I do. You're a bunch of bastards."

Said Steve Bell, a radio and TV newscaster: "When it came to Indians, there was no politicking, only genuine feeling."

Jackie, however, got into an acrimonious legal squabble with a group of Indians over a tiny parcel of beachfront land that is entirely surrounded by her cherished hideaway. Between 1980 and 1990, she fought in both the probate and land courts to deny the Wampanoags access to a tract of beachfront land 264 feet long and 225 feet deep that the tribe considered sacred. All during those years, she posted security guards at the beach, barring tribe members from going in and conducting pageants, which were reenactments of Wampanoag legend.

According to the story handed down, a Wampanoag tribal chief named Moshup and his wife, Old Squant, fled to the sand dunes there more than two centuries ago to escape the white man, who they believed would slaughter them. Tribe members believe Moshup and his wife died and were buried on the site.

The Wampanoags have a rich and colorful history. When the pilgrims celebrated their first Thanksgiving in 1621, a year after they had established the first permanent settlement in New England, the Indian Chief Massasoit and some of his braves were invited to the feast.

Massasoit was a member of the Wampanoag tribe, which then inhabited a large area in southeastern Massachusetts, from what is now Boston down to Narragansett Bay, including the coastal area of Plymouth where the Pilgrims had landed.

Shortly after the landing, the Pilgrims entered into a pact with the Wampanoags. The Indians would remain friendly to the settlers, teaching them their techniques of hunting, fishing, and agriculture and, in turn, the Pilgrims would protect the Indians—a treaty that lasted fifty-four years, after which hostilities broke out between the Indians and white men. Historians have said that if the tribe had been hostile and unwilling to share their knowledge, the early colonists might not have survived.

Ironically, the generosity of the Wampanoags set into motion the forces that led to their near extinction as a tribe. Nearly four centuries later, there were fewer than five hundred left in the entire area, about two hundred fifty on the mainland and the same number on Martha's Vineyard. Only ninety remain in Gay Head. Their native language is almost extinct with only a few words remaining. "The songs that we sing are about the closest we come to preserve the language," said Cameron Cuch, now eighteen and a descendant of the tribe.

Through her attorney, Alexander D. Folger, Jackie contended that she had endured a life of violence and risk and was entitled to a place where she could have peace, quiet, and minimum exposure to danger. Permitting so many people to cross her property, Folger said, would threaten the seclusion she was seeking. The Vanderhoop clan of the Gay Head Wampanoags, who claim the land is the site of the tribal legend, countered with bitter comments that throughout American history Indians, unable to defend their property rights, slowly but all too surely lost everything they had ever owned.

In 1989, Mrs. Thelma Weissberg, a great granddaughter of the original Vanderhoop family, bitterly assailed Jackie. "A woman like that," she said, "who owns all that land, why would we be bothering her?"

Finally a settlement was reached. In March of 1990, Jackie agreed to cede to the Wampanoag group a parcel of land slightly larger than the one sought, about two acres with a two-hundred-fifty-foot ocean frontage, located three hundred yards west of the disputed property. She would give them $120,000 in court costs in exchange for the area they had wanted, and the Wampanoags would relinquish all rights to it. Even though the new tract is surrounded by Jackie's property, tribe members would be permitted to enter and leave without hindrance.

In 1985, Jackie was the fiftieth wealthiest woman in America, but the only one on the list, compiled by *Good Housekeeping* magazine, with a job to which she went regularly. (Topping the list was Margaret Hunt Hill and her sister Caroline Hunt Schoelkopf, daughters of H.L. Hunt, the oil-billionaire who died in 1974. Others were Estée Lauder, whose cosmetics company was said to be worth more than $700 million; Yoko Ono, widow of John Lennon, $150 million, and Mary Kay Ash, whose cosmetics fortune was estimated at $100 million.

Jackie's financial worth at the time was about $25 million, most of it coming from the settlement of Onassis's estate. But it hasn't remained at that level.

Estimates now put Jackie's net worth at between $150 to $200 million, including:

- Her Gay Head estate, valued in the millions.
- The Manhattan apartment, worth close to $4 million.
- Her home on the Kennedy compound in Hyannis Port.
- A country estate in Bernardsville, New Jersey, which she bought for $200,000 in 1974 and was assessed at $888,600, in 1991. In 1992, Jackie sold the ten-acre property, which is surrounded by rolling hills and horse farms, to John and Caroline for the nominal price of about $100. According to the *Bridgewater Courier-News,* in New Jersey, the sale was reportedly made for tax and estate-planning purposes.
- A $50,000-a-year job.
- Art, jewelry, antiques, cars, and other personal possessions whose worth nobody can calculate.

A large sum is available for investment in cash-producing instruments, such as stocks and bonds, and certificates of deposit. According to a financial consultant whose clients include many persons with large fortunes, the rich generally invest much of their funds in tax-free municipal bonds, which in 1993 generated about five or five and one-half percent annually for the higher-rated issues, and much more if the investments were made in the early 1980s when the rates were significantly higher. No need to do arithmetic, which could be far from accurate. The bottom line is that Jackie's cash flow is ample.

Two men were mainly responsible for the accretion of Jackie's personal worth. One was André Meyer, banker and art collector who advised her on stock market investments in 1975. Said Edward Klein in *Vanity Fair* magazine: "He took Jackie's nice fortune . . . and made it into a nicer fortune."

The second was Maurice Tempelsman, who advises her on investments in the precious metals markets. Jackie reportedly made huge profits by selling gold futures in the commodities market when the price was at an historic high. In the market, an investor contracts to buy a certain amount of a commodity at a particular price. If the price rises, the investor sells his or her option to buy, and reaps a profit. Jackie reportedly bought gold options when the price was about $100 an ounce, and sold them when, fueled by inflation, the price soared to more than $800 an ounce in the early 1980s.

If retreating to the "booming blue sea" of her childhood visions is Jackie's best-loved way of achieving peace and quietude, and working as an editor best satisfies her creative urge, being a grandmother is the profoundest emotional experience of her later years.

When Caroline was pregnant with her first baby, Jackie's close friend Doris Cerutti, owner of Cerutti Children Enterprises, an elegant clothing store at 807 Madison Avenue in Manhattan, told her that the approaching new turn in her life would be "a truly incredible thing." Jackie and Doris Cerutti have known each other ever since Caroline and John were small. Jackie had taken them to the Cerutti store to be outfitted when she moved to New York from Washington in 1964.

"I told her that she will surprise even herself about how she feels toward the new baby," Doris said. And she told me that Jackie was looking forward with great anticipation to the new role. "There is no question that she will love every minute of being a grandmother and no question that she will dote on the baby."

Son-in-law Ed Schlossberg told me: "She couldn't be a better grandmother."

And when I dropped in to see Doris Cerutti soon after Rose was born, she told me, "Jackie is simply terrific. She babysits for Caroline and Ed, either in their apartment or hers, she feeds her, takes her for strolls and kisses her just about all the time."

Jackie changed the baby when necessary but forgot some of her baby-raising skills in the first few months, Doris revealed. One day, when Rose was about three months old, she gave the baby her bottle and put her over her shoulder to burp her. But she had neglected to put a diaper over her T-shirt. Rose obliged with a loud burp, which was accompanied by a great gob of milk that sent Jackie hastily to her closet for another shirt.

Once in August of 1989, Caroline and Rose, then seven weeks old, were visiting Jackie at Gay Head. Jackie's mother, Janet Auchincloss, then eighty-three and in the late stages of Alzheimer's disease, was there too. Jackie introducing her mother to Rose for the first time, put the baby in her lap. "This is your great-granddaughter, baby Rose," she said.

Janet just looked at the infant, showing no understanding of what was being said. Said a servant who was present: "She knew there was a baby, but couldn't understand why it was there or who it belonged to."

Caroline and Jackie, observing the poignant scene, were close to tears. When the baby was taken away, Janet's face suddenly brightened. For a few moments her mind cleared. Turning to Caroline, she said: "You look very pretty, dear. You're Caroline, aren't you? And this is your new baby. She's lovely."

Caroline smiled. "She's beautiful. She looks just like you."

The children have a nanny, but often, when the weather is pleasant, Jackie will walk half a mile to the Schlossberg apartment and take over. While Ed is working at his office at 641 Avenue of the Americas and Caroline is bustling around town doing errands, Jackie will head for Central Park two blocks away with the two older children.

Wheeling a stroller in which dark-eyed Tanya, age four, sits placidly, and with Rose walking alongside, she attracts no more attention than any other grandma. No heads turn as Jackie enters the park wearing dark slacks, long-sleeved white shirt and a man's tie with a zigzag pattern. She also sports large sunglasses and a silk scarf tied around her head.

At the carousel, she buys tickets for everyone—ninety cents per person per ride—waits for her change from a twenty-dollar bill, counts it carefully, and goes aboard. Rose mounts a horse; Jackie, Tanya on her lap, sits on the ornate bench alongside as the music starts and the merry-go-round turns. The second time around she and Tanya ride a horse.

Afterward, they troop to the statue of Hans Christian Andersen, where Rose and Tanya clamber into the bronze lap of the Danish writer of much-loved fairy tales as Jackie, knuckle in mouth, watches apprehensively. Nothing bad happens. The children climb down, the outing continues.

Rose and Tanya skip ahead but Jackie lets out a loud Indian war whoop and they scamper back.

After that comes ice cream. Rose and Tanya get cones, which the younger girl soon drips over her face and shirt. Jackie buys a frozen, low-fat, low-calorie treat on a stick. Then, after about three hours, they stroll back home.

Said Ted Leyson, a free-lance photographer who had spotted the group: "She [Jackie] was a little kid again. When she did that Indian whoop thing, you could see she just loved it."

18

∞

Crusader

In maturity, Jacqueline Onassis has displayed a unique capacity for growth and change. That she has become deeply involved in civic causes is a fact that few people, perhaps not even Jackie herself, would have foreseen.

Looking back on her life, we can see that her involvement in these crusades was not an epiphany. There was no sudden awakening, no switch turned on to reveal new values. Her early interest in the political process and what it could accomplish, her empathy with the poverty-stricken miners of West Virginia, her secret trip to Cambodia to open a new dialogue between Prince Sihanouk and the United States (as discussed in chapter 6)—all were signs of an evolving social conscience.

Her values today are an extension and a widening of her goals three decades ago, but now she aims for them with a greater intensity.

When she was redoing the Executive Mansion, she was quietly persistent; now she is whipped into a frenzy at what she considers abominations committed against the urban environment. She is on the telephone cajoling, pleading with, charming others to join her; she writes scores, if not hundreds, of letters; she is unafraid of the richest and most powerful forces who may be arrayed against her.

In her earlier years, she was tolerant of the women in Washington, Paris, and New York whose social lives revolved around parties and other social events. She herself was a dedicated partygoer, especially after the death of Onassis in 1975.

The older Jackie is scornful of women who idle away their days and evenings. At a publishing party for a book she had edited for Doubleday, she looked around at a cocktail crowd of well-dressed women and said, half to herself and half to Charlotte Curtis of *The New York Times*: "They don't do anything, do they?"

She herself *does* things. Many things.

"I am passionate about architecture," she said. "We are the only country in the world that trashes its old buildings. Too late we realize how very much we need them."

She acted upon that passion by joining a demonstration to save a treasured landmark and traveled to Albany to testify before a joint committee of the Senate and Assembly.

And she tackled—and helped beat—a powerful investment banking firm and an equally powerful real estate developer in a battle that had a striking parallel to the "war"—his word—that President Kennedy had waged against big business in 1962.

The lesson of that bruising fight had not been lost on Jacqueline.

Exactly a quarter century earlier, Jack Kennedy led a charge which, in the end, left some industrialists bruised and defeated. On April 10, 1962, Roger Blough, chairman of the United States Steel Corporation (then the formidable "Big Steel"), told the president in the Oval Office that his company would announce a six-dollar-per-ton increase.

Kennedy was enraged. Just four days before, an understanding had been reached between the United Steel Workers of America and the industry calling for a small wage increase but ruling out a price rise, although no agreement had been officially signed. Immediately after Blough's announcement, four other major producers followed Big Steel's move.

"My father always told me that all businessmen were sons-of-bitches but I never believed it until now," fumed the president. The increase would trigger an inflationary spiral, increasing the cost of homes, tools, and machinery, erode the incomes of people living on fixed incomes, and add $1 billion to the cost of national defense.

Jack, with Bobby at his side, counterattacked. The President denounced the steel industry at a televised press conference. Bobby, as attorney general, announced that the Justice Department would immediately convene a grand jury to investigate the possibility that the producers were violating criminal laws against price fixing; dozens of telephone calls were made to powerful men in the industry; a veiled threat was leaked that the administration might seek means of breaking up Big Steel into smaller units.

In three days, the steel producers caved in. Prices were rolled back to where they had been.

Jackie launched her own battle against powerful interests in the summer of 1987 when one of the city's fiercest real estate battles in decades erupted.

The banking firm of Salomon Brothers, in partnership with Mortimer B. Zuckerman's Boston Properties, a real estate development company, proposed to construct a 2.1 million-square-foot office, retail, and apartment complex at the 3.4 acre site of the New York Coliseum at Columbus Circle. The project included two towers, one sixty-eight stories, the other fifty-eight. The existing structure at the southwest corner of Central Park would be demolished.

The City Planning Commission and the Board of Estimate, then the city's legislative body, approved the project. Mayor Edward I. Koch said it was a fine idea, sure to pour tax money into the city's chronically shriveled treasury.

Despite the approvals already won, despite Mayor Koch's stance, Jackie spearheaded the opposition to the Coliseum project whose plans for twin towers would not only cast a mile-long shadow over the lower part of Central Park but would also significantly worsen Manhattan's air pollution problem because of the exhaust emissions from the vehicular traffic it would attract.

Studying the plans, Jackie discovered the extent of the menace city dwellers were facing. Shortly after noon, "The Shadow," as the project was quickly dubbed, would cause the playing fields, walkways, and benches in the lower part of Central Park to darken as though a solar eclipse had occurred. Trees, lawns, children's playgrounds would be chilled.

By midafternoon, the pond where children, and many grownups too, sail remote-controlled boats, the Wollman skating rink, and soon Fifth Avenue and beyond would be cast into gloom. "The mere prospect of such a massive building at the border of Central Park drives certain people almost speechless with outrage," wrote John Taylor in *New York* magazine.

Jackie Onassis was one of them. "I have never seen her so angry," a friend confided. "She was absolutely furious. Remember that movie, in which the guy cries out that he's mad as hell and won't take it any more?* That was Jackie!"

Jackie called on her powerful neighbors and friends to join the crusade to ban "The Shadow." She enlisted former Secretary of State Henry Kissinger, commentator Walter Cronkite, feminist leader Betty Friedan, authors Brendan Gill and E. L. Doctrow, actresses Celeste Holm and Candace Bergen, and the latter's husband, film direc-

---

* The film was *Network.* The "guy" was Peter Finch.

tor Louis Malle; former New York City Mayor John Lindsay; and the famed architect I. M. Pei.

The battle they fought was over principles that went far deeper than a zoning dispute. For them the war was an emotional one with resonances that went far beyond the controversy. It was a metaphor for a conflict between good and evil—between good civic values and avariciousness on the part of developers. Kent Barwick, president of the Municipal Art Society, said: "This building . . . has come to stand for excessiveness in New York. By the time this is over, you'll see the reemergence of the popular voice in what happens in this city."

The developers counterattacked furiously. Jackie, along with eight hundred other influential opponents of the project, was sent a stinging eight-page letter signed by Edward H. Linde, Mort Zuckerman's partner in Boston Properties.

The letter scornfully attacked the critics for embracing "this season's cause célèbre," and accusing them of distorting the facts about the proposed complex. Wrote Linde: "Their [the critics'] contentions are untrue, they are erroneous, they are based on emotionally appealing myths, not facts." The lawsuit, he contended, was both "groundless and unfair" because the "shade" that the buildings would cast would not last as long or go as far as the opposition contended.

Despite the furor raging around the project, John Gutfreund, then chairman of Salomon, Inc., refused to budge. His company would not only be the principal owner of the complex but would occupy more space in it than any other tenant. Gutfreund said the project would cement the city's standing as the financial hub of the entire world. "Our heritage is in New York," said Gutfreund, and we are looking forward to our new home in the Coliseum site."

Not so fast, Jackie contended.

Standing before microphones at a news conference on

July 29, 1987, in the offices of the Municipal Art Society at 457 Madison Avenue, of which she is a trustee, Jackie barely contained her fury. "It's a monstrous idea," she said. "It's time to stop the overbuilding in New York City by drawing the line at Columbus Circle and reducing the size of the monstrous building that has been proposed there." (The taller of the two towers would be 925 feet high.)

"We are drawing the line at Columbus Circle. It's our responsibility to voice concern when we feel the city's future is in danger."

In 1987, the conflict moved into the courts. The Society brought suit in State Supreme Court to stop the project, and won. The developers filed new plans lopping 173 feet off the taller of the two towers.

Not enough, said the opponents, who now sued the developers in the United States District Court on the grounds the complex would violate the Federal Clean Air Act.

Jackie and her forces won, but the developers appealed and the ruling was overturned. By this time, however, Salomon had pulled out of the project and Mort Zuckerman was hesitating, partly because of the depressed real estate market, partly because his foes might appeal to the U.S. Supreme Court.

By late summer of 1993, the Coliseum project as originally envisioned, was dead. If, in the future, something is constructed on the site, it will surely be far different from the original concept.

The forces of good had prevailed; Jackie was given full credit for her contribution by the Municipal Art Society.

It was a great victory but not her first crusade. Jackie became initially interested, and ultimately excited by, urban environmental issues when the magnificent Grand Central Terminal building on 42nd Street in Manhattan was threatened.

The Grand Central case began in 1968 when the New York City Landmarks Preservation Commission designated the huge terminal and the property it occupies as a landmark, thus barring any further construction on the property and any alteration of the exterior without the approval of the Commission.

Five months later, Penn Central, owner of the terminal, announced plans to lease its air rights above the terminal to a developer who was to build a fifty-three-story office tower above Grand Central.

But in 1968 and 1969 when the developer submitted two design proposals for the tower the Commission ruled both unacceptable. The railroad and the developer went to court, contending that the city, through the Commission, was taking their property for public use without compensation, in violation of the due process and equal protection guarantees of the Constitution.

The State Supreme Court held the rejection of the proposals unconstitutional, but the Appellate Division reversed, holding by a 3–2 vote that the Commission's action had not unconstitutionally deprived the owner and developer of their property. New York's highest court, the State Court of Appeals, affirmed the ruling unanimously.

The railroad appealed to the U.S. Supreme Court. At issue was whether the New York City Landmarks Commission was entitled to designate the terminal as a landmark and bar construction of the office tower.

Jackie, approaching fifty on April 27, 1977, joined the battle and protested construction of the tower above the terminal. Office workers streaming from the surrounding buildings for lunch gaped as Jackie mounted a makeshift rostrum in front of the building and pleaded for their support. "You must help me," she cried. "This building is part of our heritage. It must not be deserted." Flanking her on the platform were leaders of the drive to bar construction of the tower.

Jackie devoted full time to the cause. And the cause prevailed. On June 27, 1978, the U.S. Supreme Court ruled that nothing could be built in the air space above the terminal because any such construction would significantly alter its status as a historic landmark.

In 1980, St. Bartholomew's Episcopal Church on Lexington Avenue and 50th Street announced that it had accepted a proposal by Howard Ronson, a British developer, to raze its parish or community house adjoining the church and replace it with a 59-story office skyscraper.

Jackie went once more unto the breach. She became cochair, with writer Brendan Gill, of the Committee to Save St. Bartholomew's.

She went head-to-head with the rector, Rev. Thomas Bowers, who wanted the tower because it would provide a badly needed infusion of money. The church, he said, urgently needed repairs which would cost $7.5 million. With collections down, the parish, despite its wealthy flock, could be broke in a decade. Further, he claimed, the additional funds would help the church go forward with varied projects, now on hold, to help the poor and deprived.

Jackie and her committee argued that the project directly violated New York City's landmark laws. Proponents countered by having sympathetic legislators introduce a bill in the state legislature to exempt all religious institutions.

As in the Columbus Circle fight, this one, too, transcended a clash of opponents over zoning. It was a battle over historical preservation and the needs of Mammon. The Rev. Mr. Bowers considered Jackie such a powerful enemy that he invited her to tea at the rectory and sought to have her drop her opposition. It was a cordial meeting, but Jackie stood firm. The tower must not go up. The church reduced the height of the building to forty-seven stories. The answer was still no.

On February 8, 1984, Jackie boarded a special train called "Landmark Express II" to Albany, along with about one hundred civic leaders, representatives of neighborhood organizations, architects, planners, preservationists, and religious leaders. It was her first visit to the state capital, and it was a triumphant one. "The magical Jackie Onassis cast her spell on the Capitol, enchanting Governor Mario Cuomo . . . and sweet-talking the legislators on her crusade to save New York City landmarks," wrote the *New York Post*.

Jackie fever swept through the state capitol's marbled halls as she whirled through a full day of meetings and conferences, lobbying against the "St. Bart's bill," which would allow the church to proceed.

Testifying before a joint Senate-Assembly committee, she said in impassioned voice, "The future of New York City is bleak if landmark laws no longer apply to religious institutions. I think that if you cut people off from what nourishes them spiritually or historically then something inside of them dies." After her appearance, she left the hearing room to loud applause to make her argument to key lawmakers in their offices.

The bill was defeated but St. Bart's fought on in the courts, and the case dragged on for seven more years. Finally, in March of 1991, the church gave up after the U.S. Supreme Court refused to hear its constitutional challenge to its designation as a landmark.

Like Grand Central Terminal, the church and its parish house still stand alone.

These were her three most important crusades, and Jackie played major roles in them all.

19

co

Her Passing

Late Wednesday afternoon, May 18, Ted Kennedy received a telephone call in Washington from his nephew John Kennedy, Jr. He listened for a few seconds, then barked a few orders to his staff. While standing at his desk, he phoned New York Hospital—Cornell Medical Center, spoke less than half a minute, and rushed to the airport to take the shuttle to New York. A taxi transported him to Jackie's apartment at 1040 Fifth Avenue in Manhattan.

More than two hundred reporters and television correspondents huddled under umbrellas in a soft rain, littering the sidewalk with cigarette butts, coffee containers, and candy wrappers.

When the senator arrived, the press crowded around him, shoving microphones, tape recorders, and cameras at him. A weary smile crossed his face; the same set, humorless smile always appears when he talks to newspeople while discussing family matters. Brushing back his hair, wet from the rain, he said he had spoken to Jackie from Washington but had nothing new to report. "We just had a little conversation," he said. "She just wanted to rest."

Two days earlier, Jackie had checked into the hospital.

She had felt somewhat disoriented, shaky and extremely weak, and she was wracked by chills.

All along, Jackie's spokesperson, Nancy Tuckerman, had been issuing bulletins that were mildly encouraging, certainly giving no hint of the gravity of her condition. Consequently the newspaper and television accounts led everyone to believe that, while Mrs. Onassis was doubtlessly quite ill, she had a good, if not excellent, chance of being among the 40 percent of non-Hodgkin's lymphoma victims who survive for five years or more.

"I was not trying to be deceptive," Ms. Tuckerman said later. "I said what I thought was appropriate. We were trying to protect her and the children, because they could not make the visits [to the hospital and home] with ease."

And so the rapid pace of events of the next two days puzzled, then shocked the world.

The type of lymphoma from which Jackie suffered proved extremely aggressive, and her doctors found that it had not responded to the chemotherapy she was receiving. Steroids, which had been added to the corrosive chemicals, were not working. By the time she arrived at the hospital on Monday, the malignancy had already spread to her liver and brain.

The Stich Radiation Therapy Center, in an annex adjoining the main hospital building, housed a radiation unit called a linear accelerator, which can attack deep tumors within the body without damaging adjacent tissues. Radiation therapy from this machine was beamed into Jackie's brain. The radiation, combined with drug therapy, weakened her immune system, and she developed pneumonia, which doctors began treating with massive doses of antibiotics.

By this time the cancer had metastasized extensively. A computerized tomography examination, commonly known as a CT or CAT scan, revealed that the malignancy had spread to her liver. At that point doctors had to tell Jacqueline that medical science had failed, and there was nothing else they could do.

Jacqueline accepted the verdict as stoically as she had every other downturn in her life.

"I want to go home," she told the doctors. "I want to die at home with my family."

Jackie may have known the gravity of her condition as early as February when, the *New York Times* reported, she signed a living will that expressly stated that aggressive medical treatment to keep her alive was not to be used if doctors determined that her condition was hopeless. And so she received no more antibiotics after she left the hospital.

The family began to gather.

Her sister, Lee Radziwill Ross, arrived from California and left the apartment in tears after thirty-five minutes, then returned a half-hour later. Other relatives came: her nephews Michael Kennedy; William Kennedy Smith, who had been acquitted of rape charges in Palm Beach; Chris Lawford, son of Jack's sister Pat; niece Maria Shriver and her mother, Eunice. Even Ethel Kennedy, a longtime enemy, came with two of her daughters and told reporters, "She needs everyone's prayers."

Soon after 11 A.M., Monsignor George Bardes of St. Thomas More Church on East 89th Street in Manhattan arrived at Jackie's apartment. He heard her confession, gave her communion, and administered the sacrament of the Annointing of the Sick, provided to critically ill members of the Roman Catholic Church. It was at St. Thomas More that, on December 11, 1988, Jackie, looking radiantly youthful, had witnessed the christening of her first grandchild, Rose.

Monsignor Bardes, Jackie's parish priest, had been summoned at 8 A.M. A gracious, friendly man, now retiring after more than a half century in the priesthood, he had become very friendly with Jackie over the years. He shook his head sadly as he left her home. "I never wanted this to happen," he told reporters and walked slowly back to the church in the rain.

By noon, crowds had gathered across Fifth Avenue, peering from behind the lined-up television trucks. Fifteen policemen were now at the scene, setting up barricades to keep the crowds back and traffic moving.

More friends kept coming, each jostled by the media upon arrival and departure. Carly Simon, the singer who was Jackie's neighbor at Gay Head, remained an hour. "I love her very much," she said in a tear-choked voice. Victoria Reggie, Ted's second wife, came, but Joan did not. More nieces and nephews came by ones and twos as the day went on. Late in the evening Darryl Hannah, John's current girlfriend, visited.

Two sons of Ethel Kennedy, Rep. Joseph Kennedy II and Robert, emerged in the afternoon. Young Bobby's eyes were red-rimmed, and Joe told the reporters, "She is very, very sick, and it's very sad. There's a lot of love in her room and in her apartment."

Close friends whom Jackie had personally requested to come to her bedside were Rachel (Bunny) Mellon, a friend of many years who is married to the wealthy Paul Mellon; Jayne Wrightsman, a Palm Beach neighbor and widow of the oilman Charles Wrightsman; and Joe Armstrong, former publisher of *Rolling Stone* magazine.

In the apartment, the visitors spoke in hushed tones in the large library and, a couple at a time, went into the sickroom. Jackie lay quietly, her face chalk-white, her body shrunken after having lost twelve pounds during the treatments. She was able to speak to each of them and to hold their hands.

Caroline, John Jr., and Ed Schlossberg were in and out of the room constantly. Maurice Tempelsman never left her side.

At 2:30 P.M. the media began stampeding toward the entrance of the apartment house. John and Caroline came out, followed by Ed. John's face was grave; Caroline's was expressionless, recalling the little six-year-old child with the dead eyes who came to play at Hickory Hill after her father, the president, was murdered, and who would not smile or even cry. Bobby, himself wracked by grief, said then that when he saw the blank look on Caroline, he wanted to cry.

In Washington, President Bill Clinton and First Lady Hillary Rodham Clinton received frequent bulletins about Jackie's condition. White House sources said both were visibly upset.

Even into the evening hours, Nancy Tuckerman issued statements indicating that Jackie was in no immediate danger. "It is just another phase of her illness, which she's facing with great fortitude," she said. But after a while she stopped taking calls from the media.

Ted, apparently believing Jackie could survive longer, left the house at 8:30 P.M.

But soon after 9 P.M. Jackie lapsed into a coma.

At 10:15 P.M., May 19, 1994, a little more than two months before her sixty-fifth birthday, Jacqueline Kennedy Onassis died, with her family surrounding her bedside.

Next morning, John, in one of the finest moments of his young life, stood at the door of his mother's home and in a firm voice said:

Last night, at around ten fifteen, my mother passed on. She was surrounded by her friends and her family and her books and the people and things that she loved.

And she did it in her own way and in her own terms, and we all feel lucky for that, and now she's in God's hands.

There has been an enormous outpouring of good wishes from everyone, both in New York and beyond. And I speak for all of my family when we say we're extremely grateful. Everyone's been very generous. And I hope now that, you know, we can just have these next couple of days in relative peace.

At 1:30 P.M. the next day, a coffin covered by a simple gray blanket was delivered at the service entrance of the Fifth Avenue apartment by a silver hearse from the Frank E. Campbell funeral home. Six men in dark suits took it into the building and up to the fourteenth floor.

All evening long on Sunday, May 22, thousands of people came to the entrance of the Fifth Avenue apartment building, fanning out to 84th Street and up to 86th and across the avenue. Some remained only a few moments, but most stayed for hours, weeping and seemingly unable to leave. So many flowers were placed on either side of the door that house personnel had to clear the area to prevent obstruction of the sidewalk.

At six that evening, a private wake was held in the apartment. Mike Nichols, the film writer and director; his wife, newscaster Diane Sawyer; Maria Shriver's husband, Arnold Schwarzenegger; and about 150 others pushed through the crowd to enter the building. A cloth of antique silk covered the closed mahogany coffin that contained Mrs. Onassis's body. Monsignor Bardes said: "My brothers and sisters, we believe that all the ties of friends and affections that we know as one goes through life do not unravel after death." Father Rafael Jiminez de la Sopa, who was a lifelong friend, uttered prayers both in Spanish and English.

Later, John Jr., Caroline, and Darryl Hannah appeared on the railed terrace of Jackie's apartment facing the park. When the throng caught sight of them, a great roar went up. From somewhere in their midst a lone male voice began to sing "The Battle Hymn of the Republic." He had completed the first line, "Mine eyes have seen the glory of the coming of the Lord" when others took it up, and soon a great chorus of sound welled up, climaxing with "Glory, glory, hallelujah." It was Bobby Kennedy's favorite hymn, and it had been sung as his body was borne across Memorial Bridge to be buried not far from his brother on the slope beneath the Curtis-Lee mansion in Arlington Cemetery.

Before dawn the next day, crowds began gathering in front of the limestone Church of St. Ignatius Loyola, pressing against the police barricades. The church had been selected for the funeral services because it could accommodate fifteen hundred persons, while St. Thomas More had room for only three hundred fifty.

On Sunday, invitations had been delivered by messenger to seven hundred guests, the first of whom began arriving soon after 8:30 A.M. Among them were First Lady Hillary Rodham Clinton and Lady Bird Johnson, widow of former president Lyndon B. Johnson. All the members of the extended Kennedy family were seated in the front pews. Others included longtime friends, political figures, celebrities from the world of art, music, and entertainment, and individuals who had been close to Jackie most of her life, such as the hairdresser Kenneth Batelle; the former Rams football star Roosevelt Grier; Pierre Salinger, Jack Kennedy's former press secretary; and the architects I. M. Pei and Philip Johnson.

The funeral mass was not televised, but reporters and television commentators could hear the services over the church's public address system.

Promptly at 10 A.M. the body of Jacqueline Onassis was placed in a hearse and driven slowly to the church, where it was received by eight honorary pallbearers inside the doors.

John Jr. rose from his front-row pew and went up to the pulpit and in a strong voice told the mourners over the body of his mother in the coffin covered by green ferns and a spray of baby's breath: "Three things come to mind over and over again and ultimately dictated our selections [of what would be spoken at the mass, ed.].

They were her love of words, the bonds of home and family, and her spirit of adventure."

He chose a passage from the Book of Isaiah, who is generally considered one of the greatest of the prophets. It was an inspired choice. Isaiah was a city dweller who was also an aristocrat. Yet "in spite of his aristocratic birth and breeding, Isaiah sympathized with the proletarian aspects of the prophetic school," according to *The Bible Designed to Be Read as Living Literature.** John read: "The Lord God will wipe away the tears from all our faces."

The eulogy was given by Edward Kennedy, who, twenty-seven years before, had struggled against tears as he spoke over the coffin of his brother Robert at St. Patrick's Cathedral in New York. This time his voice was steady and strong as he talked about the former president's widow.

He began with an anecdote that made many of the mourners smile. "Last summer," he said, "when we were on the upper deck of the boat at [Martha's] Vineyard, waiting for President and Mrs. Clinton to arrive, Jackie turned to me and said, 'Teddy, you go down and greet the president.' But I said, 'Maurice is already there.'

"And Jackie answered, 'Teddy, you do it. Maurice isn't running for reelection.' "

He went on to say:

> She was a blessing to us and the nation, and a lesson to the world on how to do things right, how to be a mother, how to appreciate history, how to be courageous.
> No one else looked like her, spoke like her, wrote like her, or was so original in the way she did things. No one we knew ever had a better sense of self. . . .

* Simon and Schuster, New York, 1943, p. 413.

No one ever gave more meaning to the title of first lady. The nation's capital city looks as it does because of her. She saved Lafayette Square and Pennsylvania Avenue.

Jackie brought the greatest artists to the White House, and brought the arts to the center of national attention. Today, in large part because of her inspiration and vision, the arts are an abiding part of national policy.

And then, during those four endless days in 1963, she held us together as a family and a country. In large part because of her, we could grieve and then go on. She lifted us up, and in the doubt and darkness, she gave her fellow citizens back their pride as Americans.

Afterward, as the eternal flame she lit flickered in the autumn of Arlington Cemetery, Jackie went on to do what she most wanted—to raise Caroline and John, and warm her family's life and that of all the Kennedys. . . .

Her love for Caroline and John was deep and unqualified. She reveled in their accomplishments, she hurt with their sorrows, and she felt sheer joy and delight in spending time with them. At the mere mention of their names, Jackie's eyes would shine and her smile would grow bigger.

She once said that if you "bungle raising your children, nothing else much matters in life." She didn't bungle. Once again, she showed how to do the most important thing of all, and do it right. . . .

I often think of what she said about Jack in December after he died. "They made him a legend when he would have preferred to be a man." Jackie would have preferred to be just herself, but the world insisted that she be a legend, too.

She never wanted public notice, in part I think because it brought back painful memories of an unbearable sorrow, endured in the glare of a million lights.

In all the years since then, her genuineness and depth of character continued to shine through the privacy and reach people everywhere. Jackie was too young to be a widow in 1963, and too young to die now. . . .

She made a rare and noble contribution to the American spirit. But for us, most of all she was a magnificent wife, mother, grandmother, sister, aunt, and friend.

She graced our history. And for those of us who knew and loved her, she graced our lives.

Caroline Schlossberg chose her mother's lifelong love of Cape Cod as her memorial. She had discovered a book in Jackie's room, Caroline said, presented to her in 1946, at the age of fifteen, when she had won first prize in a literature contest at Miss Porter's School in Farmington, Connecticut. *The Harp-Weaver and Other Poems* was by Edna St. Vincent Millay, who also went to Vassar and was alive at the time (she died in 1950). The last lines of "Memory of Cape Cod" were:

The winds died down. They said, leave your pebbles on
    the sand and your shells too and come along.
We'll find you another beach like the beach at Truro.
Let me listen to the wind in the ash.
It sounds like surf on the shore.

The eighty-minute service ended with "America the Beautiful" sung by Jessye Norman, the Metropolitan Opera star. The coffin was borne down the church steps and placed in a hearse that led a seven-car motorcade up Park Avenue to the Triborough Bridge and LaGuardia Airport. Preceded by three police cars waiting there, the cortège went to the Marine Air Terminal, where a luggage conveyer hoisted the coffin aboard a plane provided by USAir. John, Caroline, Hillary Clinton, Lee Radziwill Ross, Ethel Kennedy, Maria and Arnold Schwarzenegger went aboard, and at 12:40 P.M. the twin-engine aircraft roared down the runway toward Washington.

At Arlington National Cemetery, only about a hundred mourners were permitted at the grave site where Jacqueline would lie next to her husband. It was Jackie who had chosen the site in 1963 after recalling that one day, after she and Jack had visited the spot several years earlier, he had remarked: "I could rest here forever." The president's body lay beneath a simple black granite stone inscribed: JOHN F. KENNEDY—1917–1963.

Here, thirty years before, Richard Cardinal Cushing, his gray, lined face tense with emotion, had handed Jacqueline a lighted taper that she touched to the tip of the eternal flame. Instantly it blazed brightly. A bugler had sounded taps and riflemen had fired a twenty-one-gun salute. An honor guard had folded, in crisp, military fashion, the commemorative flag that had covered the coffin and handed it to her.

On that November day, the ground had been starkly barren; now trees had grown around the site, where a memorial had been erected. To the left of Jack Kennedy's grave there was now a newly dug grave, covered by Astroturf. To the right lay their son, Patrick Bouvier Kennedy, who died of hyaline membrane disease after forty-eight hours of life; below and to the left was an unnamed baby daughter who did not survive childbirth in 1956. Some hundred yards away was the grave of Robert Kennedy, marked by a white cross.

President Bill Clinton met the special plane carrying the coffin and rode with the procession to the grave on the grassy slope. The burial service was brief and simple, lasting only eleven minutes.

President Clinton, who stood behind John Jr., Caroline, and Tempelsman, also cited Jacqueline for "soothing a nation grieving for a former president" and for her mothering of her two children and her passionate devotion to culture.

"God gave her very great gifts," the president said, "and imposed upon her great burdens. She bore them all with dignity and grace and uncommon common sense. In the end, she cared most about being a good mother to her children, and the lives of Caroline and John leave no doubt that she was that, and more. . . .

"With admiration, love, and gratitude, for the inspirations and the dreams she gave to all of us, we say goodbye to Jackie today."

One of the most touching moments was the emergence, at long last, of Maurice Tempelsman, who until the final days remained in the shadows, rarely allowing himself to be photographed with Jackie, though the two had been intimate companions for more than a dozen years. In a dark suit, his shoulders slumped, his face somber, he stepped forward.

He chose to read a poem called "Ithaka," by C. P. Cavafy.* Ithaka is one of the main islands in the Ionian Sea west of Greece.

> Keep Ithaka always in your mind.
> Arriving there is what you are destined for.
> But do not hurry the journey at all.
> Better if it lasts for years,
> so you are old by the time you reach the island,
> wealthy with all you have gained on the way,
> not expecting Ithaka to make you rich.

John and Caroline knelt, kissed their mother's coffin, and moved slowly on. John knelt at his father's grave and touched the black granite stone. He and several family

---

* From Collected Poems, translated by Edmund Keeley and Philip Sherrard (Princeton University Press, 1992).

members walked to the grave of Robert Kennedy, knelt, and crossed themselves.

The mourners drifted away.

Jacqueline Kennedy Onassis had been buried with the grace and dignity with which she had lived her life.

The journey had ended.

The brief, shining moment that was Camelot was over.

Coda

THE COMMONLY HELD belief is that Jacqueline Kennedy Onassis was a woman of unfathomable mystery. She herself fostered that opinion by cultivating a Mona Lisa image, never revealing what lay behind her enigmatic smile. But the events of her life have shown quite clearly that she was not a complex puzzle at all.

Cut through the myths, which, like tangled jungle undergrowth, have obscured her real self; slash through the interminable buzzing of gossip, rumor, innuendo, and false "facts," and we find that Jackie was a woman who passed through difficult phases of her life and emerged, at long last, as reasonably well adjusted in her maturity.

Raised in luxury, Jackie chose to live no less luxuriously, and she did. She sought a marriage based on love, and she got it. She developed a mission as first lady of the United States and fulfilled it. She was shaken at a too-early age by tragedies, was almost overwhelmed by them but eventually recovered. She found another man whom she loved for a brief time and enjoyed a period of emotional tranquility. After he died, she had a renewed fling at jet-set life, then, realizing its emptiness, formed an attachment with another man with whom she felt warm and comfortable, and she maintained a loving relationship with her two children.

Jackie worked hard to achieve a delicate balance between power and celebrity. She knew full well that she had the former, which she believed, quite correctly, was essential to helping her achieve the goals she sought. And she knew that, at the same time, she had celebrity, which she could not or would not give up.

Her social life was not nearly as hectic as it was in earlier years, curtailed by choice even before her lymphoma was discovered. The syndicated gossip columnist Liz Smith called her "semi-retired to private life in New York." Liz quoted Jackie as saying that she would like to click her ruby slippers together "and wish myself off to Kansas," as Dorothy did in *The Wizard of Oz*.

As she moved into her mid-sixties, she chose the places she went with great care, declining more invitations than she accepted, with polite notes, most of them handwritten. Virtually all of the events she did attend were publishing parties and lunches, dinners and benefits centering on her special causes.

She was always present at the JFK Memorial Library at an anniversary or special event, as she was in late October 1993, when the museum, closed for a year, was reopened with a new exhibit designed by Ed Schlossberg.

On the yacht sailing from Martha's Vineyard that summer, Jackie had personally asked President Clinton to attend, and he had accepted. Much of the extended Kennedy family was there too, including Caroline and John Jr., the late president's sisters Eunice, Patricia, and Jean, the new ambassador to Ireland, Ethel Kennedy, Rep. Joseph Kennedy, Dr. William Kennedy Smith, and hundreds of former JFK staff members.

After Clinton's brief speech, in which he noted that President Kennedy had renounced isolationism in favor of reaching out to the world in all ways, she grasped his hand and said, "That was wonderful!" She was not always gracious to presidents. She barely tolerated Lyndon Johnson, despised Richard Nixon, ignored Ronald Reagan and George Bush, and showed unmistakably how she felt about Jimmy Carter. On October 20, 1979, Carter attended the dedication of the JFK Library. Approaching Jackie, he kissed her on the cheek. "She recoiled as if bitten by a snake," noted Richard Burke, then senior aide to Ted Kennedy.

As a child, though she looked fragile and doll-like, she was a daredevil. She still was as she neared sixty-five. She would ride her horses at Middleburg, Virginia, where she was a member of the Orange County Hunt Club, through the wind and the rain, when her mount could easily have lost its footing and sent her crashing. She had fallen from a horse at least a half-dozen times, but had never been hospitalized until November of 1993, when she took a nasty tumble on a farm in Upperville, New Jersey.

Said Police Chief Dave Simpson, "She was unconscious for some time." She was rushed to Loudoun Hospital Center in Middleburg and remained there under observation for a day. Then, bruised but otherwise unhurt, Jackie rested at her home nearby for several days.

She swam in shark-infested waters off St. Kitts Island in the Caribbean with no fear. In the winter of 1991, she reportedly dived into the water from Tempelsman's yacht and encountered a real-life "Jaws." The shark circled Jackie, who was unaware of the danger until Tempelsman shouted a warning from the deck. Jackie swam as hard as she could toward the vessel as Maurice ordered a crewman to get a rifle and destroy the shark. While, as always, a spokeswoman for Jackie would not confirm or deny the report, she did say, "It is something that was very predictable. Jackie has always been willing to take a chance in the water."

Neither had her sense of humor dimmed. At a Literary Lions dinner in the New York Public Library honoring great American authors, she and John Sargent, her former boss at Doubleday, were chatting with the curator of a special, and very costly, collection. Glancing at the beautifully set tables, each with a lighted candle, she said to Sargent, "Wouldn't it be something if those candles started a fire that burned all these wonderful books?" The woman curator turned pale; the collection was adjacent to the dining area. Jackie giggled and winked at Sargent. All evening long, the curator didn't take her eyes off the candles.

Mario Buatta, a noted interior designer who has worked for Lee Radziwill and was a friend of Jackie's, tells about the evening he split his pants and Jackie threatened to reveal his misfortune to an assemblage of famous people.

Buatta, who had gained some weight, was invited to a party in Jackie's apartment to celebrate Lee Radziwill's birthday. "I had a nice suit," he said, "which was a bit tight but I thought I could get away with it." He couldn't. He sat gingerly on a silk-upholstered chair and was dismayed to hear the sound of ripping fabric. It wasn't the upholstery.

"I didn't dare get up," he said, "until the buffet dinner was announced, when I did a kind of dance, twirling this way and the other away from people's view of the tear. I got a plate of food, then sat on a loveseat. Jackie came over to sit beside me.

"Well, I had to confess my plight, and she listened sympathetically. In a little while, Placido Domingo got up to sing, after which I told Jackie that I had to leave.

" 'Better not,' she told me. 'Because if you do, I'll tell everyone you split your pants.' " Buatta stayed.

There were no more mountains to climb. She had scaled the highest peak, found excitement and tragedy too, and, said Buatta, who reflects the thoughts of many of her closest friends, wanted only to lead a relaxed life, at her own self-directed pace. And, he added, she was succeeding extremely well.

For a woman who had been through so much, seen and

experienced so many glories and such depths of despair, she had, at long last, set her course. She knew what she did and did not want. She was in total control of herself, channeling her resources into interests of her own choosing, doing what she wished and not what people expected of her. Said Buatta, "She was close to achieving total serenity, and when young John finally marries and settles down, the serenity would have been complete."

Even before her illness, she had gradually narrowed her circle of intimates, with her children at the center of the ever-shrinking ring. She wanted her loved ones to be closest, and they responded. Early in January 1993, after learning she had lymphoma, she told Maurice, who burst into tears, then called Caroline and John to her apartment. There, in the large living room, she gave them the stunning news. Mother and children hugged each other and wept, according to a source, who also reported that young John had taken an apartment nearby to be close in case Jackie needed him.

Jacqueline Kennedy Onassis was a woman who lived by the culture of two generations. She was a woman of the 1950s, when family values, centering on the home and children, were the dominant themes in American life. Perhaps that was why housewives who grew to maturity in that generation came by the hundreds to weep at her home. One, Millie Gentile, told Andrea Peyser of the *New York Post*: "I was raising my children, like she was. She was more or less my age. Her children are close to the age of mine. Somehow, I felt she was like us."

And then, as time passed, she became yet another role model for women: a woman of the eighties and nineties, a working woman who showed by her example that a woman need not waste her education and intelligence after the children were grown but could embark on a productive career. "If Jackie can do it, why can't I?" many millions of women said, and they did.

She was surely one of the world's most celebrated

women, if not the most famous of them all, and yet, though she never wanted it, the mantle of legend was draped over her shoulders. Just before she fell ill, the comedian Steve Martin, in an article he had written about her in the *New Yorker* magazine, discussed fame: "There is nothing good about it," Martin wrote. "What's so demoralizing is that it has nothing to do with me. It could be Oliver North. It could be Jack Ruby. It has nothing to do with my work. It becomes more and more abstract all the time. It has to do with recognition and a weird kind of laying on of hands. It's not that your presence lets them get in touch with their fantasies. It's that your presence lets them get in touch with reality."

A friend sent the article to Jackie. And in her tiny script, she wrote in the margin: "That's the truth."

Though unwillingly, Jackie won enduring fame.

Rudyard Kipling once wrote: "Some women'll stay in a man's memory if they once walked down a street." Jackie has walked down many streets in many countries. And she has left a mark that will never be forgotten.

A Garland of Tributes to Jacqueline Kennedy Onassis

Jacqueline Kennedy Onassis was a model of courage and dignity for all Americans and all the world. More than any other woman of her time, she captivated our nation and the world with her intelligence, her elegance, and her grace. Even in the face of impossible tragedy, she carried the grief of her family and our entire nation with a calm power that somehow reassured all the rest of us.

As First Lady, Mrs. Onassis had an uncommon appreciation of the culture that awakened us to all the beauty of our own heritage. She loved art and music, poetry and books, history and architecture, and all matters that enrich the human spirit. She was equally passionate about improving the human condition. She abhorred discrimination of all kinds. And, through small, quiet gestures, she stirred the nation's conscience. She was the first First Lady to hire a mentally retarded employee here at the White House. And she made certain for the first time that minority children were all welcome in the White House nursery.

She and President Kennedy embodied such vitality, such optimism, such pride in our nation. They inspired an entire generation of young Americans to see the nobility of helping others and to get involved in public service.

—President Bill Clinton, *statement, May 20*

We are joined here today at the site of the eternal flame, lit by Jacqueline Kennedy Onassis thirty-one years ago, to bid farewell to this remarkable woman whose life will forever glow in the lives of her fellow Americans.

Whether she was soothing a nation grieving for a former president, or raising the children with the care and the privacy they deserve, or simply being a good friend, she seemed always to do the right thing, in the right way. She taught us by example about the beauty of art, the meaning of culture, the lessons of history, the power of personal courage, the nobility of public service, and most of all, the sanctity of family.

God gave her very great gifts and imposed upon her great burdens. She bore them all with dignity and grace and uncommon common sense.

In the end, she cared most about being a good mother to her children, and the lives of Caroline and John leave no doubt that she was that, and more. Hillary and I are especially grateful that she took so much time to talk about the importance of raising children away from the public eye, and we will always remember the wonderful, happy times we shared together last summer.

With admiration, love, and gratitude, for the inspirations and the dreams she gave to all of us, we say goodbye to Jackie today. May the flame she lit, so long ago, burn ever brighter here and always brighter in our hearts. God bless you, friend, and farewell.

—PRESIDENT CLINTON, *at graveside ceremony, May 23*

The nation owes a great debt to Jacqueline Kennedy Onassis. And the nation has lost a treasure, and our family has lost a dear friend. . . . If she taught us anything, it was to know the meaning of responsibility—to one's family and to one's community. Her great gift of grace and style and dignity and heroism is an example that will live through the ages.

As a mother, she was selflessly devoted to her children

and never wavered in the value she placed on being a mother, and more recently a grandmother. She once explained the importance of spending time with family and said: "If you bungle raising your children, I don't think whatever else you do matters very much." She was a great support to me, personally, when I started talking with her in the summer of 1992 about the challenges and opportunities of being in this position, and how she had managed so well to carve out the space and privacy that children need to grow into what they have a right to become.

—FIRST LADY HILLARY RODHAM CLINTON

She showed us how one could approach tragedy with courage.

—FORMER PRESIDENT JIMMY CARTER

Jackie Onassis brought great dignity and grace to the White House and was, indeed, a charming and wonderful first lady. Barbara and I join her many friends and admirers around the world in mourning her loss.

—FORMER PRESIDENT GEORGE BUSH

Few women throughout history have touched the hearts and shaped the dreams of Americans more profoundly than Jacqueline Kennedy Onassis.

—FORMER PRESIDENT RONALD REAGAN

She was very kind to me when my husband was shot, and we didn't know whether he was going to live or not. . . . She wrote and called me—wrote me a very sweet, sensitive note and called me. She couldn't have been nicer to me at that time when I really needed it.

—NANCY REAGAN

In times of hope, she captured our hearts. In tragedy, her courage helped salve a nation's grief. She was an image of beauty and romance and leaves an empty place in the world as I have known it. We shared a unique time, and I always thought of her as my friend. I feel a poignant sense of loss, and a larger one for the nation.

—LADY BIRD JOHNSON

When you look back at Jackie, she appears to be the traditional first lady, yet when you think about it she was revolutionary. She changed the White House and established an identity for herself that was completely different from the president. That's quite a trick for a first lady. She's always been a woman for her time.

—SALLY QUINN, *author*

In a time of gilt and glitz and perpetual revelation, she was perpetually associated with that thing so difficult to describe yet so simple to recognize, the apotheosis of dignity. . . . Always there was this one person, with her world-famous face and her flawless posture, the last vestige of a charmed life that seemed to envelop us all for a time and then broke to bits, leaving her to pick up the pieces. Now even she is gone.

—ANNA QUINDLEN, *The New York Times*

She was a widow. A mother. A legend. One of those people you never truly expect to die. She was Jacqueline Kennedy Onassis, Jackie O. She was sixty-four when she chose to go home to die in dignity, within the privacy of her own home, surrounded by the only people who ever counted to her—her children, friends, and family. She is a permanent part of our history and our culture. And, all her life, she taught us how to behave.

—MIKE BARNICLE, *The Boston Globe*

Jacqueline Bouvier Kennedy Onassis remained the most famous and the most private of women. She didn't comment. She didn't write her memoirs or do interviews about her disappointments. Call it distance. Call it shyness. Call it reserve, aloofness. Choose your word on the continuum of privacy. May I suggest dignity? At this end of an era, Jacqueline Bouvier Kennedy Onassis did it her way. She died with dignity.

—ELLEN GOODMAN, *The Boston Globe*

She obviously had considerable talent, considerable ambition and brains. You have to see her life as a significant and poignant mark in the evolution of women. She was the beautiful, sad heroine of our time.

—BETTY FRIEDAN, *author*

She was as witty, warm and creative in private as she was grand and graceful in public.

—BILL MOYERS

She was always there—for all our family—in her special way. She was a blessing to us and to the nation—and a lesson to the world on how to do things right, how to be a mother, how to appreciate history, how to be courageous.

No one else looked like her, spoke like her, or was so original in the way she did things. No one we knew ever had a better sense of self. . . .

She never wanted public notice—in part I think, because it brought back painful memories of an unbearable sorrow, endured in the glare of a million lights.

In all the years since then, her genuineness and depth of character continued to shine through the privacy, and reach people everywhere. Jackie was too young to be a widow in 1963 and too young to die now. . . .

She made a rare and noble contribution to the American spirit. But for us, most of all she was a magnificent wife, mother, grandmother, sister, aunt, and friend. She graced our history. And for those of us who knew and loved her—she graced our lives.

—SENATOR EDWARD KENNEDY (D-MA)

I think that after Eleanor Roosevelt, first ladies were invisible. Women, in general, weren't very visible. Then, when Jackie burst on the scene, she made women visible again—in the public eye and in the new medium of television. And she was talented and accomplished in her own right as well as being her husband's partner.

—SENATOR BARBARA MIKULSKI (D-MD)

In choosing the readings, we struggled to find ones that captured my mother's essence. Three attributes came to mind over and over. They were the love of words, the bonds of home and family, and her spirit of adventure.

—JOHN F. KENNEDY, JR.

But now the journey is over. Too short, alas too short. It was filled with adventure and wisdom, laughter and love, gallantry and grace. So farewell, farewell.

—MAURICE TEMPELSMAN

NOTES ON SOURCES

THOUGHTS, FEELINGS, AND ATTITUDES attributed to Jacqueline Kennedy Onassis in this book have either been written or stated by her, or related by her to others, many of whom are quoted. Specific sources for statements made, which the author felt necessary to cite, are given here. Notes are omitted for chapters where the sources are cited in the text.

1: The Woman Who Invented Herself

Had kinky hair: Anderson and Boxendale, p. 169; *Women's News Service*, Sept. 15, 1969; confidential sources.

Whispery voice an artifice: Sources given in text. Others: "Why scream at me?" and "You son of a bitch" anecdotes: Kelley, *Jackie, Oh!*, pp. 148, 149; quarrel with Onassis: David and Robbins, *Jackie and Ari*, p. 99.

John Baker comments: Author interview, *Publishers Weekly*, Apr. 10, 1993.

James Brady comments: Author interview.

Cassini comment: *In My Own Fashion*, p. 304.

Jackie cheapness: Gallagher, *My Life With Jacqueline*

Kennedy; Heymann, *A Woman Named Jackie*; Kelley, op. cit., passim.

Nuns at RFK rites and Ethel anecdote: Taylor and Rubin, *Jackie, a Lasting Impression,* p. 148;

2: The Importance of Being Jackie

"More than a match for European royalty": Giglio, p. 272.

Quigley, Carter statements: author interviews.

Photos of naked Jackie: Heymann, p. 527; Birmingham, *Jacqueline Bouvier Kennedy Onassis,* pp. 167–68; *Screw, Hustler* magazines, *Boston Herald, New York Post,* sundry other newspapers.

Jackie as a fashion leader: Edith Head quoted in Cassini, p. 298; *Philadelphia Inquirer,* July 23, 1989; Brady comment; author interview.

Pat Nixon's clothes contrasted with Jackie's: David, *Lonely Lady,* p. 116.

Jackie and hemlines: Bender, *The Beautiful People,* p. 44.

Miss Porter's school uniforms: Birmingham, op. cit., p. 16.

Mink inappropriate: Cassini, op. cit., p. 46.

Curtis survey: Bender, op. cit., p. 46.

JFK "went through ceiling": West, *Upstairs at the White House,* pp. 211–12.

Gods and goddesses: Bender, op. cit., p. 46.

Continue to be fashion leader: *Philadelphia Inquirer,* July 23, 1989.

3: Love Her, Love Her Not

Sources noted in text.

4: Young Jackie, Young Jack

Most reliable sources for Jackie's early life are in *Jacqueline Bouvier Kennedy Onassis* and *A Woman Named Jackie,* in addition to Davis, *The Kennedys* (McGraw-Hill, 1984) cited in text.

For John Kennedy's early life, best sources are Kenneth P. O'Donnell and David F. Powers, with Joe McCarthy, *A Hero for Our Time.* Little, Brown, 1972; Richard J. Whalen, *The Founding Father.* New American Library, 1964; Rose Kennedy, *A Time to Remember.* Doubleday, 1974; Leo Damore, *The Cape Cod Years of J.F.K.* Prentice-Hall, 1967.

Inga Arvad, dismissed as "Inga-Binga," has been assigned only a footnote in JFK's life, yet she was much more important. Anyone seriously interested in the personal life of John Kennedy should consult the JFK personal papers, correspondence, 1933–1950, Box 4A, in the JFK Library, from which these passionate letters are quoted.

5: The Truth About the Marriage

The Mary Pinchot Meyer affair is still a murky chapter in JFK's life. Felsenthal, in *Power, Privilege and the Post,* pp. 188–89, states flatly that JFK was in love with her but offers no corroboration. The likelihood is that the beautiful Vassar graduate was just another woman in JFK's list of conquests. Heymann cites their "closeness," including a time when the president and Pinchot smoked marijuana in the White House in July 1962 (p. 375) but stops short of saying that JFK was in love with her. The never-reticent Kitty Kelley says Mary was one of the many women who enjoyed Washington interludes with Jack Kennedy, calls the affair a "romance" (pp. 118–20) and also cites the marijuana episode. Kelley says Mary confided to her friend James Truitt, a journalist, that she was in love with the president but does not say Kennedy returned the affection. Apparently in Kelley's lexicon "romance" is not love but an affair.

Mary Lynn Kotz's statements expanding on her coauthorship of the memoirs of J.B. West were made to the author.

"Black Jack" Bouvier's advice to Jackie: Anderson and Boxendale, op. cit., pp. 170, 172.

Frances Spatz Leighton's statements expanding on her coauthorship of the memoirs of Mary Barelli Gallagher and Traphes Bryant, *Dog Days at the White House,* were made in the course of several interviews with the author.

Kennedy's reaction after death of baby Patrick: Dave Powers, author interview.

Jackie calling the era Camelot: White, *In Search of History,* pp. 520–25. Teddy White told author: "I've done a lot of interviewing in my time, but this one was the toughest. The woman was so devastated, so completely overcome by the events, that no words can come close to describing it." Teddy then took a long swallow of a drink (at the American Society of Authors and Journalists dinner at which he was honored as "author of the year," and this author had the honor of presenting him with the plaque), shook his head, and turned to another subject.

What love implies: Symonds, *The Dynamics of Human Adjustment,* pp. 542–50.

6: Jackie and Politics

Bored into total silence: Martin, *A Hero for Our Time,* p. 100.

Schlesinger statement: Schlesinger, *A Thousand Days,* p. 17.

Translating books: *Ibid.,* p. 103.

Bartlett statement: Heymann, op. cit., p. 347.

Jackie's campaigning skills: Author interviewed journalists who covered the campaign for primary source information on just how skillful Jackie was. Most agree her contribution to JFK's campaign has been seriously underrated. See also Anthony, *First Ladies,* pp. 588–89, and Martin, op. cit., pp. 142–43. She captivated audiences in ethnic neighborhoods by addressing them in flawless Spanish, French, or Italian. However, because of her inexperience, Jackie committed a number of gaffes, funniest of which was the time she was drafted to "warm up" an audience in Kenosha, Wisconsin, before the candidate came out. Unprepared, Jackie thought that a song would put the crowd in a good frame of mind. "Let's all sing 'Southie Is My Home Town'," she said. The throng looked at her, bewildered. "Southie" is practically a national anthem in South Boston but totally unfamiliar to Kenoshans.

Mission to Cambodia: *McCall's* magazine, June 1968.

Influence on American culture: Sorensen, Kennedy, p. 430.

7: Days of Glory

Clifford comment: *Counsel to the President,* p. 261.

Jackie afraid of Mamie: David and David, *J.F.K., The Wit, The Charm, The Tears,* p. 113.

Walton comment: Goddard, *John Fitzgerald Kennedy . . . As We Remember Him,* p. 106.

Bernstein anecdote: Bernstein, OH, JFK Library.

Mamie outraged: West, op. cit., p. 196.

Paintings, objets d'art arriving: Salinger, *With Kennedy,* p. 366.

Chair incident: *Ibid.* pp. 307–308.

Press conference: *Ibid.*

Isabelle Shelton story: *Scranton Times,* Dec. 7, 1972, distributed by the North American Newspaper Alliance.

Excellent sources for Jackie's restoration of White House: Mary Van Rensselaer Thayer. *Jacqueline Kennedy: The White House Years.* Popular Library edition, 1967, 1968, 1971. Also consulted were files of *The New York Times, Washington Post, Washington Star, Boston Globe,* and *The Boston Herald.*

Letter to Clifford: Thayer, op. cit., p. 291.

8: Fears for Her Sanity

Jackie's state of mind after the assassination was drawn from interviews with Lemoyne K. Billings, Kenneth P. O'Donnell, author and journalist Joe McCarthy, and others who are noted in the text. Specific citations are:

Birmingham, op. cit., discusses Jackie's deep despondency on pp. 122–23, and expanded on her friends' fears in interview with author.

Overshadowed by William Manchester's superb account of the assassination, op. cit., is Jim Bishop's minute-by-minute story of the event, *The Day Kennedy Was Shot.* See also Tom Wicker's story of the assassination in *The New York Times,* Nov. 23, 1963, for the best on-the-spot reporting of the assassination.

Hugh holds Jackie: Several sources including Anderson and Boxendale, op. cit., p. 180.

Dialogue with West: West, op. cit., pp. 277–78, 277–79.

Cushing statement: Kelley, op. cit., p. 20.

Jackie's testimony: Volume 5, President's Commission on the Assassination of President Kennedy, pp. 178–81.

"I'm a freak": John Thomas Church, *Jackie Onassis,* pamphlet published by *National Mirror,* New York, 1978.

Jackie and Caroline on beach: Dallas and Ratcliffe, *The Kennedy Case,* p. 328.

Jackie in deep depression: Martin, op. cit., pp. 570–71.

"Crazy Aunt Beale": Birmingham, op. cit., p. 122.

Baldwin statement: *Billy Baldwin Remembers,* pp. 109–113.

Details of Caroline's early life: Author interviews with sundry sources, including friends, family employees, visits to school, restaurants, etc.

Jackie's tribute: *Look* magazine, Memorial Issue, Nov. 17, 1964.

Would not have hired Manchester: Kelley, op. cit.; Lyndon B. Johnson Library.

9: A Greek Bearing Gifts

Rough football game: author interview, Salinger.

Letters to Gilpatric: *Time,* Feb. 23, 1970.

Onassis's life has been extensively chronicled. Two reliable sources are Willi Frischauer, *Onassis.* Meredith, 1968, and Frank Brady, *Onassis: An Extravagant Life,* Prentice Hall, 1977.

The marriage and relations with Caroline and John: Sundry interviews in Greece with friends and associates of Onassis and Christina.

"I hate this country": Kelley, op. cit., p. 271; Heymann, op. cit., p. 486.

Building Skorpios: *London Daily Express,* Oct. 19, 1968, article by Willi Frischauer.

"Mummy, mummy, they're so pretty!" *Time,* Nov. 1, 1968.

Ari and John Jr.: author interview with friends of Onassis.

Church's views: AP, Oct. 21, 1968; UPI, Oct. 22, 1968.

Interview with Iranian journalist: *Scranton Times,* May 25, 1972, AP story.

10: The Truth About That Marriage

In Greece, author Jhan Robbins talked with scores of relatives, friends, business associates, as well as enemies, of Jackie and Ari, while this author conducted interviews in the U.S. Both came away from these talks with the conviction that the two seemingly mismatched people had a deep affection for each other in the early years of their marriage. Pearl Buck, in *The Kennedy Women,* also describes a happy, contented couple. "He loves her" statement is on p. 93. It should be noted that Ms. Buck's book was written in 1970, two years after the marriage, before the highly publicized animosity that was to color the relationship in the public's mind had set in.

Maria totally in love: Stancioff, *Maria,* p. 142.

"Most charming performances": Stassinopoulos, *Maria Callas,* p. 294.

Juan Cameron statement: author interview.

Onassis devastated after Alexander's death: David and Robbins, op. cit., pp. 132–33.

"Body turned against itself": Stassinopoulos, op. cit., p. 24.

"Adultery is a national sport": Stancioff, op. cit., p. 143.

Jackie and Christina at Ari's bedside: *Sundary Mirror,* London, May 11, 1975.

11: Jackie's Children—Caroline

Ted Jr.'s problem with alcohol: *The New York Times,* Dec. 10, 1991; David, *Good Ted, Bad Ted,* pp. 204–205; *Ladies' Home Journal,* March 1992.

The story of Caroline's personal life obtained from the following sources: author's visits to Concord and Concord Academy, which included interviews with townspeople, classmates, and school officials; Dave Powers, who provided much helpful material over the years; files of London newspapers, which were jammed with articles about Caroline's stay there in 1975; reporters at *The Daily News* who told of her brief experience there as a reporter; many visits to Harvard and Columbia where friends and classmates talked freely of her Cambridge and law school years; Ed Schlossberg, who was a valuable source on Caroline's pregnancy and their children; the editor of her book and the residents of Chester, Massachusetts, where Caroline and Ed have a vacation hideaway.

12: Jackie's Children — John

"John-John" story: Told to author by Dave Powers.

"Restless and disruptive": *People* magazine, March 20, 1989.

Sandy Boyer on John's acting: author interview.

Connie Chung interview: courtesy NBC.

Maria Cuomo "Blew my chance . . .": *McCall's*, June 1989.

O'Neill, Smathers, Powers comments on John and politics: author interviews.

"I'm John's mother": confidential source.

13: Close-up

All material in this chapter was obtained from dozens of interviews with family members, friends, and neighborhood tradespeople, plus author's observations. Jackie's apartment, her dinner parties and guests were described in detail to the author by friends who had visited and dined there. All talked freely about their experiences but requested anonymity.

14: Her Mysterious Significant Other

Tempelsman as Jackie's "significant other" is documented in the following: *Vanity Fair,* Aug. 1989; Watney, *Jackie O.,* p. 371; *USA Weekend,* Oct. 4–6, 1991; *New Idea,* May 6, 1993.

Helene Gaillet comment: Birmingham, op. cit., pp. 224–25.

Facts about Tempelsman: Author reporting, numerous interviews with colleagues in the diamond industry; also *Insight* magazine, Aug. 12, 1991; Birmingham, Heymann, Watney, op. cit., passim; selected issues of *Star* and *National Enquirer;* Kwitney, *Endless Enemies,* pp. 8–9; author visits to Hyannis Port and Martha's Vineyard where interviews were conducted with residents, restaurant and marina owners, etc.

Tempelsman and Lazare Kaplan: author interviews with spokesman for Kaplan company.

Jackie not a domineering woman: *Vanity Fair,* August 1989.

Jackie and Sacraments: Birmingham, op. cit., pp. 192–93.

15: Working Woman

RFK's disinterest in minorities: His OH, JFK Library.
Wofford comment: author interview.
Letitia Baldridge: Tish had been something of a loose cannon during the Camelot years, efficient but prone to off-the-wall comments at press conferences. Once she told reporters, with a straight face, that if there wasn't enough wall space for the great paintings the first lady was seeking to hang, they would be hung in front of the other paintings. The joking remark, duly reported in the media, caused much acerbic comment and numerous phone calls and letters to editors. Another time she infu-

riated the newly elected president when she told the media that Mrs. Eisenhower had not yet been invited to visit the White House, whereupon the *Washington Daily News* published a headline saying that Jackie "was not disturbed" by the missing invitation to Mamie. Jack, aware that he had been elected by the narrowest of margins and anxious to win as much GOP support as he could, told his aides: "Shut this goddamned woman up before she opens her mouth again!" Upstairs, he ordered Jackie to ban Tish from giving any more press conferences. Three-year-old Caroline, overhearing the wrangle, asked Maud, her British nanny: "What did that goddamn lady do to make Daddy so mad?"

16: Jackie and the Kennedys

Luella Hennessey Donovan comments: author interview.

Jackie mimicking Rose: Gail Cameron (*Rose*, Putnam's, 1971), pp. 175–76, citing Gallagher, op. cit.

Jackie hated touch football: Sparks, *The $20,000,000 Honeymoon*, p. 215, quoting Ted Sorensen.

JFK's spectacular catch: Rogers, *When I Think of Bobby*, p. 74.

Jackie on Ethel: Taylor and Rubin, *Jackie, A Lasting Impression*, p. 35. David, *Ethel*, pp. 11–13. Phone anecdote was told to Sparks by friends of Lee Radziwill.

Close to Maria Shriver, Caroline and John's current lifestyles: *McCall's* magazine, Aug. 1985, and Sept. 1987.

17: A Woman of Independent Means

Most of the description of Gay Head estate and community reaction came from author interviews on Martha's Vineyard. Also consulted were files of *People* magazine, *Newsweek*, *The Boston Globe*, *Boston Herald*,

Christian Science Monitor, Newsday, and *Vineyard Gazette.* Good accounts of Gay Head are in Kelley and Heymann, op. cit., passim.

Estimates of Jackie's wealth: Vanity Fair, Aug. 1989; *Los Angeles Herald Examiner,* July 7, 1989; Heymann, op. cit., p. 604; interviews with real estate experts and accountants.

Jackie as grandmother: Schlossberg comment: author interview; *Daily News,* April 26, 1992; Jan. 28, 1989; *National Enquirer,* Jan. 24, 1989; Doris Cerutti was an excellent source.

Jackie at Viking: *McCall's* magazine, Feb., 1976; author interviews with staff.

Viking, cold reception and resignation: Watney, op. cit., pp. 370, 376; Liz Smith syndicated column, Oct. 17, 1977.

Jackie at Doubleday: author interview with editors and visits to office.

Michael Jackson comment: *Toronto Star,* Jan. 12, 1988.

Baker interview: *Publishers Weekly,* op. cit.

Betty Friedan comment: *The New York Times,* Sept. 15, 1993.

18: Crusader

The extensive files of the Municipal Art Society in New York City were invaluable sources for the controversies over preserving New York City's historical landmarks and for Jackie's role in the disputes.

Charlotte Curtis comment: *The New York Times,* Feb. 25, 1986.

John Taylor comments: *New York* magazine, Oct. 5, 1987.

Jackie in Albany: files of *The New York Times, New York Post,* other newspapers.

Liz Smith comment: *Daily News,* April 2, 1991.

Bibliography

ANDERSON, ALICE E., AND HADLEY V. BOXENDALE. *Behind Every Successful President.* New York: S.P.I. Books. 1982.

ANTHONY, CARL SFERRAZZA. *First Ladies: The Saga of the Presidents' Wives and Their Power. 1789–1961.* New York: William Morrow, 1990.

BASS, JACK. *Taming the Storm: The Life and Times of Judge Frank M. Johnson, Jr.* New York: Doubleday, 1993.

BALDWIN, BILLY. *Billy Baldwin Remembers.* New York: Harcourt Brace Jovanovich, 1974.

BENDER, MARILYN. *The Beautiful People.* New York: Coward-McCann, 1967.

BIRMINGHAN, STEPHEN. *Jacqueline Bouvier Kennedy Onassis.* New York: Grosset & Dunlap, 1978.

BISHOP, JIM. *The Day Kennedy Was Shot.* New York: Bantam, 1969.

BOLLER, PAUL F., JR. *Presidential Wives: An Anecdotal History.* New York: Oxford University Press, 1988.

BRADLEE, BENJAMIN C. *Conversations With Kennedy.* New York: W. W. Norton, 1975.

BRADY, FRANK. *Onassis: An Extravagant Life.* Englewood Cliffs, N.J.: Prentice Hall, 1977.

BRADY, JAMES. *Superchic.* Boston: Little, Brown, 1974.

BRUSSEL, JAMES. A., M.D. *The Layman's Guide to Psychiatry.* New York: Barnes & Noble, 1961.

BRYANT, TRAPHES, WITH FRANCES SPATZ LEIGHTON. *Dog Days at the White House.* New York: Pocket Books, 1978.

BUCK, PEARL S. *The Kennedy Women.* New York: Pinnacle Books, 1972.

BURKE, RICHARD E., WITH WILLIAM AND MARY HOFFER. *The Senator: My Ten Years With Ted Kennedy.* New York: St. Martin's, 1992.

CASSINI, OLEG. *In My Own Fashion.* New York: Simon and Schuster, 1987.

CHURCH, JOHN THOMAS. *Jackie Onassis.* New York: National Mirror Pamphlet, 1979.

CLARKE, GERALD. *Capote: A Biography.* New York: Simon and Schuster, 1988.

CLIFFORD, CLARK, WITH RICHARD HOLBROOK. *Counsel to the President.* New York: Random House, 1991.

CLINCH, NANCY GAGER. *Kennedy Wives, Kennedy Women.* New York: Dell, 1976.

DALLAS, RITA, R.N., WITH JEANINA RATCLIFFE. *The Kennedy Case.* New York: G.P. Putnam's Sons, 1973.

DAVID, LESTER. *Good Ted, Bad Ted: The Two Faces of Edward M. Kennedy.* New York: Birch Lane Press, 1993.

———. *The Lonely Lady of San Clemente: The Story of Pat Nixon.* New York: Thomas Y. Crowell, 1978.

———. AND IRENE DAVID. *JFK: The Wit, The Charm, The Tears.* New York: Paperjack, 1988.

DAVIS, L.J. *Onassis, Aristotle and Christina.* New York: St. Martin's, 1986.

DEMPSTER, NIGEL. *Heiress: The Story of Christina Onassis.* New York: Grove Weidenfeld, 1989.

FAIRLIE, HENRY. *The Kennedy Promise: The Politics of Expectation.* New York: Doubleday, 1973.

FELSENTHAL, CAROL. *Power, Privilege and the Post: The Katherine Graham Story.* New York: G.P. Putnam's Sons, 1992.

GALLAGHER, MARY BARELLI. *My Life With Jacqueline Kennedy.* New York: David McKay, 1969.

GIGLIO, JAMES N. *The Presidency of John F. Kennedy.* Kansas City, Kansas: University Press of Kansas, 1991.

GUTHRIE, LEE. *Jackie: The Price of the Pedestal.* New York: Drake Publishers, 1978.

HEYMANN, C. DAVID. *A Woman Named Jackie: An Intimate Biography of Jacqueline Bouvier Kennedy Onassis.* New York: Lyle Stuart, 1989.

KWITNY, JONATHAN. *Endless Enemies: The Making of An Unfriendly World.* New York: Cogdon and Weed, 1984.

LIEBERSON, GODDARD, ED. *John Fitzgerald Kennedy . . . As We Remember Him.* New York: Macmillan, 1965.

LILLY, DORIS. *Those Fabulous Greeks: Onassis, Niarchos and Livanos—Three of the World's Richest Men!* New York: Cowles Book Company, 1970.

ROGERS, WARREN. *When I Think of Bobby: A Personal Memoir of The Kennedy Years!* New York: HarperCollins, 1993.

SALINGER, PIERRE. *With Kennedy.* Garden City, New York: Doubleday, 1966.

————. *An Honorable Profession: A Tribute to Robert Kennedy.* Garden City, New York, Doubleday, 1968.

SMITH, SALLY BEDELL. *In All His Glory: The Life of William S. Paley.* New York: Simon and Schuster, 1990.

SORENSEN, THEODORE C. *Kennedy.* New York: Bantam Books, 1965.

SPARKS, FRED. *The $20,000,000 Honeymoon: Jackie and Ari's First Year.* New York: Bernard Geis Associates, 1970.

SPOTO, DONALD. *Marilyn Monroe: The Biography.* New York: HarperCollins, 1993.

STANCIOFF, NADIA. *Maria: Callas Remembered.* New York: E.P. Dutton, 1987.

STEIN, JEAN AND GEORGE PLIMPTON. *American Journey: The Times of Robert Kennedy.* New York: Harcourt Brace Jovanovich, 1970.

STASSINOPOULOS, ARIANNA. *Maria Callas, The Woman Behind the Legend.* New York: Simon and Schuster, 1981.

SULLIVAN, MICHAEL JOHN. *Presidential Passions: The Love Affairs of American Presidents from Washington and Jefferson to Kennedy and Johnson.* New York: Shapolsky Publishers, 1991.

SYMONDS, PERCIVAL M. *The Dynamics of Human Adjustment.* New York: St. Martin's Press, 1990.

VANDEN HEUVEL, WILLIAM AND MILTON GWIRTZMAN. *On His Own: RFK 1964–1968.* Garden City: Doubleday, 1970.

THAYER, MARY VAN RENNSSALAER. *Jacqueline Kennedy: The White House Years.* New York, Popular Library, 1967.

WATNEY, HEDDA LYONS. *Jackie O.* New York, Tudor Publishing Co., 1990.

WEST, J.B. WITH MARY LYNN KOTZ. *Upstairs at the White House: My Life with the First Ladies.* New York: Coward, McCann & Geoghegan, 1972.

WHITE, THEODORE A. *In Search of History: A Personal Adventure.* New York: Warner Books, 1978.

Index

Alderman, Ellen, 132, 150
Allen, Woody, 200, 200n
American Journey, 182
Anatomy of an Illness, 202n
Anthony, Carl Sferrazza, 61
Archer, Jeffrey, 193, 195
Aristide, Father Jean-Bertrand, 208
Arlington National Cemetery, 12, 82
Armstrong, Joe, 238
Arvad, Inga, 35–39
Ash, Mary Kay, 221
Ataturk, Kemal, 105
Atget, Eugene, 198
Arlington National Cemetery, 245
Athanassion, Archimandrite Polykarpos, 114
Auchincloss, Hugh Dudley, 32, 42, 48, 80
Auchincloss, Janet Lee Bouvier, 13, 29–31, 79, 153, 223

Baker, John F., 4, 8, 201
Baldridge, Letitia, 191, 204
Baldwin, William, 91
Balenciaga (designer), 109
Bardes, Monsignor George, 237–38, 240
Barnicle, Mike, 258
Bartlett, Charles, 39, 59–60
Barwick, Kent, 230
Battelle, Kenneth, 18, 241
Battista, Giovanni, 122
Baudelaire, Charles, 52
Beale, Edith Bouvier, 77, 94
Beck, Mr. and Mrs. Dave, 211n

Behind Every Successful President, 3
Belafonte, Harry, 68
Bell, Steve, 219
Bender, Marilyn, 18, 22
Bergen, Candace, 169, 229
Bernstein, Leonard, 69, 97, 102
Billings, Lem, 57, 77, 91, 94, 125, 213
Birmingham, Stephen, 32, 46, 64, 79, 188, 196
Bissell, Judith, 33
Blough, Roger, 227
Bolton, Oliver, 108
Bouvier, Jacqueline. *See* Onassis, Jacqueline Bouvier Kennedy
Bouvier, James, 31
Bouvier, Lee. *See* Radziwill, Lee Bouvier
Bouvier, Michael, 31
Bouvier, William S., 77
Bouvier III, John Vernon, 29–34, 43, 48, 53, 77
Bowdoin, Judith and Helen, 33
Bowers, Rev. Thomas, 233
Boyer, Sandy, 155
Bradlee, Benjamin C., 21, 81
Bradlee, Tony, 51
Brady, Frank, 110
Brady, James, 10, 17–20
Brearley School, 133
Brown University, 154
Bryant, Traphes, 50, 53–54
Buatta, Mario, 251–52
Buck, Pearl, 121–22, 129
Buckley, James, 190

Bundy, McGeorge, 93
Buren, Martin Van, 72
Burke, Richard E., 212, 250
Burton, Richard, 16
Bush, Barbara, 24, 257
Bush, George, 250, 257

Cacoyannis, Michael, 177
Cafarakis, Christian, 112
Callas, Maria, 107, 122–23, 125–27, 130
Calloway, Cab, 199
Call the Darkness Light, 197–98
"Camelot," 56
Cameron, Juan, 125, 136, 144
"Campaign Wife," 61
Cannon, Laurie, 139
Carney, Tom, 142
Carter, Jimmy, 58, 250, 257
Carter, John Mack, 16
Carter, Rosalynn, 58
Casals, Pablo, 65
Cassini, Igor, 33
Cassini, Oleg, 10, 17
Cavafy, C. P., 246
Central Park (New York, N.Y.), 229–31
Cerutti, Doris, 223
Cézanne, Paul, 71
Charles, Prince of England, 200–201
Cher, 16
Chevalier, Maurice, 3
Chung, Connie, 157
Churchill, Winston, 104
Clark, Dr. William Kemp, 80
Cleveland, Frances Folsom, 29
Cleveland, Grover, 29
Clifford, Clark, 15, 46n, 66, 71, 76
Clinch, Nancy Gager, 3
Clinton, Bill, 71n, 181, 239, 242, 245–46, 249, 255–56
Clinton, Chelsea, 181
Clinton, Hillary Rodham, 24, 58, 239, 241, 242, 245, 256–57
Cohn, Roy, 127, 128
Coliseum project, 229–31
Collegiate School, 153
Columbia University School of Law, 132, 143

Columbus, Christopher, 72
Comerford, Frank, 138
Concord Academy, 5, 134
Connally, Gov. and Mrs. John B., Jr., 79, 86–89
Considine, Shaun, 10, 174
Cousins, Norman, 202, 202n
Cravath, Swaine & Moore, 103–4
Cronkite, Walter, 218, 229
Cuch, Cameron, 220
Cuomo, Maria, 154
Cuomo, Mario, 201
Curtis, Charlotte, 21, 227
Cushing, Richard Cardinal, 84, 245

Daily News, 140
Dallas, Rita, 89
Dancing on My Grave, 200
Davis, Bette, 68
Davis, John H., 32
Death of a President, 194
De Gaulle, Charles, 23
de la Sopa, Father Rafael Jiminez, 240
Diaghilev, Sergei, 52
Diana, Princess of Wales, 14, 15, 24
Doctorow, E. L., 229
Dog Days at the White House, 50
Domingo, Placido, 251
Donavan, Luella Hennessey, 78–79, 208
Doubleday & Company, 4, 170, 195, 199–200
du Pont, Henry Algernon, 72
Durante, Jimmy, 47
Dutton, Fred, 218

Eisenhower, Dwight D., 19, 34, 44, 67n
Eisenhower, Mamie, 24, 67, 70
Elizabeth II, Queen of England, 15, 42, 173
Esquirol, Joseph A. Jr., 159

Fabulous Onassis: His Life and Loves, The, 112

Farrow, Mia, 200
Fausto, Rt. Rev. Msgr. Vallainc, 118
Fay, Paul B. (Red), 42, 57
Feiffer, Jules, 218
Fejos, Paul, 35
Felsenthal, Carol, 51
Feminine Mystique, The, 48, 101
Finch, Peter, 229*n*
Fischer, Albert III, 216
Folger, Alexander D., 220
Fonda, Jane, 24
Ford, Betty, 24
Ford, Gerald, 15
Fountain of Age, The, 203–4
Frank E. Campbell funeral home, 240
Fraser, Sir Hugh, 140
Friedan, Betty, 48, 101, 203–4, 229, 259

Gaillet, Helene, 178
Galbraith, John Kenneth, 17, 146, 169
Galella, Ron, 133
Gallagher, Mary Barelli, 11, 53, 81, 209
Gallup Poll, 24
Garbo, Greta, 106
Gardiner, Julia, 29
Garland, Judy, 23
Gay Head (Martha's Vineyard), 215–21
Gentile, Millie, 252
Georgetown University, 43
Gershman, Dr. Katherine, 208
Giglio, Dr. James F., 14
Gill, Brendan, 229, 233
Gilpatric, Roswell, 103
Givenchy (designer), 109
Glenn, John, 102
Glen Ora, 45*n*
Good Housekeeping, 25
Goodman, Ellen, 259
Goodwin, Doris Kearns, 95
Graham, Katherine, 218
Grand Central Terminal building, 231–32
Gravas, Costa, 131
Graziani, Benno, 49

Grier, Rosie, 241
Growing Up Kennedy, 7
Guinzburg, Thomas, 191–92, 193
Gutfreund, John, 230
Guthrie, Lee, 124

Haag, Christina, 155
Hamill, Pete, 177
Hamilton, Charles, 104
Hannah, Daryl, 163, 208, 238, 240
Harlech, Lord, 103, 103*n*
Harper & Row, 194
Harp-Weaver and Other Poems, The (Millay), 244
Harriman, W. Averell, 90
Hartington, Marquess of, 103
Harvey, Jacques, 112
Hayes, Helen, 23
Hayes, Rutherford B., 71
Head, Edith, 17
Healing and the Mind, 203
Herrera, Caroline, 146
Heymann, C. David, 46, 50*n*
Hill, Clinton J., 88
Hill, Margaret Hunt, 221
Hogan, Dr. Michael, 173
Holm, Celeste, 229
Holton Arms, 33
Honduras, President of, 12
Hornblower family, 216
Hume, David, 153
Hunt, H. L., 221
Husted, John, 34, 40

In Our Defense: The Bill of Rights in Action, 150
International Brotherhood of Teamsters, 211*n*
"Ithaka" (Cavafy), 246

Jackie Oh!, 46
Jackson, Michael, 199
Jacobsen, Hugh N., 218
Jenkins, Holman, Jr., 179
Joel, Billy, 218
John F. Kennedy Library, 13, 146, 156, 249–50
Johnny, We Hardly Knew Ye, 112
Johnson, Lyndon B., 61*n*, 153, 241, 249

Index

Johnson, Lady Bird, 19, 90, 257–58
Johnson, Philip, 241
Jordan, Vernon E., 181, 218
Joseph Campbell and the Power of Myth, 200
Joseph P. Kennedy Foundation, 140, 207

Kabat-Zinn, Jon, 203
Kahn, Otto, 95
Kalb, Marvin and Bernard, 63
Kefauver, Estes, 44
Kellerman, Roy, 88
Kelley, Kitty, 46
Kelly, Beth, 208
Kennedy, Caroline. *See* Schlossberg, Caroline Kennedy
Kennedy, Courtney, 213
Kennedy, David, 77–78, 144, 212
Kennedy, Edward M., 24, 136, 146, 160, 181–82, 212, 235, 242–44, 250, 259
Kennedy, Ethel, 12, 43, 77, 92, 102, 132, 144, 210–12, 237, 245, 249
Kennedy, Jacqueline Bouvier. *See* Onassis, Jacqueline Bouvier Kennedy
Kennedy, Joan, 7, 24, 206, 210, 212, 238
Kennedy, Joe, Jr., 161, 207–8, 238, 249
Kennedy, John F., Jr.
  birth 45
  childhood/youth, 71*n*, 152
  education, 153–54, 159
  girls he has dated, 162–64
  at graveside service, 260
  interviews given, 157–58
  and mother's death and funeral, 238–42, 245–246
  and mother's final illness, 235
  possibility of political career, 160–63
  relationship with Kennedy cousins, 206–8, 213
  relationship with Onassis, 117–18
  work, 159–60
Kennedy, John Fitzgerald
  assassination and funeral, 79–90
  debate with R. Nixon, 62
  inauguration, 67–68
  infidelities of, 49–54
  marriage to Jackie, 5, 41, 46–56
  meeting Jackie, 39–40
  relationship with Inga Arvad, 35–39, 38*n*
  steel companies and, 227–28
  war years, 38–39
Kennedy, Joseph P., 7, 36, 49, 64, 68, 103, 111*n*, 126
Kennedy, Kara, 133
Kennedy, Kathleen, 103
Kennedy, Kerry, 213
Kennedy, Michael, 136, 237
Kennedy, Patrick, 132, 162
Kennedy, Patrick Bouvier, 55, 64, 107, 245
Kennedy, Robert F., 12, 48, 80–92, 83*n*, 102*n*, 110, 162, 182, 218, 239, 241, 242, 245
Kennedy, Robert F., Jr., 78, 143, 238
Kennedy, Rose, 7, 24, 146, 206–8
Kennedy, Teddy, Jr., 132, 207
Kennedy, Victoria Reggie, 181, 206, 238
Kennedys: Dynasty and Disaster, 1948–1983, The, 32
Kent, Rosemary, 4, 20
Kerry, John, 137
Kharazmi, Maryam, 119
Khrushchev, Nikita, 15, 23
Kipling, Rudyard, 253
Kirkland, Gelsey, 200
Kirkpatrick, Jeane, 24
Kissinger, Henry, 168, 229
Klein, Calvin, 169
Klein, Edward, 232
Klingman, Howard, 36
Knickerbocker, Cholly, 33
Koch, Edward I., 191, 229
Kominates, Nikos, 117
Kopechne, Mary Jo, 64
Kotite, Tony, 163
Kotz, Lynn, 82
Kotz, Mary Lynn, 52
Krock, Arthur, 34
Kubiak, Hieronym, 83*n*

La Caravelle, 96

Lafayette, Marquis de, 31
Lambrey, Maureen, 142
Last Tsar: The Life and Death of Nicholas II, The, 200
Lauder, Estée, 221
Lawford, Christopher, 213, 237
Lawford, Patricia, 50, 93, 213, 237, 249
Lawford, Peter, 68, 93, 200, 213
Lawford, Sidney, 145
Lawford, Victoria, 213
Lax, Dr. Henry, 172
Lee, Spike, 218
Leighton, Frances Spatz, 50, 53
Lennon, John, 221
Leonard, John, 193
Lerner, Alan J., 102
Leyson, Ted, 225
Life magazine, 22
Lincoln, Abraham, 71, 82
Linde, Edward H., 230
Lindsay, John, 230
Livanos, Athena (Tina). *See* Onassis, Athena (Tina) Livanos
Livanos, Stavros, 106
Lobel, Evan, 169
Lodge, Henry Cabot, 40
Look, 97, 194, 195
Loren, Sophia, 16, 25
Loudon Hospital Center, 250

MacDonald, Torbert, 57
Maclaine, Shirley, 177
MacNamara, Robert J., 102
Madonna (singer), 15, 23, 163
Malle, Louis, 230
Manchester, William, 84n, 194
Manott, Charles, 157
Mansfield, Jayne, 49
Mansfield, Mike, 73
Marilyn Monroe: The Biography, 50n
Markel, Helen, 192
Marshall, Burke, 146
Martha's Vineyard, 215–21
Martin, Mary, 23
Martin, Ralph G., 57, 62, 94
Martin, Steve, 253
Mathias, Charles, Jr., 177

McCarran, Patrick, 58
McCarthy, Joe (author), 21, 112
McCormack, John W., 14, 73
McCoy, Tim, 38
McCullough, E. R., 211n
McCusker, Donald, 126
McGovern, George S., 137, 176–77
McGovern, Maureen, 207
McHugh, Godfrey, 55
McIlvain, Isabel, 147
McMillan, Rev. Donald A., 145
McNamara, Robert S., 168, 218
Meir, Golda, 14
Mellon, Paul, 238
Mellon, Rachel (Bunny), 217, 238
Mercadier, Dr. Mercedes, 129
Merman, Ethel, 68
Meyer, André, 222
Meyer, Cord, Jr., 51
Meyer, Mary Pinchot, 51
Michael, Prince of Greece, 128
Mikulski, Barbara, 260
Millay, Edna St. Vincent, 244
Miller, Melody, 208
Miller, William "Fishbait," 5
Miss Chapin's School, 29
Miss Porter's School for Girls, 19, 33, 244
Mojica, Aline, 206
Monroe, Marilyn, 49, 200
Moonwalk, 199
Morales, Mrs. Villeda, 12
Morgenthau, Robert N., 132
Morrissey, Thomas, 173
Mortimer's, 170
Moyers, Bill D., 200, 202, 203, 259
Mudd, Roger, 169
Municipal Art Society, 231
Munro, Sally, 163

Naco, Frank, 200n
Namath, Joe, 169
National Geographic Society, 75
National Society of Interior Designers, 75
Nehru, Jawaharlal, 23
Nelson, Doris, 80
Nelson, Mary, 96
New York City Landmarks Preservation Commission, 232

New York City Office of Economic Development, 158
New York Coliseum, 228–30
New York University School of Law, 158–59
Niarchos, Charlotte Ford, 122
Nichols, Mike, 102, 169, 240
Nixon, Pat, 17, 24, 76
Nixon, Richard, 17–18, 44, 62, 249
Nomikos, Markos, 107
Norman, Jessye, 244
Nureyev, Rudolph, 169

O'Brien, Lawrence F., 73
O'Donnell, Kenneth P., 93, 111, 189–90, 212
Olivier, Sir Lawrence, 68
Onassis, Alexander, 106, 117, 126
Onassis, Aristotle Socrates
  courtship of Jackie, 107–12
  criminal charges against, 111
  death of son, 126
  donation to clean up Beale house, 94n
  early life, 104–5
  illness and death, 128–30
  marriage to Athena (Tina) Livanos, 106–7
  marriage to Jackie, 6–7, 112–15, 123
  private island, 16, 113–14
  relationship with Maria Callas, 107, 122–27
Onassis, Athena (Tina) Livanos, 106–7, 115
Onassis, Christina, 106, 115–17, 128–31
Onassis, Jacqueline Bouvier Kennedy
  appearance, after age sixty-five, 173
  arguments in public, 5–6
  beauty regimen, 173, 174
  birth of Caroline and John, Jr., 45
  campaigning for JFK, 60–61
  college education, 33–34
  courtship by Onassis, 108–10
  daily life, 170–72
  death, 239
  death of baby Patrick, 55, 64
  early education, 30, 33, 244
  eating habits, 169–70
  employees, stinginess with, 11
  engagement to JFK, 42
  engagement to John Husted, 34
  exercise regimen, 173–74
  family events, absence from, 206–8
  family football games and, 209
  fashion, sense of style, 19
  fashion trends, impact on, 17–19
  feminism and, 101, 203–5
  financial worth, 221–22
  as First Lady, 57–58, 64–65, 66–67
  funeral, 240–47
  generous nature of, 12–13
  gifts placed in JFK's casket, 55
  as a grandmother, 222–25
  hairdresser, 173
  hands, appearance of, 173
  home, Cape Cod, 206, 213
  home, Georgetown, 45, 90, 91
  home, Glen Ora, 45n
  home, Hickory Hill, 43
  home, Martha's Vineyard, 215–21
  home, New York City, 93, 167–68
  home, White House, 66, 70
  horseback riding, 174, 250
  illness with lymphoma, xi–xiii, 170, 233–39, 252
  imperious attitude, 12
  interior decorating styles, 44–45, 67, 71–76, 92, 168, 216
  interviews given, 4, 8, 119–20, 194, 201–3
  invitation to Clintons, 181, 242
  invitation to Kennedy family, 213
  JFK's assassination, 78
  JFK's death, grief/depression, 78, 89–97
  JFK's funeral, 55, 79–82
  JFK's marital infidelities and, 49–54
  job offers, 190–91
  legal actions/lawsuits, 129–30, 194–95, 219–21

letters to Gilpatric auctioned, 103
marriage to JFK, 41, 46–56
marriage to Onassis, 104, 113–14, 118–19, 121, 124–29, 188
media, attitude towards, 6–10
media coverage, 15–17, 101, 104–5, 118–20
meeting JFK, 39–40
meeting Michael Jackson, 199
meeting Onassis, 109
men she has dated, 102–4, 176–78
miscarriage, 44, 60
as a mother, 89–92, 132–33, 164, 190, 213. See also Kennedy, John F., Jr.; Schlossberg, Caroline Kennedy
newspaper column by, 60–62
nude photographs of, 17
oral history by, 13
parents' divorce, 30–31
personal expenditures, excessive, 10–12, 19–22, 46
plastic surgery, 172–73
as a political wife, 60–63
politics, attitudes towards, 57–60
prenuptial agreement with Onassis, 112–13
public opinion polls, 24–26
relationship with Ethel Kennedy, 12, 92, 210–12
relationship with her mother, 13
relationship with Joan Kennedy, 212
relationship with Joe Kennedy, 64, 187
relationship with Kennedy family, 206, 212–13
relationship with Onassis children, 115–17
relationship with other presidents, 249–50
relationship with RFK, 79, 80–92, 189–90, 218
relationship with Rose Kennedy, 210–11
relationship with Ted Kennedy, 207, 212
relationship with Tempelsman, 176, 177, 181–82, 186–88, 217, 222, 238, 242, 246, 250, 252, 260
RFK's death, grief/depression after, 110–12
sense of humor, 110, 250–51
social conscience of, 59–62, 226–27
social life, 102–4, 169, 174, 248
swimming, shark-infested waters, 250
urban civic causes, 228–34
Vatican's comments on, 118, 188
visits to JFK Memorial Library, 249
visits to JFK's grave, 208
visit to Cambodia, 63–64, 226
visit to Onassis's yacht, 47
visit to West Virginia, 12, 60, 226
voice, characteristics of, 3–7
Warren Commission testimony, 85–89
White House restoration project, 66, 69–76
work, Doubleday & Co., 4, 170, 195–202
work, Viking Press, 192–94, 196
work, Washington Times Herald, 34
yoga/meditation, study of, 171, 202
Onassis, Penelope, 105
Onassis, Socrates, 105
O'Neill, Thomas P., III, 162
Orange County Hunt Club, 250
Ono, Yoko, 221
Ormsby-Gore, Sir William David, 103
Oswald, Lee Harvey, 82, 83n

Parish, Mrs. Helen (Sister), 70
Parker, John L., 105
Parker, Sarah Jessica, 163
Parker-Bowles, Camilla, 200
Parkland Memorial Hospital (Dallas, TX), 80
Paul, Weiss, Rifkine, Wharton and Garrison, 146
Pearce, Mrs. Lorraine, 75
Pei, I. M., 230, 241

Pender, Robert Beebe, 213
Penn Central, 232
Peyser, Andrea, 252
Philadelphia Inquirer, 17
Phillips Academy, 154
Pinchot, Gifford, 51
Platt, Henry, 177
Playmen, 16
Plimpton, George, 102, 169, 182
Portrait of a President, 194
Powers, Dave, 58, 84, 90, 112, 138, 140–41, 152, 162
Prashker, Betty, 196
Presidential Medal of Freedom, 153
President's Commission on the Assassination of President Kennedy, 85–89
Profiles in Courage Award, 156, 160

Quigley, Brian, 15
Quindlen, Anne, 258
Quinn, Anthony, 102, 177
Quinn, Sally, 258

Radcliffe College, 139
Radzinsky, Edward, 200
Radziwill, Lee Bouvier, 30, 93, 97, 107, 182, 237, 245, 251
Radziwill, Prince Stanislas ("Stash"), 93, 182
Rainie, Harrison, 7, 213
Randall, Tony, 197
Rankin, J. Lee, 85, 86–89
Reagan, Nancy, 12, 24, 257
Reagan, Ronald, 249–50, 257
Redford, Robert, 16
Reed, James, 94
Reeves, Dr. Thomas C., 50n
Reggie, Victoria. *See* Kennedy, Victoria Reggie
Reston, Richard, 217
Richardson, Ashley, 163
Ringwald, Molly, 163
Rochas, Helen, 123
Rohatyn, Felix, 177–78
Rolling Stone Magazine, 238
Ronson, Howard, 233
Roosevelt, Eleanor, 24, 58

Roosevelt, Franklin Delano, Jr., 107
Rosebush, James S., 12
Rusoff, Marly, 8

Saint David's Catholic School, 153
Salinger, Pierre, 5, 72, 97, 102n, 241
Salomon Brothers, 228–30
Sargent, John, 195–96, 250–51
Sawyer, Diane, 240
Schiff, Dorothy, 190–91
Schlesinger, Arthur, Jr., 59, 62, 102, 168
Schlossberg, Alfred, 145
Schlossberg, Caroline Kennedy
  birth, 45
  childhood/youth, 113, 135–42
  children, 147–49
  co-authored a book, 149–50
  education, 95, 132–44
  engagement to Edwin Schlossberg, 142–44
  JFK's death, reaction to, 89–91, 95–96, 239
  marriage to Edwin Schlossberg, 7, 147–49
  and mother's death, 238–39, 240, 244–46
  relationship with Kennedy family, 206–8, 212–14
  relationship with Onassis, 117–18, 125
  work, 149–51
Schlossberg, Edwin, 7, 142–47, 249
Schlossberg, John Bouvier Kennedy, 149
Schlossberg, Mae, 145
Schlossberg, Rose Kennedy, 7, 147, 223, 224, 237
Schlossberg, Tatiana Celia Kennedy (Tanya), 149, 223, 224
Schlossberg, Edwin A., 142, 238
Schoelkopf, Caroline Hunt, 221
Schwarzenegger, Arnold, 15, 157, 213, 240, 245
Schwarzenegger, Maria Shriver, 157, 213, 237, 245
Shall We Tell the President?, 193
Shelton, Isabelle, 75

Index

Shriver, Anthony, 206
Shriver, Eunice, 78, 206, 237, 249
Shriver, Maria. *See*
    Schwarzenegger, Maria Shriver
Shriver, Sargent, 206
Sihanouk, Prince Norodom, 23, 63, 226
Sills, Beverly, 218
Simon, Carly, 207, 218, 238
Simpson, Dave, 250
Sinatra, Frank, 23, 68, 177
Singleton, Becky, 192
Smathers, George, 44, 48, 161
Smith, Dr. William Kennedy, 208, 237, 249
Smith, Jean, 93, 145, 208, 249
Smith, Liz, 195, 249
Smith, Steven, 93
Sorenson, Theodore C., 65, 146
Spada, James, 200
Sparks, Fred, 126
Spellman, Francis Cardinal, 12
Spoto, Daniel, 50n
Springsteen, Bruce, 15
St. Ignatius Loyola Church, 241
St. Matthew's Cathedral, 82
St. Patrick's Cathedral, 10, 12
St. Thomas More Church, 237, 241
Stallone, Sylvester, 15
Stassen, Harold, 51
Stassinopoulos, Arianna, 123, 126, 127
Stein, Jean, 182
Steinem, Gloria, 204
Stevenson, Adlai, 44
Stich Radiation Therapy Center, 236
Stravinsky, Igor, 65
Streisand, Barbra, 16
Stringfellow, Ethel, 30
Summers, Anthony, 50n
Swanson, Gloria, 7
Symonds, Dr. Percival M., 56

Tartiere, Gladys and Raymond, 46n
Taylor, Elizabeth, 14, 15, 25
Taylor, John, 229
Tempelsman, Lily, 183–84
Tempelsman, Maurice, 155, 176–88,
217, 222, 238, 242, 246, 250, 252, 260
Thatcher, Margaret, 14, 24
Thayer, Mary Van Rensselaer, 46n, 76
Thomas, Albert, 86
Thomas, Evan, 194
Tilden, Samuel J., 71
Times to Remember, 7
Tippet, Officer J. D., 82
Tuckerman, Nancy, 8, 10, 177, 236, 239
Tyler, John, 29

United States Steel Corporation, 227
United Steel Workers of America, 227
Upstairs at the White House, 52

Valentino (designer), 109
Vanderhoop clan, 220
Vanity Fair, 22
Vassar College, 19, 33
Viking Press, 191, 195
Vogue, 22

Wallace, Mike, 218
Wallace, Robert, 61
Walsh, Dr. John, 54
Walters, Barbara, 24, 169
Walton, William, 68, 177
Warhol, Andy, 4
Warren, Chief Justice Earl, 85
Washington, George, 72
Washington Times Herald, 34
Weissberg, Mrs. Thelma, 220
Welch, Raquel, 25
West, Chief Usher J. B., 12, 22, 52–53, 70, 81
White, Theodore A., 55
White House restoration project, 66, 69–76, 243
Wilde, Oscar, 52
Windsor, Duke and Duchess of, 16
Winfrey, Oprah, 24
Winterthur Museum, 72
Woman Named Jackie, A, 46
Worcester Cercle Français, 58
Wrightsman, Charles, 238

Wrightsman, Jayne, 72, 76, 238
Wyeth, Andrew, 65

Yarborough, Ralph, 80

Zaroulis, Nancy L., 198
Zuckerman, Mortimer B., 228–31